Fair Pay

Thomas H. Patten, Jr.

Fair Pay

The Managerial Challenge
of Comparable Job Worth
and Job Evaluation

 Jossey-Bass Publishers

San Francisco • London • 1988

FAIR PAY
The Managerial Challenge of Comparable Job Worth and Job Evaluation
by Thomas H. Patten, Jr.

Copyright © 1988 by: Jossey-Bass Inc., Publishers
350 Sansome Street
San Francisco, California 94104

&

Jossey-Bass Limited
28 Banner Street
London EC1Y 8QE

Library of Congress Cataloging-in-Publication Data

Patten, Thomas H., Jr., date.
  Fair pay.

  (Jossey-Bass management series)
  Bibliography: p.
  Includes index.
  1. Job evaluation—United States.   2. Pay
equity—United States.   I. Title.   II. Series.
HF5549.5.J62P38   1988   658.3′222   88-42796
ISBN 1-55542-120-2

Manufactured in the United States of America

The paper in this book meets the guidelines for
permanence and durability of the Committee on
Production Guidelines for Book Longevity of the
Council on Library Resources.

JACKET DESIGN BY WILLI BAUM

FIRST EDITION

Code 8853

The Jossey-Bass
Management Series

To my loving wife, Jule

Contents

Contents

Tables and Figures

Chapter 6

Tables and Figures xv

Appendix

—— Preface ——

I think socioeconomic change moves forward as forcefully as a train traversing the track. Trains can become derailed, stopped, or slowed down. But they move under momentum, and, more often than not, roll on to their destination.

Comparable job worth might well be viewed as a train chugging uphill but near the summit and ready to roll down the track at a fast speed very soon. If this scenario is realistic, the challenge for corporate management in America is whether it wishes to wave a flag from the caboose or to play a role as locomotive engineer and blower of the whistle as the train presses on to its destination in pay equity. However, policy-level executives, line and staff managers, and even human resource managers, who should be alert to developments in comparable job worth, do not seem to realize what is going on and how the public sector is moving very rapidly to implement male-female pay equity. Corporate management needs to know what is taking place and to decide what it wants to do before the trip is over. This book addresses this important need and is the first book of its kind: it provides a managerial perspective by a professor of management and human resources and an active pay consultant to corporate managers who are about to be directed to solve the multifarious problems of fair pay.

My purpose is to inform private-sector management of the comparable job worth challenge and the new roles of job evaluation

in dealing with pay equity demanded by women in industry. I want
to help management to cope with the challenge and implement
new, appropriate policies.

This book will allow busy policy-level executives to learn
about the managerial, legal, legislative, labor union, collective
bargaining, and strategic business issues framing the comparable
job worth panorama. It will provide middle managers in line and
staff positions with useful information on how to understand why
comparable job worth remains a persistent problem among
American women in their employ. I set forth and explain techniques for solving the problems involved in pay equity for these
readers because they will be expected to take corrective action.
Human resource managers will find the book a current source of
ideas, coping methods, and cases and facts—as well as a review of
legislative developments. It will help them in staying up to date,
formulating policies, and designing workable practices.

Whether the reader is at work in industry, government, the
health care industry, the labor movement, education, the legal
profession, management consulting, or even the armed forces or
large religious organizations, there is material in *Fair Pay* that will
shed light on why comparable job worth is a matter that must be
addressed and resolved.

My highest hope is that my treatment of the topic might jolt
American management into realizing that pay equity is virtually a
fact of life in much of the public sector and that it is spreading to
the remainder of the economy quite rapidly. Corporate management seems completely unaware of the momentum—and unpre-
pared to act. It needs to know and to be ready. This book should
assist readers in meeting these needs because it provides an up-to-
date managerial treatment of the problem.

Overview of the Contents

The book begins with a careful examination of the many meanings
of comparable job worth and concludes that, stripped of confusing
connotations and fuzzy ideology, this concept means pay equity.
Managers are organizational gatekeepers who can bring about pay
equity at surprisingly low costs. Women have historically been

subjected to—and have largely accepted—minority status that has included differential and unfair treatment in the world of work. They and various supportive groups in contemporary society are now actively engineering important socioeconomic changes to stamp out sex-based pay discrimination. Through litigation women have obtained greater equity than ever before, although the U.S. Supreme Court has not yet endorsed comparable job worth. The changing composition of the Supreme Court may not be an impediment to a change in such endorsement if a case with the right fact pattern is presented to it.

Although the judiciary is at present not sending out new signals to corporate America, certainly the state legislatures and local government are doing so. The level of comparable worth activity there borders on the frantic, though somehow this is not being noticed in boardrooms and corporate offices, where the main concerns of business today are seen as foreign competition, the size of the deficit, the vicissitudes of the stock market, *glasnost,* global risk assessment, and the like. Yet state legislative activity on comparable worth has not been unnoticed by women's groups, labor unions, civil rights advocates, academics, and others whose focus of attention is less diffuse than that of corporate management. Unions have been using collective bargaining to further comparable job worth, and some pacesetting companies have quietly used job evaluation unilaterally—on their own—to resolve persistent problems of pay equity. Are these the preferred solutions to the problem? If they are not, what strategy is appropriate in a free society such as ours?

There are some new appreciations of job evaluation that have come about as a result of the struggle for pay equity since the 1960s. Job evaluation now has some new faces and facets. It certainly has been revived from the doldrums of the pre-1960 era. The totality of these developments leads one to conclude that pay equity will come tomorrow—as soon as the 1990s. Such an assertion may seem indefensible to readers who are not on top of the fast-moving trends in comparable job worth and who would expect such fundamental change to come along at the pace of a glacier. But that is what this book is all about. Moreover, I hope that it heightens awareness and interest on the part of American management and is put on the business reader's list of "must" reading.

How This Book Came About

I have been interested in the field of compensation for more than thirty-five years and have followed the growth of the comparable job worth issue very closely from 1976 to the present. In these years I have benefited greatly from personal contacts with some of the most knowledgeable attorneys in the employment law field in Pittsburgh, Cleveland, Chicago, Detroit, Minneapolis, Los Angeles, Fort Worth, Denver, and Washington, D.C. More limited contact with Donald J. Treiman of UCLA and Alvin O. Bellak (formerly of the Hay Group) has also been helpful. Time off for research granted by the School of Labor and Industrial Relations at Michigan State University during the fall quarter of 1986 when I was on the faculty there helped me prepare an outline for the book and read widely in source materials. A graduate seminar on comparable job worth that I taught in the summer quarter of 1986 while at SLIR-MSU provided me with an opportunity to concretize what I really thought about the subject and to invite criticisms from an astute group of doctoral and master's degree candidates, several of whom were practitioners in human resources.

Gene L. Houser, chair of the Department of Management and Human Resources, and Ronald W. Eaves, dean of the College of Business Administration, of the California State Polytechnic University in Pomona, gave me consideration in course scheduling and complete freedom of action to bring this book to completion during 1987-88.

Most of the writing was done in my home in Kaunakakai, Molokai, Hawaii, during the summer of 1987. Susan M. Foster of Claremont, California, ably performed all the word processing. William H. Hicks and Mary L. White of Jossey-Bass were constant supporters, and their encouragement and follow-up were crucial to completion of the book.

Claremont, California   Thomas H. Patten, Jr.
September 1988

The Author

Thomas H. Patten, Jr., is professor of management and human resources at the California State Polytechnic University, Pomona, California, where he has served on the faculty of the College of Business Administration since 1984. In March 1988 he was appointed director of research in the college, as well. He received his A.B. degree *cum laude* in sociology from Brown University (1953) and his M.S. (1955) and Ph.D. (1959) degrees from Cornell University, specializing in human resource management, organizational behavior, and social and labor legislation.

Patten's research, consultation, and writing have covered almost all aspects of human resource management. He is one of the foremost experts in the world on such topics as wage and salary administration, job evaluation, compensation forensics, performance appraisal, organizational development and executive teambuilding, and management education. He is the author of more than ninety articles and author or editor of nine books, including three editions of the well-known bibliography on compensation planning and administration published by the American Compensation Administration.

Patten's career includes eight years with the Ford Motor Company in various positions in the personnel and organization staff and twenty-two years of teaching and research at the University of Detroit and Michigan State University. Simultaneously, he has served as a court-appointed master in chancery and expert witness and consultant in some of the leading cases in America involving alleged sex discrimination in employment, the improper conduct of wage and salary surveys, and unjust discharges stemming from improper performance appraisal. In this forensic work he has, in various cases, been retained by defendants (employers) and plaintiffs (unions, employee classes, and individuals). These experiences have provided him with a balanced set of insights into the comparable job worth controversy.

Patten is listed in *Who's Who in America* and is a member of a large number of professional and honorary associations, such as the Academy of Management, the American Compensation Association, the Industrial Relations Research Association, and Phi Beta Kappa.

—— Fair Pay ——

1

Comparable Job Worth: Confronting Discrimination and Inequity in Public and Private Organizations

Comparable job worth is surely one of the most important challenges that management will face in the next decade. But American industrial management seems afraid of the problem from cost and human resources standpoints and hopes it will either go away or be left indefinitely in the realm of legal casuistry. Challenges need to be confronted, though; ostrich postures will not solve managerial or other problems.

Sex-based wage discrimination of all types is gradually being eliminated in the United States, and comparable job worth is as inevitable in private industry as it has become in the public sector. America has been moving for three decades in the direction of being an open society that permits the free mobility of people based upon their ability to contribute and perform. The comparable job worth challenge should be seen as a part of this movement and more than anything else as a powerful, indomitable demand for pay equity.

Discrimination against women in the various America labor markets has over the years developed two major aspects, exclusion and low pay. These two aspects are closely connected. The exclusion of women from many jobs and occupations pushes women into labor markets separate from those dominated by men, fenced-off markets in which supply and demand decree lower rates of pay. The main attack on exclusion is through affirmative action programs and an organizational policy of equal employment opportunity.

1

Under affirmative action, employers draw upon and implement plans to recruit women and minority men into occupations in which their presence has historically been low. The main attack on low wages is through pay equity and the implementation of fairness in compensation systems. The goal is to encourage employers to raise the pay in jobs where women predominate and thus to close the wage gap between men and women by direct action (Bergmann, 1986).

Since World War II, more and more women have entered the American labor force without closing the pay gap with men. The result has been to create an employee rights issue that is in line with such other new issues in contemporary compensation administration arising from labor force and workplace changes as skill-based pay, gainsharing, two-tier wage structures, performance bonuses, and innovative pay-for-performance systems. However, comparable job worth is seen by managers as the greatest threat to the legitimacy of the traditional American hierarchy and pay systems in management (Kanter, 1987).

Most of the changes in pay planning and administration taking place today are attempts by employees to improve organizational performance while controlling payroll costs. Organizational change is not, for the most part, a goal even if it is an unintended side effect of the new pay plans, and it is often resisted by managers. The fact of the matter is that most of the various forms of the new contribution-based pay also tend to shake up the managerial hierarchy, challenge traditional authority relations, and weaken the meaning of organizational status. But the threat of comparable job worth, from the standpoint of executives, is the massive organizational readjustments it may bring about even more than the cost of equalizing pay across certain jobs (Kanter, 1987).

Performance- or contribution-based pay is highly compatible with the principle behind comparable job worth: to ensure equivalent pay for jobs that create equivalent value for the organization. Measures of social status in the company—such as the market price used to hire for certain positions, the location or standing of the job in an organizational hierarchy, or the prestige acquired by typical job incumbents—should be less important to managers than the actual contributions made to carrying out organizational purposes if we adopt a comparable worth principle (Kanter, 1987).

Business organizations are gradually coming to accept the necessity of gearing pay to performance and giving employees a share of the extra value or gain they produce. But they are also trying to confine these rewards so that the jobs themselves do not have to be repositioned in the hierarchy of status structures. In this way management can preserve some of the old status order while overlaying a few new features on it. However, the old status order becomes upended when comparable job worth is implemented. The latter represents real change and therefore becomes a serious challenge to managerial comfort (Kanter, 1987).

Comparable job worth is thus a multifaceted issue that transcends compensation matters narrowly conceived. It can be viewed from economic, social, cultural, psychological, historical, legal, philosophical, political, and moral perspectives. It has a definite managerial focus involving for its implementation various strategic, policy-level, operational-level, motivational, organizational behavior, organizational development, and applied behavioral science dimensions. The challenge of comparable job worth may also be viewed in a contingency context, because although a strategy is needed to cope with the problem, any particular strategy chosen should be shaped to fit mandates from top management and the corporate culture. Comparable job worth clearly involves contingent culture change, and everything we know about effective change agentry clearly would apply to meeting the challenges presented when an organization's reward system is the object of attention.

Concepts of Comparable Job Worth

Having set forth the important idea that comparable job worth is a significant organizational challenge to management today, I now turn to some basic concepts. The key to an understanding of the various facets of comparable job worth is approaching the subject with an open mind. The common denominator to all concepts of comparable job worth is systemic unfair levels of pay in a business or other establishment. Insofar as neither policy-level executives nor operating managers are ever inclined to argue in favor of systemic unfair pay, I think an understanding of the concepts of comparable job worth is easy to create if pay equity is kept in mind as the central idea governing the meaning of the concepts.

To begin with, most organizations try to pay their employees in line with the principle of unequal pay for unequal work in proportion to the inequality. Stating the fundamental organizational pay goal in this way affirms the commonly observed phenomenon that American working people want their paychecks to reflect the differential importance of work to which they are assigned. Quite apart from this, employees doing work of the same degree of importance—that is, various people doing work carrying the identical job title—may want their paychecks to reflect a difference in the level of performance, length of service (also called seniority), a shift differential (that is, premium pay for the afternoon or night turn or watch), or for overtime or for the occasional conduct of exceptionally dangerous tasks (for example, stevedores who load dynamite in the holds of a ship). All of the aforementioned refinements in pay may be demanded beyond base pay, and none of these is technically considered part of job evaluation. They are merely a collection of pay expectations that go along with the customary demand for fair levels of pay according to the contingencies involved. Comparable job worth goes even deeper and causes us to firm up our concepts and be more rigorous in our thinking.

There are four very distinct concepts of comparable job worth afloat in America today. They are (1) equal pay for equal work, (2) equal pay for similar work, (3) equal pay for equal worth, and (4) pay parity. These are sometimes lumped together as notions of pay equity, representing four different theories of sex-based compensation discrimination (Lorber and others, 1985). Each concept is discussed in turn.

Equal pay for equal work is the least controversial and most widely accepted approach to simple pay equity. This concept applies to sex-segregated jobs where a position held predominantly by women (conventionally defined as 70 percent occupied by women) and a position held predominantly by men (also conventionally defined as 70 percent dominated by one gender, men in this instance) are of *substantially equal* content, even though the jobs in question may have different titles. The jobs are not identical in content, only equivalent, such as the work performed by many male hospital orderlies and by female nurse's aides. The basic factors that are used for comparing the substantial equality of the jobs are the traditional job evaluation factors of skill, effort, responsibility, and working conditions. For the jobs in question to be considered equal, they must be substantially equal on each and every one of the aforementioned traditional job evaluation factors.

The Equal Pay Act, an amendment to the Fair Labor Standards Act of 1938, has since 1963 required that employers pay equal wages for work that is substantially equal unless the employer can show that a difference in wages is attributable to some factor other than sex. Similarly, Title VII of the Civil Rights Act of 1964 also requires equal pay for equal work under the same standards as those of the Equal Pay Act. Thus, it can be said that equal pay for substantially equal work has been the law of the land for about a quarter of a century.

The second concept, equal pay for similar work, is harder to grasp and has not been fully explicated as yet in litigation. There is a hairline difference between jobs that meet the substantially equal test on the one hand and those that fall short of it but are nevertheless similar in job content as well as skill, effort, responsibility, and working conditions on the other. The only way to suggest what the differences may be between "similar" and "substantially equal" is to appeal to one's sense of legal casuistry and tolerance for nicety in making distinctions between, for example, a male-dominated occupation like public health sanitarian and a female-dominated occupation such as a public health nurse. An empirical job analysis might show that these two jobs have tasks that are not greatly different and the skill, effort, responsibility, and working conditions are similar but not substantially equal. However, the distinction seems strained, overly rational, and unlikely to be spun into a clear general principle.

The third concept is equal pay for equal *worth*, which is probably the notion that comes most readily to the minds of managers when they hear or see the words comparable job worth. Advocates of equal pay for equal worth believe that sex-segregated jobs should be paid the same when those positions have equal worth as measured by an approach to compensation planning of one type or another. For example, the "difficulty" of the job could be measured by job evaluation, or the "value" of the job could be arbitrarily determined by managerial judgment and fiat. In either of these approaches a comparison is made of the worth of jobs whose content is different. Then the pay of the subject job and comparison job are equalized. Thus, if it is determined that the difficulty or value of a female-dominated power keyboard operator job is equal to that of a male-dominated job in an entirely different job family or occupation, such as local delivery van driver, under the doctrine of equal pay for equal worth, the two jobs would be paid at the same level. The equalization of pay across occupational lines without slavishly assigning rates of pay based upon labor-market information or traditional gender differentials is perhaps the most popular interpretation of what comparable job worth means.

The fourth concept of comparable job worth is narrowing the pay gap between large groups of men and women by achieving pay parity. The advantage in pay that men had over women in America in 1985 was very large: women's annual pay in full-time work averaged 68 percent of that of men (Bergmann, 1986). There is little doubt that much of this wage gap can be attributed to factors other than sex discrimination in employment. Nevertheless, labor-market studies not limited to statistical analyses of the causes of the male-female wage gap support the belief that women have suffered extensive and damaging discrimination in labor markets (Aaron and Lougy, 1986). Persons who rally around the pay parity concept of comparable job worth are insisting that we will not achieve the latter until statistics reported by the federal government show the average earnings of females equal to the average earnings of males on a nationwide basis regardless of any characteristics distinguishing the work of the two sexes. Of all the concepts of comparable worth, pay parity appears to be the most insupportable by management because it seems to be more of an ideology than a serious argument deserving of support as a tool of pay equity.

The semantic problems of understanding comparable job worth are undoubtedly formidable and very much get in the way of dealing with the remaining issues of sex discrimination in pay in America. Yet we should not lose sight of the fact that the common denominator of the problem is attainment of pay equity. What manager is prepared to argue in favor of systematic unfair pay?

Characterizing Divergent Views: Two Polar Points

The comparable job worth drama in America today is a rejection of part of the cultural heritage of the past and a challenge for managers of all ages and persuasions to consider. I turn next to two opposite points of view on the subject and summarize the divergencies according to the interpretation of why the male-female wage gap exists, the understanding of how labor markets operate, the explanation of the role of job evaluation in setting wages, the estimation of how comparable job worth could be implemented, and the prediction of the effects of comparable job worth in the future if it were implemented. I turn to the views of the supporters of comparable job worth first and then juxtapose the opponents' views.

Supporters interpret the male-female wage gap as disappearing if one adjusts for hours worked, education, and age, leaving discrimination as the explanation for the remainder of the differential. Opponents agree that about one-half the wage gap can be explained statistically and that adjustments should be made not only for hours but also for experience and time spent outside the labor force. Furthermore, the remainder may reflect female preferences for certain jobs or the ignorance of investigators but do not necessarily reflect discrimination.

In regard to understanding how labor markets operate, supporters of comparable job worth believe institutional factors are important in wage setting. Internal labor markets are used in hiring and promotion, crowding women into certain occupations. The supply and demand for female workers and wage flexibility play only a small role in the insulated internal labor markets within which women are found. Thus, the opportunity for competition to eliminate discrimination is very limited. However, opponents take the puristic view that wages are determined primarily by supply and demand: wages are flexible, and labor markets adjust so that supply equals demand. Furthermore, opponents argue that the corporate goal of maximizing profits leads employers rationally and automatically to eliminate discrimination. The opponents appear to be theoretical and classical; the supporters are empirical and institutional, looking carefully at the practices of management.

Supporters explain that traditional approaches to job evaluation can measure the value of jobs to employers and can establish the ordinal, if not cardinal, ranking of job values. Opponents assert that job evaluation is so inherently subjective that the only reliable indicator of the value of a job is the wage an employer is willing to pay a person to fill it. In reality, job evaluation is largely subjective in practice, but much of the subjectivity inherent in the administration of job evaluation can be controlled by experienced compensation analysts who personally try to be as objective as possible about their work in building job structures.

Supporters of comparable job worth believe it will be applied on a firm-by-firm basis. These applications can be carried out through bilateral collective bargaining or through the unilateral use of tailor-made job evaluation studies. In the public sector, the latter types of studies are presently under way and are being used in wage setting. Private industry can and should follow suit. Once having made such job evaluation studies, corporations or other organizations should decide upon the sizes of comparable worth pay adjustments and go ahead and implement them. However, opponents totally disagree with this prognostication of how comparable job worth will come about and raise the heavy specter of government intervention and mandate. To them comparable job worth is tantamount to mandatory job evaluation in both the public and private sectors, possibly economywide. They perceive the creation of burdensome new legislation or the court's arbitrary interpretation of existing law, authorizing either the wholesale intervention by executive agencies through regulation or through the judiciary by means of wage-setting litigation. Bilateral free collective bargaining or employer freedom to unilaterally solve the problem of pay equity would fall by the wayside.

Turning to predictions of the effects of comparable job worth, the supporters believe that there would be significant changes in the relative wages of jobs. But there would be only small effects on labor costs, even if pay equity is brought about by "leveling up," that is, by increasing the wages of persons in the female-dominated jobs to equal those in the comparable male-dominated jobs. There would be little job displacement and little effect on economic efficiency. Moreover, the cost of eliminating discrimination is never a valid excuse for inaction. Job segregation would decrease because as wages in traditionally female jobs increased, men would probably be encouraged to enter those occupations. On the other hand, opponents predict that higher wages in traditionally female jobs would discourage women from moving out of those categories. There would be large increases in wages in millions of jobs and great overall increases in labor costs. This, in turn, would reduce economic efficiency, increase prices, and create major disemployment effects, especially for low-wage unskilled workers.

Institutional and Academic Views

These conflicting views are difficult to support with the kind of empirical evidence management likes to have. It is very hard to argue against the opponents because their views are a mixture of theory and ideology, and they are interested in maintaining the status quo with which they are comfortable. On the other hand, in this role the supporters of a new concept are necessarily agents of planned social change. Any proposal to consciously alter the status quo must combat inertia as well as the rationalizations, opposition, and entrenched power of those who fear change or simply do not want it. We should therefore not be surprised that the notion of fair pay for jobs of different content but equal value has been politicized and become an important social movement in recent years. Also, no one should be dismayed that various professional organizations and academic observers of the comparable job worth movement have divergent or (even at this late stage in the evolution of the subject) crescive—that is, gradually developing—views. I turn to these next.

The American Compensation Association (ACA), which is the premier professional organization in the compensation field with more than 10,000 members, has had an active Task Force on

Comparable Job Worth in the 1980s and through its newsletter
regularly reports on progress in pay equity legislation in Congress.
The ACA has taken note particularly of the politics of comparable
job worth, but, as an organization, has never taken an official
position on the subject. I would characterize its position as watchful
waiting that could turn at any time into an official published
position should Congress or the federal government enact legislation that might be signed into law or made an executive order. It
is carefully following developments at the state level, where almost
thirty states are now conducting or have already completed studies
to identify any sex discrimination in their pay systems and where
fifteen states have already made pay adjustments following such
studies.

The American Society for Personnel Administration, which
is the world's largest association for human resource professionals
with more than 34,000 members, has analyzed the concepts of
comparable job worth in depth and commissioned one of the best
monographs on the subject published to date, namely that by
Lorber and others (1985). In 1985 the ASPA board stated its belief
that properly designed and administered compensation programs
afford the greatest opportunity to ensure that bias will not enter into
setting pay and that the adoption of legislation or regulations
embracing the concept of comparable worth is unnecessary and
inappropriate given the American economic system. The ASPA also
believes that the market should play a key role in determining wages
and that the courts should not be involved in wage-setting
procedures, that business and other organizations should be allowed
to establish internal hierarchies of jobs with or without formal
systems of job evaluation and pay administration as long as these
systems are nondiscriminatory, that current job evaluation methods
are more art than science and are inherently flawed by imprecise
measurement and judgment, that there is no evidence better job
evaluation systems are either forthcoming (or required), and that
small employers and business owners (which constitute 80 percent
of the business in America) neither need nor can afford formal
systems of job evaluation. The ASPA is firmly committed to equal
pay for equal work, to the principles of affirmative action, and to
continue efforts to ensure that all persons are afforded equal

opportunity to compete for every job. It considers the aforementioned as the appropriate solutions to the issues of compensation disparity that underlie the comparable job worth controversy. Basically, it is in favor of focusing resources on the realization of free mobility into all jobs for all qualified persons.

Moving from the views of the ACA and ASPA to academia, we also find deep-seated differences of opinion. In the earliest published symposium of the important academic works on comparable job worth, we find that Milkovich (1980) is the most open-minded on the question of whether job evaluation and analysis may in the future be capable of yielding a universal taxonomy or set of guidelines for determining comparable job worth. For a variety of reasons, Schwab (1980), Hildebrand (1980), Northrup (1980), and Livernash (1980b) reject the notion of comparable job worth. Schwab (1980) argues that job evaluation is not likely to be helpful in identifying job worth in any way that differs from the market and that any assumption that pay differences between employees is due to job evaluation or any other single pay procedure is probably incorrect. Job evaluation achieves an important organizational objective, although not the one it is thought to address—that of arranging jobs in a hierarchy determined by worth through job content. Specifically, Schwab suggests that practical job evaluation is used by organizations to establish wage rates for nonkey jobs (where the market is difficult to assess) from variables (called compensable factors) that are related to key job wage rates (where market forces can be more readily determined).

Hildebrand (1980) argues that job evaluation is a reflection of a wage hierarchy and a wage curve derived from the labor market; therefore, comparable job worth cannot be harmonized with job evaluation because the theory has been formulated to exclude the external market. He also asserts that a system of job evaluation must be adapted to conditions prevailing in external labor and product-service markets to be compatible with the survival and profitability of the firm. Hildebrand's overly rationalistic argument against comparable job worth (by which he appears to have in mind only the concept of male-female pay parity) is that it will bring about a dreary scenario of unemploymment, poverty, and welfare dependency for women, particularly those under the age of twenty-five and from minority groups. Pay equity will mean the price of low-productivity women workers will go up without a corresponding increase in their productivity. As a result, employers will be induced to lay off part of the female group to hold down the enforced rise in their costs. For the low-paid women working in numerous small firms, the imposed rise in labor costs will cause either much bankruptcy or voluntary closure, resulting in their losing their jobs. In larger firms the rise in labor costs will create an incentive to substitute capital and revise plant or shop organization to replace women or, alternatively, to raise hiring standards so that fewer workers of either sex who are more productive can replace them. Female youngsters will be large losers of job opportunities. Discouraged women workers whose job opportunities have gone will withdraw from the labor force.

Like Hildebrand, Northrup (1980) perceives comparable job worth as a social movement that proposes a job evaluation and pay administration system that is unrelated not only to the external labor market but also to the internal labor market of the firm. To him, comparable job worth would raise the wage level and would require the establishment of a government agency to be the final arbiter of wages. Such an agency would become overburdened and probably would not be able to provide lasting results in the way companies, unions, and employees can when they negotiate to solve their own problems in pay and other domains in human resource management.

Livernash (1980b) concludes that any attempted implementation of comparable job worth will encounter substantial difficulties and have disruptive and undesirable consequences. He believes problems begin with the ambiguous character of the concept and its lack of an operational definition. To him, comparable job worth is based on a rejection of traditional job evaluation plans and labor-market rate standards and would substitute in their place some undetermined form of bias-free or value-free job evaluation. Support for such an approach fails to appreciate the realities of how job evaluation procedures actually operate and would eventually bring about all the harsh consequences enumerated by Hildebrand. There is a viable alternative to comparable job worth: the accelerated promotion of women, the strengthening of training and promotion policies and practices, and the creation of a positive and open climate for employee relations.

Practitioners' Views

Turning from compensation academics to compensation practitioners, we find that the latter have a significantly different stance. In a recent survey of thirty-six wage and salary administrators in the Midwest, compensation specialists endorsed several definitions of comparable job worth. Almost 75 percent of the respondents argued that their organization's compensation policies were compatible with the principles of equal pay for work of comparable worth. A majority endorsed continuation of past practices of job evaluation and the use of surveys of labor markets in setting wage levels. Most of the respondents stated they would revise their job evaluation plans to restore equity in the event of demonstrated pay inequities (Mahoney, Rosen, and Rynes, 1984).

The compensation specialists also endorsed several strategies for assessing the objectivity of current compensation policies. However, there was little agreement about the most effective strategy for restoring pay equity in situations where bias has been identified. About 32 percent of the respondents reported that redefining or reweighing compensable factors and implementing a single job evaluation system for all positions in the organization were promising approaches for redressing compensation inequities. Only 2 percent favored elimination of job evaluation procedures in favor of market surveys as the way of bringing about pay equity.

Many compensation administrators in industry are inclined to interpret the comparable job worth debate today solely in terms of the male-female earnings gap. Compensation specialists tend to believe that concepts of comparable worth are irrelevant in the determination of earnings received by women. Instead, they assume that wage rates are justified as determined by labor-market data, and concepts of worth are denigrated as being too subjective and arbitrary. They basically argue that the male-female earnings gap is a result of employment patterns of men and women and that women should seek employment in higher-paying occupations.

Mahoney, Rosen, and Rynes (1984) believe that the issues of a male-female earnings gap and the principle of equal pay for jobs of equal (or comparable) worth can and should be differentiated. The comparable job worth principle has been advanced for decades by compensation specialists, and it clearly underlies and provides the philosophical justification for the compensation practices of job evaluation and the use of market surveys. We have sought an understanding of how to provide unequal pay for unequal work in proportion to the inequality for decades, which suggests that the concept of worth reaches back beyond the current debate and remains a type of continuing challenge. Therefore, an appropriate response to the issue today of comparable job worth calls for a philosophical discussion and thorough examination of current compensation practices in America, including the development of a socially acceptable measure of a job. To date, little debate or new thinking has emerged, and compensation specialists and behavioral scientists have not taken advantage of the opportunity for conceptual development (Mahoney, Rosen, and Rynes, 1984). While it is quite clear that compensation practitioners acknowledge the existence of a salary gap between the average earnings of male and female workers, they disagree about the factors contributing to the salary differences. Female compensation administrators are more likely to attribute salary differences to sex bias in hiring and staffing decisions and in the pricing of jobs. Compensation specialists of both sexes agree that shorter career ladders in traditionally female jobs are a major contributor to the male-female pay gap.

Compensation specialists also agree that the movement toward reducing pay differences will be pushed by women's political groups, but that these groups currently lack the political clout necessary to significantly change the relevant corporate compensation policies. Instead, encouraging women to pursue nontraditional, higher-paying career paths appears to be the approach favored by compensation professionals for reducing the pay gap. Very little enthusiasm is shown for upgrading salaries for traditional women's occupations. Dramatic changes in compensation policy aimed at reducing the male-female pay gap are perceived as likely to increase business costs, weaken American business's position relative to foreign competitors, and contribute to the loss of jobs in industries staffed largely by women. However, some compensation specialists believe that policy changes resulting in higher salaries for female-dominated jobs are likely to attract more men to these occupations (Mahoney, Rosen, and Rynes, 1984).

Politicization of the Issue

For women's social action groups, comparable job worth has become the issue of the 1980s that will be transformed into the solution of the 1990s in the form of pay equity. There has been no letup in American women's desires for equal opportunity in employment and career mobility, despite the statement of President Ronald Reagan that comparable job worth is a "cockamamie idea" or the comment by Clarence M. Pendleton, Jr. (late chairman of the U.S. Commission on Civil Rights) that it is "the looniest idea since Looney Tunes." Demeaning the words *comparable job worth* will not cause the idea to die or social movements supporting the goal to break up and vanish. If anything, belittling the concept probably solidifies its proponents behind it. Exactly what have women's political groups accomplished to date in the quest for comparable job worth?

The Influence of Labor Markets

Women are disproportionately employed in certain occupations in which wages are relatively low. As we have seen, a male-female pay gap also exists. Statistical evidence shows that there are human capital differences between the sexes that account for part of this gap. Yet a considerable part cannot be explained away by these differences. In fact, women who make heavy investments in human capital receive a reward for that investment that is far inferior to the reward men obtain (Bergmann, 1986).

Some observers have argued, as I have previously stated, that the pay in female-dominated jobs is low because they are filled to a large extent by women who are the victims of discrimination. If it is true that labor markets are biased against women, it can be argued further that discrimination is perpetrated by using the market as a basis for paying females in female-dominated occupations and males in male-dominated occupations. The remedy to this problem would be to break with tradition and pay women according to comparable job worth, that is, to compensate them based upon the intrinsic value of jobs. In this instance, the latter would be established by the comparison of one female-dominated job to another, more highly paid job predominantly held by males. Some economists theorize that upward pay adjustments of this type attempt to "trick the market," which is very difficult to accomplish because labor markets are governed by inexorable forces (Ehrenberg and Smith, 1988).

The difficulties economists see with the concept of comparable job worth in the "naturalistic" contexts of labor markets can even be illustrated by an example in which gender does not enter. Consider the labor-market dynamics for college professors in the fields of computer science (CS) and English, irrespective of gender. Let us suppose that at the same point in time, the demand and supply curves for both are initially at the same level. The same single-rate wage prevails in the labor market for the CS professor and the English professor, both are being hired, and both are of equal quality in educational preparation (input) and performance (output). As so described, the employment situation of these professors theoretically embodies comparable job worth. Both types of professors require the same amount of training or education (represented by the receipt of the Ph.D. degree), and both are required to engage in the same activities, namely, teaching and research. Unless we would be willing to assign different values to the teaching and research produced in different academic fields (or increase the theoretical value of the CS job because the greater transferability of computer science skills would allow the computer specialist to more readily find alternative employment in industry), we could probably agree the two jobs are of comparable worth to the college employer. Thus, if the two jobs are equal in the ways mentioned, equal pay would be justified according to the concept of comparable job worth.

Let us assume time passes and the demand for CS professors rises as a result of the increasing numbers of students who want to take CS courses. Simultaneously, the demand for English professors falls because fewer students desire to take elective courses in

English. At the old equilibrium wage rate there is an excess demand for CS professors and an excess supply of English professors.

How should the college respond? It can let the labor markets work naturalistically by allowing the salary of CS professors to rise significantly and that of English professors to fall. As a result, the number of CS professors employed would increase, and the employment of English professors would decline.

Another possibility is for the college to maintain the pay of the two groups of professors at the old wage level. The college could respond to the excess demand for CS professors and the excess supply of English professors by lowering hiring standards for the former and raising them for the latter. In theory, because the average quality of English professors would then exceed the quality of CS professors, the wages paid per "quality-unit" would now be higher for the computer scientists. Therefore, true comparable worth— equal pay for equal-quality employees performing comparable jobs—would not be achieved. Also, in this situation, professional employment levels and the array of course offerings would not be altered to meet changing student demands. The college would, in effect, be failing to meet students' needs.

Still another response by the college would be to significantly raise the pay level of all professors. Although this would not eliminate the shortage of CS professors, it would theoretically exacerbate the excess supply of English professors. The college could react to this by drastically reducing the employment of English professors and reducing course offerings in that subject. The excess supply again would permit the college to raise hiring standards for English professors so that their average quality would rise anew. The result of all this would render the wage per quality-unit of English professors less than that of CS professors, thereby again preventing the achievement of comparable job worth.

According to Ehrenberg and Smith (1988), the message one takes away from this example of the changing pay of CS and English professors is that it is difficult to "trick the market." When faced with changing relative demands in the labor market, either pay differentials for the two types of professors must be allowed to increase or quality differentials will arise. In neither case is comparable job worth achieved. The value of a job cannot be

determined independently of market conditions, and comparable
job worth is to be deplored because it theoretically interferes with
the way labor markets naturalistically function. It is a trick—
possibly a deception—or even a ruse. Certainly, it is unnatural.

Economists have also used regression analysis in attempting
to winnow out the extent that sex discrimination affects pay levels,
and I turn to this next, first explaining what regression is and then
how it applies. (The appendix provides more information on the
role of regression analysis in the evaluation of pay equity.)

Regression Analysis

The degree of relationship between any two variables, such as a
predictor and criterion, is the extent to which they vary together (or
"covary") in a systematic manner. The degree to which they are
linearly related is indicated by some measure of correlation, the
most popular of which is the Pearson Product Moment Correlation
Coefficient (r). As a measurement of relationship, r varies between
plus and minus 1.00. When r is 1.00, the two sets of scores are
perfectly and systematically related to each other. But correlation by
itself does not allow us to predict one set of scores (criterion scores)
from another set of scores (predicator scores). Regression analysis
builds upon correlation and enables us to predict the scores of
interest (Cascio, 1982).

The conceptual basis for regression analysis can be understood by considering the characteristics of a typical bivariate scatter
diagram consisting of predictor and criterion scores. Such a
"scattergram" can by inspection yield useful information about the
linearity of the predictor-criterion information. (Shortly, I present
a comparable job worth example that illustrates how this usefulness
is obtained.) When the relationship between two variables can be
described by means of an equation of the general form $y=f(x)$, which
means simply that y is a function of x, then prediction becomes
possible. Put another way, for every value of x, a value of y can be
generated by carrying out appropriate mathematical operations on
the value of x. Thus, if x is the predictor, y (the criterion) can be
predicted if we can specify the function f, which serves to relate x
and y.

The most familiar of all functional relationships is the equation for a straight line, which is commonly used in the compensation field when building a wage or salary structure by means of job evaluation. This equation is $y=a+bx$. Since r always measures only the degree of linear relationship between two variables, the interpretation of the equation describing a straight line (which is the basis for the general linear model) is called a *regression line*. The interpretation is as follows: For every unit increase in x, there is an increase in y that may be determined by multiplying x by a regression coefficient b (the slope of the straight line $\Delta y/\Delta x$, which indicates the change in y observed for a unit change in x), and adding a constant a (indicating the point at which the regression line crosses the x axis). When this type of functional relationship is plotted for all the items in a sample (such as all the male and female salaries in a number of jobs), then the result will be a straight line or linear function.

Let us turn from this simple explanation of regression analysis to an uncomplicated real-world example of how it can be applied in job evaluation to the study of comparable job worth, as was done by the state of Minnesota in 1979. The reader should gain from this an idea of how data from job evaluations can be analyzed using regression to determine whether discriminatory wage differentials may exist (Ehrenberg and Smith, 1988).

Minnesota retained the Hay Group, a prominent compensation and human resource management consulting firm, to evaluate the jobs in state government. Initially 188 positions were evaluated in which at least 10 workers were employed and which could be classified as either male- or female-dominated. Each position was evaluated by trained job evaluators and awarded a specified number of Hay plan points (called HPs) for each of the four factors included in this version of the Hay job evaluation plan: know-how, problem solving, accountability, and working conditions. The scores for each factor were then added to obtain the total HPs or job evaluation score for each job. These scores ranged from 100 to more than 800 points for the 188 jobs in the study.

Next, the salary (S_i) for each male job and its HP score (HP_i) was plotted on a scattergram. Each dot on the x axis of the scattergram shown as Figure 1 represents a male job, and this figure dis-

Figure 1. Estimated Male Comparable Job Worth Salary Equation.

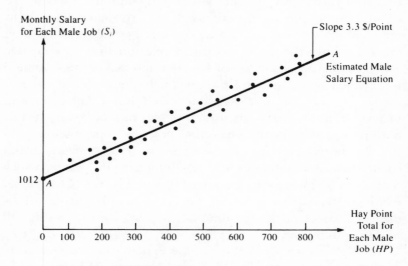

Source: From *Modern Labor Economics*, 3rd ed., Ronald G. Ehrenberg and Robert S. Smith. Copyright © 1988, 1985 by Scott, Foresman and Company. Reprinted by permission.

plays a plot of the monthly salary for each job against its *HP*s on the *y* axis. An inspection of the figure shows that for the most part jobs with higher scores receive higher pay.

The points arrayed in the figure obviously do not lie on a straight line. An infinite number of lines could be drawn through these points, but which one would fit best? Usually we choose that line for which the sum (across data points) of the squared vertical distances between the line and individual data points is minimized—what is called the least-squares line. In compensation this is known as the pay-policy line (Belcher and Atchison, 1987).

The least-squares line when applied to data for the male-dominated occupations contained in the state of Minnesota study yield the estimated line

$$S_i = 1,012 + 3.3 \; HP_i$$

Thus, if male job *i* were rated at 200 *HP*s, we would predict that the monthly salary for job *i* would be $1,012 + (3.3)(200) or $1,672.

This estimated male salary equation is shown in the figure as line
AA.

How does this illustration relate to comparable job worth?
If the value of a job could be determined solely by reference to its
job evaluation score, we would expect that, in the absence of sex-
based pay discrimination, male- and female-dominated jobs rated
equal in terms of the total *HP*s would pay equal salaries (on the
average). In other words, the same pay equation used to predict the
salaries tied to male-dominated jobs could be used to provide predictions of salaries for female-dominated jobs. Any inaccuracies in this
prediction should be completely random. Therefore, a meaningful
test of whether incumbents in female-dominated jobs are discriminated against is to examine whether the salaries they are paid are
consistently less than the salaries one would predict they should be
paid given their *HP*s and the salary equation for male jobs.

Figure 2 illustrates how this comparison can be made. In this
figure each dot represents a salary-*HP* combination for a female-
dominated job. The male job salary equation, *AA* from Figure 1,
is superimposed on this scattergram. We can readily observe that
almost all the data points lie below the male salary line. The only
logical conclusion we could draw is that female-dominated jobs are
underpaid relative to male-dominated jobs with the same number
of *HP*s. For example, point *a* in the figure marks female-dominated
job S^F_{300}, rated at 300 *HP*s. However, according to the estimated
male salary line, if job *a* were male-dominated it would be paid
S^M_{300}, considerably more money. The difference in percentages between S^M_{300} and S^F_{300} is an estimate of the comparable job worth earnings gap—the extent of the underpayment for the female job. Based
on their independent analysis of the state of Minnesota's comparable
worth study *Pay Equity and Public Employment,* Ehrenberg and
Smith (1988), to whom I am indebted for this example, report that
the average comparable job worth earnings gap across all the female
occupations in Minnesota was more than 16 percent.

A simple regression analysis of the type presented above is
very useful illustratively. However, it does not go deeply enough
into the issues, such as whether the job evaluation method used is
reliable or sex-biased in some nonobvious way, whether salaries and
*HP*s are related in a nonlinear way, whether the composition of any

Figure 2. Using the Estimated Male Comparable Job Worth Salary
Equations to Estimate the Extent of Underpayment of Female Jobs.

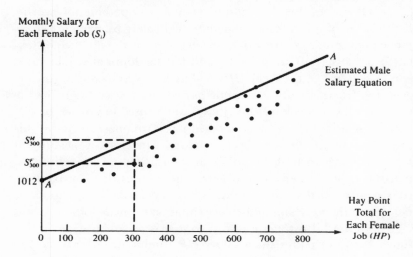

Source: From Modern Labor Economics, 3rd ed., Ronald G.
Ehrenberg and Robert S. Smith. Copyright © 1988, 1985 by Scott, Foresman
and Company. Reprinted by permission.

given total Hay point score (across the job evaluation factors called
know-how, problem solving, accountability, and working conditions) affects salaries, and whether variables other than the job
evaluation scores affect pay. Experts such as Aaron and Lougy
(1986) offer some solid and well-grounded opinion that human
capital variables and the work histories and labor force behavior
patterns of women workers definitely affect women's pay. These
factors are discussed below, but first we must consider, at least in
passing, whether multiple regression techniques can improve the
power of our analysis to winnow out the possible operation of sex
discrimination in pay.

The total variances of x and y can be large indeed. Because
there is a considerable amount of potentially predictable criterion
variance in phenomena, such as pay levels, a stronger relationship
(and, therefore, significantly more accurate prediction) is likely to
result if additional valid predictors can be found and incorporated

into the regression equations. In the real-world problems of prediction, decisions are usually made on multiple bases, not single ones. This complexity is not much of a problem conceptually because it represents only a generalization of bivariate correlation and linear regression. In the multivariate case we have one dependent (criterion) variable but more than one independent (predictor) variable. In examining multiple correlation, we consider the extent the predictors are uncorrelated (or correlated with one another), and make use of optimal b weights through the simultaneous solution of a set of linear equations. Computers can be used to carry out the necessary calculations, and any standard statistical text provides an explanation of the arcane mathematics involved (Cascio, 1982; Kerlinger and Pedhazur, 1973).

The standard statistical procedure for determining whether discrimination explains part of the male-female pay gap is to try to relate pay differences to personal or job characteristics hypothesized to influence earnings, such as job tenure, years in the labor force, or extent of education. Such unmeasured factors as luck or personality characteristics probably play a major role in everyone's economic success and career progress. But there is no reason why luck or attractive personalities should be more prevalent among men than women. Hence, we are inclined to believe that if the average pay of men with given attributes is not significantly different from the average pay of women with similar attributes, discrimination probably did not take place (Aaron and Lougy, 1986).

Yet discrimination could still have played a subtle role. Past discrimination against women in entering certain curricula or professional fields may contribute to current low earnings. Also, if women are better qualified than men on some variable omitted from the statistical analysis, then the fact that the included variables explain only the observed pay differences would suggest the presence of discrimination. Further, women's perceived employment prospects may influence decisions about childbearing and child rearing. Thus, women with relatively poor prospects in the labor market might sense correctly that they sacrifice little economically by staying home to rear children. Consequently, what appears to be a voluntary action (such as quitting a job) may be a rational accommodation to discriminatory labor markets that offer little job security or opportunity for advancement. Correspondingly, what seems to be discriminatory behavior by employers may be their rational response to behavior that they choose to use in making decisions about the hiring and promotion of women. If this train of speculation is correct, differences in pay between men and women that are statistically related to work experience or family status may to some unknown extent be explained by discrimination operating through these variables. All of this reasoning causes us to conclude that no statistical exercise or study or set of statistical studies published to date has proved definitively that any of the male-female pay gap is caused by a residual that we know for certain is discrimination (Aaron and Lougy, 1986).

Strangely, articles in the statistical, social science, and human resource management literature have continued to advocate the use of regression analysis in the investigation of sex discrimination in pay, despite the existence of a number of highly critical technical comments detailing serious problems with the regression approach. A similar phenomenon has occurred in the publications of law schools (so-called law reviews) and court opinions that have endorsed regression analysis despite a concomitant increase in the number of critiques. There is a paradox here: the use of regression analysis seems to be increasing while at the same time criticisms have become more serious and damaging. The paradox can perhaps be explained by the fact that readily available statistical packages have made it easy to apply regression analysis to pay. Meanwhile, the critiques of regression procedures are usually quite technical, requiring technical sophistication beyond that of the average user (Barrett and others, 1986).

Millions have been spent on statistical research to test the discrimination hypothesis without resolving it one way or the other. As Zellner (1979, p. 215) put it vividly a dozen years ago: "to . . . test for the existence of discrimination in the labor market by determining whether there is any wage differential left after controlling for all relevant characteristics is somewhat like trying to discover whether you left your watch in the kitchen by looking for it everywhere else first. It would be more efficient to look in the kitchen. It would be better to develop and test directly a theory of discrimination.''

Kitchen-oriented studies now exist that have suggested an alternative to the residual approach by defining discrimination as the situation whereby women need to be *more qualified* than men to receive a given wage (Finn, 1984). Roberts (1980) was the first to propose this new concept. The first economywide research using Roberts' notion found that for a given wage level the women who earned that wage had more education but less experience and less job tenure than the men employed at the same wage, a result that they interpreted as being consistent with a finding of nondiscrimination! (Kamalich and Polachek, 1982). Let us take a look at discrimination from another angle, and consider the proposition that women constitute a minority that is by definition a target of discrimination.

Women as a Minority Group

The most famous definition of a minority group is that it is a group of people who, because of their distinctive physical or cultural characteristics, are singled out for differential and unequal treatment in the society in which they live and who therefore regard themselves as the objects of collective discrimination (Wirth, 1945). Members of minority groups experience both disparate treatment and disparate impacts with respect to the material and nonmaterial culture surrounding them. The existence of a minority group in a society implies the existence of a dominant group enjoying greater power, prestige, and wealth. Minority status carries with it exclusion from full participation in the life of society. Although it is not necessarily an alien group, a minority is treated and regards itself as apart from the dominant group. From these standpoints, have women been a minority (and are they still a minority) in American society?

To understand the nature of minority status, we need to examine the objective as well as the subjective position of the persons involved. Members of a minority group are distinguishable from the dominant group by physical or cultural characteristics. If there are no such distinguishing marks, minorities blend into the rest of the population in time. They occupy a disadvantageous position in society and in contrast to the dominant group are prevented from enjoying certain economic, social, and political opportunities. These restrictions limit their freedom of choice and opportunity for self-development. The subordinate position of minority group members becomes manifest in their unequal access to educational and occupational opportunities. Also, their property rights may be restricted, and they may be deprived of the right of suffrage (Wirth, 1945).

Aside from these objective characteristics by which they are distinguished from the dominant group (and in large measure as a result of them), minorities tend to develop a set of attitudes, forms of behavior, and other subjective characteristics that further set them apart. The differential and unequal treatment—that is, the discriminations to which minority group members are subjected—causes a sense of isolation and persecution, feelings of unjust and disparate treatment and, perhaps, inferiority as well. In turn, attitudes of resignation or rebellion can develop, depending upon the length of time the minority has existed, whether their loss of rights and privileges has been negligible or severe, and the effectiveness of the social control the dominant group possesses to perpetuate the discrimination. When the sentiments and attitudes of minority group members become articulated, and when they become conscious of their deprivations and conceive of themselves as persons having rights, and when they clamor for emancipation and equality, they are likely to become a political force (Wirth, 1945).

To the individual minority group member, the most onerous circumstance is that he or she is treated as a member of a category irrespective of one's individual merits. Membership in a minority group is involuntary, and one cannot leave the group except in rare instances. Also, a minority group is not necessarily an alien group (native people are often a minority in their conquered homeland). Nor is the minority statistically determined: the people who constitute a minority may from a numerical standpoint be a majority! What matters the most about minorities are not only their objective position and the discrimination they endure, but also the corresponding patterns of behavior they develop and their self-image and attitudes toward others. The nonparticipation of minorities in the life of the larger society makes them distinguishable as a group and perpetuates their status as such (Wirth, 1945).

When the nature of the social relationship between the dominant and minority classes becomes that of exploiters and the exploited, the conflicts that arise between the two groups are those characteristic of situations of super- and subordination. The relationships become power relationships where the dominant group resorts to the sanctions of custom, law, and (possibly) force whenever persuasion, prestige, and the manipulation of economic controls do not suffice. In a secular society, such as ours, the perpetuation of a group in minority status requires the manipulation of public opinion and of economic and political power (and, if these fail, the use of various forms of harassment, possibly including physical violence). Hence, we see in sex discrimination in employment the exploitation of women by inferior pay and job assignment and unequal pay for equal work. We also see a resort by power holders to myths and stories in order to perpetuate the status quo and the use of sexual harassment and even physical abuse on occasion to reinforce discriminatory behavior patterns.

The social function of discrimination is to produce certain outcomes desired by the dominant group, namely, restriction of the power, prestige, and economic rewards of minority group members so that the dominant group has a greater share of these valued resources. Disparate treatment and impacts upon the minority group are obviously involved. Discrimination, which is objectively observable, is supported by prejudice, which is subjective. The social function of prejudice (that is, the outcome of mass prejudice by dominant group members) is to justify discrimination. In other words, we, for example, prejudge the minority group member to be unworthy of equal treatment in employment because he or she is considered inferior in work experience, occupational history, or career potential. This subjective prejudgment is carried in the mind of the member of the dominant group and applied to every encounter with a minority group member. Hence, the individual member is never seen as a person, but only as a representative of a category, which has already been prejudged as belonging in a certain inferior social place and deserving of types of unequal treatment that give superordinate power, prestige, and occupational rewards to the dominant group. In this way, prejudice opportunistically supports discrimination and becomes difficult to combat or change. Indeed, attitudes and values are very resistant to change, and the most efficacious way to combat sex discrimination is through strategies that chip away at the barriers to equality in the workplace, including equal pay for work of substantially equal value.

Prejudice begins to crumble when the stereotyped prejudgments about the minority are shown to be inaccurate and the beliefs about their inferiority, lack of qualifications, and preparation are challenged as not corresponding to reality. To combat prejudice against women in employment and the prevailing beliefs about women's pay and occupational segregation, we need to open up job placement opportunities and remove blockages to career mobility. Once the factual circumstances surrounding employment change and women enter a variety of occupations and receive pay equity, then both discrimination and prejudice will be reduced and, in time, with continued pressure aimed at breaking up stereotypes and opening up opportunities, eliminated.

In defining the term *minority group* and providing it with clear meaning, the presence of discrimination is regarded as a decisive factor. We have no evidence that a preponderance of American women have minority group feelings or consider themselves discriminated against on a group basis, although this is probably a moot point among feminists. Many American women probably do not feel themselves as objects of collective discrimination or members of a minority. Can it be argued then that women have a minority group status in our society? The answer depends on the values of the observer, whether that be a woman within or a man outside the group. A contingent answer would be true in the case of any group of persons who, on the basis of putative differential characteristics, are denied access to power, prestige, and economic rewards. If we assume that there are no differences attributable to sex membership as such that would justify placing men and women in different statuses and roles, it can easily be shown that women have constituted a minority group in America (Hacker, 1951).

Formal discrimination against women is widely recognized and takes a number of forms of unequal treatment. Historically and analogically, there are many parallels between positions and feelings toward blacks and women in American society. In the seventeenth century the legal status of black servants was borrowed from that of women and children, who were under the *patria potestas*. In fact, until the Civil War there was considerable cooperation between the abolitionist and woman suffrage movements. As Myrdal (1944) points out in his classic study of blacks in America, the problems of both women and blacks are partly the result of the transition from a preindustrial paternalistic way of life (1620–1800) to an individualistic industrial society since then (also see Hacker, 1951). There is good reason, in short, to regard American women objectively as a minority (moving increasingly perhaps into the mainstream and having greater access to power, prestige, and economic rewards than in the past), even though the preponderance of women might not see themselves subjectively as a minority.

The Women's Movement and Feminism

The idea that women should function in the economy and community as the equals of men has roots as far back as Plato's *Republic*. In the years between then and now, writers such as Mary Wollstonecraft and activists such as Susan B. Anthony and Elizabeth Cady Stanton led the fight for women's rights. Toward the end of the nineteenth century advocates of feminism concentrated on gaining the right to vote for women, which was achieved in 1920 in the United States and in 1928 in the United Kingdom. After suffrage was obtained, the movement for women's equality languished until after World War II, when Simone de Beauvoir published the *Second Sex* (1949) in France and Betty Friedan published the *Feminine Mystique* (1963) in the United States. DeBeauvoir's book spells out the customs, assumptions, educational practices, laws, literature, modes of speech, and jokes that teach girls and women that they are inferior and limited beings (in effect a minority) and that are intended to convince females to accept the places in the economy and society set aside for women only. Friedan's book excoriated the occupation of housewife with all its limitations and nineteenth-century endorsements as the only desirable career for women (also see Bergmann, 1986).

Modern feminism evolved thereafter as a political ideology that argues that men and women should have equal roles in society and that women have been denied support within the home and access to the marketplace because of discrimination and inadequate social institutions. The women's movement or feminist movement that emerged in the late 1960s pressed demands to ensure women's equality. This protest movement evolved into an organized, sophisticated political lobby, which initiates legislation and litigation and supports electoral campaigns on behalf of women's rights. These efforts have helped women define their interests, have the confidence to articulate them, and then seek attention for them in the public realm. They pushed forward the Equal Rights Amendment to the U.S. Constitution in 1972; this passed the Congress in 1972 but failed to be ratified in a majority of state legislatures. Feminists have since then been very active in the political arena to deliver the women's vote in order to elect desired candidates to public office (Klein, 1984).

A political movement, such as the women's movement, is an expression of widely shared grievances by people who have a consciousness of kind. They become subjectively a minority and see much objective evidence of discrimination. People often turn to political action when they feel that government has some respon- sibility to remedy the problems they perceive or experience. Most hopes and fears never gain a political voice, though, because people regard their problems as personal and look to themselves, their families, or their friends for solutions and not to politics, political action, and government authorities. Moreover, living under conditions that limit power, prestige, and economic rewards and being a member of a minority group do not lead inevitably to political unrest. It seems that only when people believe these problems are shared by other people like them, the group, can they attribute the source of their concerns to social conditions, such as discrimination, and look to political solutions.

Over the centuries most men and women have probably not perceived women as a minority group. Instead, women's primary affiliations have been familial, ethnic, or religious, but not gender-based. Women first needed to recognize that they were subject to differential and unequal treatment in the form of discrimination buttressed by prejudice before it became possible for a feminist movement to emerge. Women also had to surmount the inclination to think that a personal problem could be solved by working harder. They had to translate the solution into political demands, which is the stage we now appear to be at in the United States (Klein, 1984). The comparable job worth movement could be interpreted as a part of (or at least consistent with) the feminist movement and ideology. Certainly, a good part of the energy behind the lawsuits and state activities underway to pinpoint pay discrimination in public employment has been provided by the feminist movement in America today. New prejudice about women's liberation and the women in the vanguard of it has emerged for the purposes of minimizing the importance of the movement and protecting the male-dominated strongholds against entry by women. There is no reason to believe that this resistance will be effective against the inexorable change that is underway, however. Policy-level executives, line and staff managers, and human resource specialists should take action to dispel these old and new prejudices and prepare the way for removing the remaining vestiges of discrimination, especially with respect to pay matters and job evaluation.

Economic Discrimination and "Crowding"

From an economic standpoint, women working in organizations are subject to a vicious circle. They are subjected to discrimination that is not merely attributable to individual errant employers who generally prefer to pay men more than women. As we have seen, this discrimination is most likely caused by sex-segregated labor markets that confine women to a limited number of low-paying jobs. Women are proportionately overrepresented (by comparison to their overall percentage in the labor force) in clerical and service occupations. For example, according to the last U.S. Census (1980), women constituted 44 percent of all workers but filled 81 percent of clerical, 97 percent of private household, and 61 percent of other service occupations. Women were found in professional (46 percent) and sales (49 percent) jobs in approximate proportion to their overall representation in the labor force. They were underrepresented in managerial occupations (28 percent) and among operatives or people who operate equipment or machines (about 34 percent), and greatly underrepresented in crafts (6.3 percent), laboring (11 percent), and farming (17 percent) occupations (Bianchi and Spain, 1984). The overconcentration of women in certain fields is further exemplified by the ghettoization of women in professions like elementary and high school teaching, social work, nursing, library employment, and so on.

All this occupational segregation creates crowding and controls a woman's initial job assignment. The first job assignment, in turn, determines promotional opportunities and perpetuates occupational segregation. "Crowding" (or women's impact on an occupation) intensifies job segregation, reduces wages, and contributes to unemployment. All of these interrelated phenomena bring about pay discrimination and the underevaluation of women's work. Once it is perpetuated, the effect is to assign women to poor-paying and dead-end jobs. Moreover, the job segregation is likely to continue if large pay differentials are allowed to persist between female- and male-dominated occupations. Such monetary differentials discourage men from entering female-dominated jobs. Also, under prevailing circumstances, women who attempt to enter male-dominated jobs meet with hostility from men that is caused, in part, by the belief that a woman is replacing a man to whom the job rightfully belongs (almost as a kind of property ownership). If employers compensated both male- and female-dominated jobs on the basis of comparable worth, there would arguably be less impetus for males to seek traditional male jobs and less hostility toward women seeking the same jobs. Therefore, at least in theory, a policy of comparable job worth actually fosters job integration and may be more successful than a policy of equal employment opportunity standing alone (Gasaway, 1981).

Unless an organization takes deliberate action to regulate its internal labor market and human resource management policies, it will be implicitly countenancing crowding. This happens because the internal labor market of a company will generate its own formal and informal rules of operation for defining who will move up beyond entry-level jobs. In most large organizations promotional opportunities depend on the job an employee has. For some jobs, extensive promotional ladders involve the possibility of moving up a long series of positions. But other jobs have either short promotional ladders or are dead-end. Typically male-dominated occupations tend to have longer ladders than female-dominated fields. Often some of the male job ladders extend to top management; almost never do female job ladders extend to the top corporate echelon. Also, even if a woman has a job of the type from which men can be promoted up the ladder, the rules of the internal labor market of her employer may slam the door on her upward mobility (Bergmann, 1986).

Crowding and the ghettoization of jobs have the effect from the human resource management standpoint of blocking the expression of aptitudes and talents, especially of women. Some people thus have careers in work they dislike when a chance to compete for jobs of their choice should and could have been open to them. Put another way, the system of occupational sex segregation reinforces and controls the female subordination it by its nature has created. Possibly, productivity considerations valued by management have an important part in the generation and maintenance of occupational sex segregation. Thus, it is sometimes argued that if corporations and other organizations decided to desegregate their "men's jobs" and "women's jobs," there might be short-term losses in productivity. In the long run, though, desegregation should improve productivity because sex-blind policies on the utilization of human talent would cut out the dysfunctions of crowding and ghettoization (Bergmann, 1986). Human resources would be sifted, sorted, and distributed into jobs in an optimum way, not a way governed by prejudice and discrimination.

Comparable Job Worth as Foremost a Moral Issue

Equal employment opportunity and affirmative action are not long-run, automatic, self-enforcing solutions to all gender discrimination and pay equity problems. Moral issues are of central importance in solving the problem of sex discrimination in pay even though many people would like to keep them out of the comparable job worth challenge. Let us elaborate.

There are three motives for the advocacy of social change in management and in society at large that ought to be considered. First, there is self-interest, which rests on John Stuart Mill's (1965) assumption that human beings are rational actors who seek to maximize the accomplishment of their own goals and interests, especially including the economic. Corporate management is often portrayed as opposing comparable job worth because it conflicts with the advancement of its interests and may indeed be so costly as to be downright uneconomic. Earlier in the chapter we sketched this fear. Second, there is the motivation that grows out of group consciousness, as was explained many years ago by both Karl Marx (1963) and Max Weber (1958), who emphasized group solidarity as a belief that shapes action. The contemporary feminist movement has become infinitely stronger, has taken action in the political power arena, and looks very much like a permanent driving force for desegregation, the removal of prejudice, and pay equity for women. Third is ideology, which, as a concept, rests on Emile Durkheim's (1933) notion of a universal moral order that leads people to protect rights rather than their own individual interests or the concerns of their group. (For additional discussion of these points, see Klein, 1984.)

Comparable job worth from these standpoints is an ideological and moral issue. The subtle values guiding how jobs are constructed, designed, and evaluated must be brought out and challenged to determine if pay is equitable. Management, as the corporate and employment gatekeeper, must take the initiative to root out and assess how pay equity values impact upon or are impacted by an organization's culture. Data may show that pay equity exists and that a system maintenance rather than a change strategy is needed. Data may show that pay inequity exists and suggest that a decision is needed about change or retaining the status quo. A decision to perpetuate a discriminatory status quo is dangerous, unlawful, and immoral. Also, management must interpret the meaning of levels of pay for jobs in its organization for which there is information from the relevant labor markets. Policy decisions are required by management to meet the market on a high, low, or average wage level and in dealing with gender-driven rates in female- and male-dominated occupations. Such policy decisions can be deferred pending a fact-gathering study but cannot and should not be postponed indefinitely. These policy decisions are ultimately value decisions and, thus, moral issues that might collide with the logic of profit making, business necessity, and the like; but they should be confronted.

Traditionally, government has been expected to provide role models for the right way to deal with people and handle human resource management. However, today private industry is challenged and is feeling many pressures to achieve pay equity for men and women. Many firms have taken a defensive posture and point out that comparable job worth is not the law of the land, which may be technically correct depending upon which definition of comparable job worth is used. Simultaneously, many pacesetting firms have stepped up to the challenge and are quietly taking action to achieve pay equity. The sudden, forced, insensitive, government-mandated compliance with pay equity arbitrarily defined at some future date is greatly feared. A comprehensive examination of the comparable job worth challenge as set forth in this book should point the way to reasonable solutions that management can ideologically support, morally endorse, and administratively apply.

2

Legal Issues
in Pay Equity

The 1960s were watershed years for socioeconomic change in the United States, and management still has considerable indigestion from coping with the implementation of the human resource legislation of that era. Thus the 1960s are a logical modern reference point for unfolding the beginnings of the challenge of comparable job worth. During this time Congress considered 884 bills concerned with women's issues and passed only ten of them. However, two of these were landmark pieces of legislation ensuring equal pay and employment opportunities. The Equal Pay Act (EPA)—an amendment to the Fair Labor Standards Act (FLSA) of 1938—was passed in 1963. A year later Title VII, which prohibits sex discrimination in employment, among other things, was included in the Civil Rights Act (Klein, 1984).

By 1966 the National Commission on the Status of Women completed its report and recommended twenty-four areas for combating sex discrimination. Women were starting to file complaints about unlawful pay practices under the Equal Pay Act. Because of the failure of state commissions on the status of women to address these issues, a number of women in those agencies met to found the National Organization for Women (NOW) in 1966. According to Betty Friedan, a founder, the goal of NOW was to take action to bring women into the mainstream of American society *now*. Since then, NOW and many other feminist groups have led the movement for the extirpation of sex discrimination and the enactment of the Equal Rights Amendment to the U.S. Constitution. As a result of this new public concern about equality and justice for women, which is the product of a subculture of feminism and the acute sense of discrimination experienced by many women, more women's rights legislation has since been passed and more women have been elected and appointed to public office than at any other time in American history (Klein, 1984). The same may be said of women's progress in industry, though we should recall from Chapter One that this admission in no way suggests that the open society of free mobility and equality for everyone, especially women, has yet been achieved in the United States. But the crucial years between 1963 and 1988 represent progress that outstripped any prior period for which policy-level executives, line and staff managers, and human resource specialists had to deal in combating prejudice and discrimination in the workplace.

The crucial years rested on two prior decades of federal and state activities lumped under the banner of "fair employment practices" and Fair Employment Practice Committee (FEPC) activities. Many younger managers are not aware that every U.S. president from Franklin Delano Roosevelt to Lyndon B. Johnson took some kind of action in the fair employment practices area before there were generally applicable statutes on equal pay and civil rights in employment on the books. The antidiscrimination struggle had actually begun centuries before, of course, when the American creed of equal opportunity stumbled over the economic factor in its application. However, it was only in the years from 1941 to 1946 that the federal government, through the FEPC, actively assumed the role of judge and tried workers and employers for conspiring to deny equal opportunity to minority group workers in war plants and government service (Ross, 1948). Sex discrimination was not a part of this early FEPC effort covered under a presidential executive order, though.

The significant fact about the old federal FEPC was its existence rather than its accomplishments. It was unpopular with Congress and a repeated target for budget cuts. Its existence encouraged a number of states to enact "little" FEPC laws. Thus, the variety of weapons now in the arsenal of those waging legal

battles against discrimination evolved from an inauspicious patch-
work quilt background. The statutes that were to jell in the 1960s
were enacted after many failures to get federal laws passed in the late
1940s and throughout the 1950s. The new laws borrow heavily from
nonlinear unrelated statutes in regard to coverage and techniques
of enforcement. The provisions covering prescribed misconduct
have no counterparts in other earlier protective labor legislation.
Clearly, a great deal of judicial interpretation has taken place and
will continue to be needed before line and staff manager, policy-
level executives, and human resource managers acquire that
certainty of meaning essential to evenhanded enforcement of the
pertinent law (Murphy, Getman, and Jones, 1979). Let us turn next
to a close examination of the two most important laws affecting sex
discrimination in pay and the highlights of the resulting litigation.

Equal Pay Act of 1963

Although the Truman, Eisenhower, and Kennedy administrations
gave pay equity their support, Congress, as indicated previously,
took nearly twenty years to resolve its disagreements over the policy.
In 1962 the first bills taken up by the U.S. House of Representatives
and the views of the key Kennedy administration officials were to
require equal pay for work that was *comparable* by using existing
job evaluation techniques. Many unions and women's groups
supported this notion. Organized employers opposed the idea of
comparability. Now—more than a quarter of a century later—we
still see this same lineup of proponents and opponents, except the
federal government does not espouse comparable job worth,
although individual bureaucrats might unofficially support it. A
suggestion to supplant "comparable" with "equal" pay in the
legislation of the early 1960s appealed to many members of
Congress and facilitated passage of the law in 1963. However, this
was in many ways a Pyrrhic victory, because the fact that the scope
of the act was limited to women covered by the FLSA meant that
only about one-half of all working women were blanketed in
(Hutner, 1986). In 1972 amendments were enacted (under a law that
on its face had another purpose, the Educational Amendments of
1972) which expanded the EPA to include for equal pay purposes

all the executive, administrative, professional employees, and outside salespersons covered under the FLSA. These 1972 amendments meant the EPA was to cover all employees of all private and public educational institutions at all levels—preschool, elementary, and secondary schools—and all institutions of higher education (Jongeward and Scott, 1973). Owing to the large number of women employed in education, it was obvious that the amendments would have great impact on the pay of these professional women, mainly teachers, counselors, and others employed in schools.

The Equal Pay Act [29 U.S.C.A., Section 206(d)] prohibits sex discrimination in pay. No employer may discriminate between the sexes in the matter of pay where both men and women are engaged in equal work on jobs that require equal skill, effort, and responsibility and that are performed under similar working conditions. All four tests (skill, effort, responsibility, and working conditions) must be met in order for the equal pay standard to apply. The courts have ruled that the jobs in an establishment do not have to be "identical" but only "substantially equal" for an EPA comparison to be made. Employers have the full right to make distinctions in pay when it is done pursuant to a bona fide seniority system that treats men and women equally, or a merit system equally applied, or a system that measures earnings by the quantity or quality of production (such as a piecework pay plan). There can be wage differentials, but they must be based on bona fide occupational qualifications except sex (Jongeward and Scott, 1973). The EPA applies to labor organizations, unions, and employee representation committees or plans.

The remedies for sex discrimination found under the EPA are numerous and are the same as those under the FLSA. First, the pay requirements must be met. If the minimum wage or overtime compensation has not been paid, restitution must be made retroactively as well for the future. Employers are liable for liquidated damages, and back pay must be paid as required. Pay rates can never be equalized by reducing the wages of the sex receiving the higher pay. Instead, the compensation of the lower-paid sex must be raised to the higher level. In EPA cases the court, in addition to any judgments awarded to the plaintiff or plaintiffs, may allow a reasonable attorney's fee to be paid by the defendant as well as costs of the actions (Friedman and Strickler, 1987).

The EPA has benefited working women in cases where it has discouraged or eliminated pay inequity for equal work, and it has pumped billions of dollars into the paychecks of primarily lower-income women, to whom increases of 12 or 15 cents per hour were very meaningful. For the many women not doing "equal work," or those in traditionally sex-segregated jobs, or those ghettoized into such jobs by employers who saw advantages in sequestering the jobs of female employees to avoid equal work situations, the results of the EPA have not been thrilling. Needless to say, the EPA has fallen far short of what the comparable job worth proponents advocated in the early 1960s, and they look back wistfully (if not angrily) to the comparable worth notion rather than feel comfortable with the equal worth doctrine (Hutner, 1986).

Civil Rights Act of 1964, Title VII

The initial goal of the Civil Rights Act was to stop discrimination against blacks, not to fill in the gaps in coverage of the EPA. We usually think of this act in terms of the crusade against racial injustice led by Martin Luther King, Jr., A. Philip Randolph, and Clarence Mitchell, and not as a law spearheaded by feminists. In fact, the U.S. House of Representatives did not include the prohibition of sex discrimination in Title VII until almost the end of floor debate on the bill, and it was then inserted more as an accidental result of political maneuvering by white supremacists than as a concrete expression of Congressional intent to bring equal job opportunities to women. Some opponents of the Civil Rights Act added sex to such bases for discrimination as race, color, religion, and national origin in the hope that it might jeopardize passage of the bill! But the House passed the bill and it went to the floor of the Senate. There various senators raised concerns about the relationship between the sex discrimination provisions of Title VII and those of the EPA. Senator Wallace Bennett advanced an amendment to resolve this matter. He proposed that an employer may differentiate on the basis of sex in determining pay if the differentiation was authorized by the EPA. The amendment created ambiguity: Limiting sex discrimination in pay under Title VII to EPA standards made it impossible to claim sex discrimination for comparable but not equal work. Men were protected by Title VII from discrimination in pay because of race, religion, color, or national origin *and were not held to equal work standards.* Would the courts decide that the standard for women workers should be more restrictive than for men? As strange as it might seem, when case law developed in this area, the courts came down with answers on both sides of the question. Finally, in 1981 the U.S. Supreme Court decided the significant case of *Gunther v. County of Washington* by ruling that claims of sex discrimination in compensation were not limited to equal work situations. The decision did not directly address and settle the comparable job worth issue, but it has left the door open a wide crack or more (Hutner, 1986). If hope springs eternal, the *Gunther* case (and a few more recent ones) offers comfort that the issue of comparable job worth will live on and may become the law of the land when a case with the right fact pattern comes to a rapidly changing U.S. Supreme Court. It may be just a matter of time before the Supreme Court chooses to read the evidence in a way favorable to feminists, organized labor, civil rights groups, a segment of academia, state governments that are already at work in implementing pay equity, and industrial firms that are quietly but effectively imitating the pay equity activities of state governments.

Turning back to the content of Title VII as it originated and evolved, we need to be aware that of the legislation enacted by Congress to promote the goal of equal employment opportunity, none has been the basis for more litigation or the subject of more intense and wide-ranging judicial and academic scrutiny than the Civil Rights Act of 1964 [42 U.S.C., Sections 1971, 1975a-d, 2000a *et seq.*], as amended by the Equal Employment Opportunity Act of 1972 [42 U.S.C., Section 2000e *et seq.*]. The explosion of litigation that ensued from the enactment of Title VII can be traced in part to the expansive language that Congress used to define the classes of persons and employment-related decisions subject to the CRA's substantive proscriptions. Title VII prohibits employers with more than fifteen employees, unions, and employment agencies from discriminating with respect to a number of employment-related practices on the basis of five specifically enumerated classifications: race, color, religion, national origin, and sex. The unlawful employment practices are for an employer: (1) to fail or refuse to hire or to discharge an individual, or otherwise to discriminate against any person, about that individual's compensation, terms, conditions, or privileges of employment; or (2) to limit, segregate, or classify employees or applicants for employment in any way that would deprive or tend to deprive any person of employment opportunities or otherwise adversely affect the individual's status as an employer. The CRA also created the Equal Employment Opportunity Commission (EEOC), a five-member, presidentially appointed agency, to administer and interpret its provisions (Friedman and Strickler, 1987).

The EPA and Title VII duplicate each other in some respects, and courts frequently acknowledge their interrelatedness, although there has been no necessary consistency in interpreting the relationship. While Title VII covers a broader range of discriminatory wage practices based on sex, such as different rates of pay for work of comparable value, any violation of the EPA is *pari passu* also a violation of Title VII (Murphy, Getman, and Jones, 1979). Title VII forbids an employer to discriminate between men and women with reference to hiring, discharge, and compensation, and with reference to terms, conditions, or privileges of employment. The EPA pertains only to sex discrimination in pay. Under Title VII employees may not be segregated or classified in any way that would tend to deprive a woman (or a man) of employment opportunities because of sex. Employment agencies may not refuse to refer for employment or in any way classify referrals based on sex. Labor organizations may not exclude from membership or classify, segregate, or refuse to refer any individual for employment because of sex. Conditions of employment in which it is unlawful to discriminate include (but are not limited to) job assignment, layoff and recall, promotions, training, medical and insurance coverage, vacations, and overtime assignment (Jongeward and Scott, 1973).

The Pregnancy Disability Act of 1978, which is an amendment to the CRA, requires employers to treat disabilities arising from pregnancy and birth as they treat other disabilities. The Retirement Equity Act of 1983 now provides that male and female employees who make the same contributions to a retirement plan should receive equal pension benefits. Previously, pensions provided retired women were often actuarially reduced to reflect the statistical reality of females' greater longevity and the possibility that they would draw pensions longer than retired males of the same age. Taken together, the CRA and other laws on pregnancy restriction and retirement pay equalization, as well as cases concerned with equalizing sick leave for men and pregnancy leaves for women, lead us to believe that the main legal drift is toward equality of treatment for male and female employees and retirees across the board.

As with the EPA, there is one general exception to the ban on sex discrimination in the CRA, and that is in instances where a different treatment of the sexes is based upon a bona fide occupational qualification (known as a BFOQ). The latter means that a sex-based characteristic is necessary for performance of the job. BFOQs are typically interpreted very narrowly and never include race, although they may in rare instances be based on sex (Jongeward and Scott, 1973). The effect of Title VII has swept away all the state protective labor legislation restricting the hours and types of work in which women may be employed. Thus, we have seen the official end of "statistical discrimination" as a result of Title VII. Employers could no longer use facts or suppositions about women's average or general ability regarding, for example, weight lifting to keep them out of a job (that is, engage in "statistical discrimination"). Hitherto under protective labor laws women were penalized as a statistical group from working or filling a job for which they were in some instances individually qualified (Bergmann, 1986).

The CRA set up the EEOC in 1964 to receive and investigate complaints of discrimination, attempt reconciliation, and, if warranted, bring lawsuits against employers. The EEOC also issues guidelines concerning the legality under Title VII of a wide range of personnel practices. The EPA is administered by the EEOC (although this has been true only since 1978). Title VII presently covers private employers with fifteen or more employees. It allows suits by individuals and suits on behalf of classes of people. Judges can order employers to hire, promote, or reinstate persons whom they have found have suffered discrimination, can order that pay be changed, and can make back pay awards. Judges in Title VII lawsuits can also require the losing party to pay the attorney's fees of the other side (Bergmann, 1986). In both EPA and Title VII cases, U.S. District Court judges hear and decide the cases. There is no use made of juries.

Very often sex discrimination lawsuits pertaining to pay brought against an employer involve both the EPA and Title VII. One reasons for this is, of course, the broader scope of Title VII than the EPA. Second, these lawsuits seem often to involve a "let's throw the book at 'em" attitude. The range of issues may transcend unfair pay and include other human resource management policy problems that fall under the broad umbrella of Title VII. Third, there are sex discrimination lawsuits that may not be strongly founded from a legal standpoint but that are moved forward because they can signal to the managerial defendant that the plaintiffs are hostile and angry with management. For example, if the basic labor-management relationship in a unionized setting is extremely conflicted, antipathies toward management can be communicated by clogging the grievance procedure with unmeritorious complaints, sabotage (especially of the implicit type), and EPA and Title VII claims.

Executive Orders 11246 and 11375 and Order No. 4

The full gamut of sources of help to women experiencing job discrimination because of sex requires mentioning certain executive orders. Since these orders are not pertinent in any important way in the comparable job worth challenge to management, only some overall comments are made in this book.

Executive Order 11246, issued by President Lyndon B. Johnson in 1965, forbade discrimination in employment against minorities. Executive Order 11375 of 1968 included a ban on sex-based discrimination. The federal government has imposed nondiscrimination and affirmative action obligations on its contractors and their subcontractors with respect to race, color, religion, national origin, and sex. These dual obligations are contained within an equal opportunity clause that the orders, as amended, require all federal agencies to include in their contracts with private employers. The Secretary of Labor (not the EEOC) administers and enforces the provisions of the executive orders and has authority to promulgate rules and regulations considered necessary to achieve their purposes. The Secretary of Labor has delegated the responsibilities for carrying out the work under the relevant executive orders to the Office of Federal Contract Compliance Programs (OFCCP).

The Department of Labor's Revised Order No. 4, which applies to nonconstruction contractors, explains how affirmative action programs operate and how compliance is secured. The Order also covers goals and timetables for the employment of women and minorities (Jongeward and Scott, 1973; Friedman and Strickler, 1987).

It is interesting to note historically that FEPC concepts were initially moved forward into implementation by a Presidential Executive Order. This particular mechanism remains potent in the 1980s and is seen in how the OFCCP combines with the statutorily established EEOC to attack sex and other forms of discrimination in everything from large-scale to tiny business organizations today.

Overview of Leading Cases

It is proper here to turn to an overview of the most important cases litigated to date. The reader is cautioned that the highlights of cases provided next are far from a detailed, rigorous, legalistic review. Most operating and policy-level managers can benefit from gaining a feel for legal directions in pay equity cases but do not need (and probably would not like to read) an overly zealous legal review. The real-world richness of the cases and facts carry important public policy messages. Human resource management specialists and others who wish to dig more deeply will find the references covered next to be useful stopping points on a road map, the details of which will become clearer through a listing and sequencing of the cases.

The EPA and CRA are important to keep fresh in mind when reviewing case law because these two statutes are compelling within the states and among the states. No state may maintain or enact legislation that contravenes federal law. Thus, while litigation addressed to pay equity, discrimination in employment, or comparable job worth is usually brought against intrastate employers, it is most often heard in federal courts. However, the U.S. Supreme Court has agreed to hear only a very few of these cases considering the importance of the subject, leaving often contradictory lower court decisions to stand on their merits (Majeske, 1985). In this way many managers have been left befuddled by the mixed signals on comparable job worth.

The first pay equity case of considerable magnitude was filed in 1970 by the then-titled International Union of Electrical, Radio, and Machine Workers (IUE), *Rinehart v. Westinghouse Electric Corporation* [631 F.2d 1094 (3rd Cir.), *cert. denied,* 452 U.S. 967 (1981)] in the Ohio District Court. The District Court in Trenton, New Jersey, had ruled against the IUE on the grounds that the Bennett Amendment to Title VII restricted sex-based pay discrimination claims to cases where women were performing substantially the same work as men. The women in the Westinghouse lamp plant at Trenton did not claim they were doing equal work. Westinghouse had maintained sex-segregated jobs under a classification system developed in the 1930s but revised in 1965. At the time of the revision, and when sex segregation on the job was no longer lawful, Westinghouse merged the two labor grade systems, male and female, into one system that was not designated by gender. The previously sex-separated jobs were seen to be equal according to the corporation's relevant job evaluation plan. Westinghouse created additional (and lower) labor grades, separated the male and female jobs that were rated equally, and set the wage rates lower for the female-dominated jobs. The company had challenged the IUE's lawsuit on jurisdictional grounds and won at the District Court level. The Third Circuit Court of Appeals resolved the jurisdictional challenge in favor of the plaintiffs and denied the case *certiorari,* returning it to the District Court for continuance. The case was eventually settled out of court and provided for upgrading some 85 female employees and a back pay fund of $75,000 for about 600 employed at the plant from 1972 to the settlement date in January 1982. By December of 1982, Westinghouse had closed the plant, and the lamp division of which it was part was sold to North

American Philips, a unit of a well-known Dutch company (Majeske, 1985; Hutner, 1986).

Both the IUE and Westinghouse asked the U.S. Supreme Court to review the Circuit Court Decision by filing petitions for a writ of *certiorari*, a most unusual step. However, the Supreme Court decided that the *Gunther* case (discussed in detail below) was a better case for it to consider. In any event, though there was no court ruling on the Westinghouse case because of the out-of-court settlement, the Third Circuit remand held that the plaintiffs' evidence, if sufficiently documented, constituted proof of a Title VII violation. This was the basis on which the case was returned to the lower court for continuance.

The earlier sex-based discrimination cases sought relief under a number of standards, including pay equity, comparable worth, and equal worth. Courts hearing these cases in the 1970s applied the Equal Pay Act's standard of equal pay for equal work, thereby mitigating the plaintiffs' ability to plead successfully under any other standard. However, by the close of the 1970s, U.S. Circuit Courts of Appeal were rendering or had handed down decisions no longer consistently definitive on the equal-pay-for-equal-work standard within the context of Title VII. Section 703-H (or the Bennett Amendment) stated that nothing "authorized" by the EPA would be an unlawful employment practice under Title VII. Did "authorized" mean the same thing as "not prohibited"? The pivotal issue of the late 1970s in sex discrimination hinged on the answer to that question (Majeske, 1985).

The Ninth Circuit Court of Appeals heard *Gunther v. County of Washington* [452 U.S. 161, 25 F.E.P. Cases 1521 (1981)] in 1979, which was the most significant decision involving pay equity prior to the Supreme Court's decision on the same case. The plaintiffs in this case were four women employed as jail matrons at the Washington County, Oregon, jail. They guarded inmates in the female section of the jail. Males guarded men in their section of the jail and were paid at a higher rate. In their lawsuit, the jail matrons claimed that they were paid less for work substantially equal to that done by the male jailers. Also, they alleged that even if the work was not substantially equal, the wage differential was attributable to sex discrimination. The District Court found that the jail matrons' jobs did not require substantially equal effort or responsibility compared to the jobs of the male jailers and therefore dismissed the case. On appeal the Ninth Circuit upheld the District Court and that the jail matrons could not recover under the standards of the EPA. However, the Ninth Circuit also held that the jail matrons were not precluded from suing under Title VII simply because the jobs were not substantially equal. Moreover, the Circuit Court held that the District Court should have considered evidence that a part of the pay discrepancy between the male and female jailers could be ascribed to sex discrimination (Lorber and others, 1985).

The *Gunther* case went to the Supreme Court and was decided in 1981. The single issue before the Supreme Court was whether a sex-based wage discrimination claim could be maintained under Title VII for jobs that were not substantially equal; in other words, what was at stake was the Bennett Amendment's ambiguity (which was discussed earlier). The Supreme Court held that a claim of discriminatory pay is not barred under Title VII simply because the work involved in the jobs being compared is not equal. The high tribunal thus held that "not prohibited" was not the same as "authorized." Under Title VII the jail matrons had been subjected to disparate treatment and therefore discriminated against based on their sex. The high court stated that the Bennett Amendment incorporated the four affirmative standards of the EPA (namely, use of a seniority system, a merit pay system, a system for measuring the quantity or quality of production, or any factor other than sex) but *not the equal work standard of the act*. In the broadest sense, the *Gunther* decision apparently signaled that plaintiffs could now challenge pay differentials for different jobs (Majeske, 1985).

The signal was not a green light but an amber light—or possibly even a red light that appeared to be yellow. This is because the Supreme Court specifically rejected the doctrine of comparable job worth in the *Gunther* decision. In fact, the dissent to the majority opinion written by present Chief Justice William Rehnquist stated that the decision does not approve a cause of action based on a comparison of the wage rates of dissimilar jobs. Intentional sex discrimination proved by the plaintiffs in *Gunther* appears to be the crucial point in the court's decision. The jail matrons argued that their wages were deliberately depressed by the County of Washington (in Oregon) even when its pay survey of the labor market showed what they should be paid. The pay data obtained by the county plan had determined that jail matrons should be paid approximately 95 percent as much as the male jailers, but it disregarded this fact and paid the female matrons only about 70 percent as much while paying the male jailers the *full evaluated worth* of their jobs! The differential was held by the Supreme Court to be attributable to intentional sex discrimination. However, as a very astute legal observer has noted, the jail matrons had not provided direct evidence nor did the County of Washington have a formal job evaluation plan in effect at the time of the litigation (Lorber and others, 1985).

In the *Gunther* case the Supreme Court distinguished its decision from a lower Tenth Circuit Court of Appeals decision in *Lemons v. City and County of Denver* (which is discussed in more detail later but is mentioned in passing here owing to its relevancy). In the *Lemons* case, the Tenth Circuit had held that nurses employed by a public hospital who sought increased compensation based on a comparison with the pay of employees in jobs of comparable value in the same organization or community (who incidentally were tree trimmers, bookkeepers, and oilers in Denver, Colorado) could not be provided a remedy because there was not direct proof of intentional discrimination and that, indeed, the city acted in good faith (Hutner, 1986; Kurtz and Hocking, 1983). In *Gunther* the Supreme Court majority held that the lawsuit does not require a court to make its own subjective assessment of the value of the male and female jailer jobs or to attempt by statistical techniques to quantify the effect of sex discrimination on the wage rates. The high court also held in *Gunther* that it was *not* deciding in this case the precise contours of lawsuits challenging sex discrimination in compensation under Title VII (Reichenberg, 1986).

Disparate Treatment, Disparate Impact, and Business Necessity

Some clarity has actually followed from the *Gunther* decision in determining what actions constitute violations under Title VII. The two main theories of violation involve "disparate treatment" and "disparate impact." Inasmuch as these two legal theories also apply to the EPA and it is important for managers and others to understand them and their relationship to comparable job worth, before proceeding with the general drift of litigated cases we stop to explain these two theories.

Let us begin with an example of a female plaintiff who is suing an employer under the EPA and who alleges she is paid less than a male for doing substantially equal work. To meet this burden she must show that the jobs held by her and the male counterpart require substantially equal skill, effort, and responsibility and are performed under similar working conditions. Once the female plaintiff has made this initial showing of unequal pay for substantially equal work (known as a *prima facie* case), the burden shifts to the employer to show that the difference in wages is based on a seniority system, merit system, incentive system, or any factor except sex, as we have seen before several times in the book. The employer must affirmatively prove that the wage disparity is justified by one of these four defenses. However, a case brought under Title VII involves a different set of burdens.

Title VII makes it unlawful to discriminate against any member of a protected class, including women, in any term or condition of employment, including pay. Insofar as Title VII is very broad in its coverage, a substantial body of law has developed from it outside of wage discrimination. The courts have permitted two general types of employment discrimination claims under Title VII: disparate treatment and disparate impact. Under the former, a plaintiff must prove that an employer intentionally discriminated against her because of her sex. The burden is different from under an EPA claim because in EPA cases the employer's intent to discriminate need not be proved. To establish a *prima facie* case of sex discrimination under a disparate treatment theory, the plaintiff must prove facts that support an inference of intentional discrimination. This would require presenting direct or circumstantial proof of the employer's discriminatory motive. Once the plaintiff has established a *prima facie* case, the employer must articulate some legitimate, nondiscriminatory reason that justifies the practice being challenged. Unlike an EPA defense, which must be proved affirmatively by the employer, a defendant in a disparate treatment case needs only to produce some evidence that there was a legitimate basis for the employer's action. If the managerial defendant successfully rebuts the *prima facie* case, the burden shifts back to the plaintiff to prove that the employer's explanation is a pretext or alibi for discrimination. This can be done by proving that a discriminatory reason more likely motivated the employer or, alternatively, that the employer's explanation for the action taken should not be believed (Lorber and others, 1985).

Turning to the theory of disparate impact, the phenomena of interest in these cases are the employers' practices that are fair in form but discriminatory in operation. Under this theory a plaintiff must prove that a practice of the employer that is neutral on its face has a discriminatory impact on a group protected by Title VII. The burden then shifts to the employer to prove that the apparently neutral policy is justified by "business necessity" or an acceptable business reason. The plaintiff is not required to prove intent to discriminate on the part of the employer (Lorber and others, 1985).

These different standards and burdens greatly affect the success or failure of a wage discrimination action. Where a wage discrimination claim is based on an allegation of different pay for jobs that are substantially equal, the standards and burdens of the EPA apply. While theoretically a disparate treatment claim under Title VII could also be pursued even where the jobs are equal, a plaintiff would most likely want to proceed under the EPA because intentional discrimination need not be proved and the defendant's burden after a *prima facie* case is established is greater under the EPA. The central issue in litigation today is how best to proceed when the male- and female-dominated cases are *not* substantially equal in skill, effort, responsibility, and working conditions (Lorber and others, 1985). The traditional equal pay cases under the EPA have been put to rest by the doctrine of substantial equality set forth almost two decades ago in *Shultz v. Wheaton Glass Company* [421 F.2d 259 (3rd Circ. 1970), *cert. denied*, 398 U.S. 905 (1970)]. As a result, there is no need to rehash those matters in this book.

As was true with *Westinghouse* and *Gunther*, a 1979 case in Pennsylvania, *Taylor v. Charley Brothers* [25 F.E.P. Cases, 602 (W.D. Pa. 1981)], was litigated as a violation of Title VII using disparate treatment as its basis. Charley Brothers was a wholesale warehouse company supplying grocery items to retail stores. The company had divided its operation into two separate units, each segregated by sex where the work of each department was essentially the same. Female job applicants were considered for employment only in the female-dominated department, where the rate of pay was $1.70 per hour less than that of males in the other department. Prior to the lawsuit, Charley Brothers had no classification system. Job evaluations conducted subsequent to the onset of the suit demonstrated that the jobs in both departments required comparable skills and were of comparable value. The District Court in Western Pennsylvania found for the plaintiffs, ruling that the employer had violated Title VII by segregating jobs according to sex and by paying women less than men because they were women. Based on the very extensive evidence presented, the court inferred intentional discrimination on the part of the employer (Majeske, 1985).

The *Gunther* decision had not expressly ruled that intentional discrimination must be demonstrated, but it and numerous earlier cases involved allegations and factual demonstrations of purposeful discrimination based on sex. As a result, courts relying on those decisions for guidance have seemingly believed that the comparable job worth theory of recovery is not a viable cause of action unless it is based on intentional discrimination (Majeske, 1985).

Post-*Gunther* litigation has more frequently been based on the theory of disparate impact than disparate treatment. In 1980 the District Court in Georgia heard *Neeley v. Metropolitan Atlanta Rapid Transit Authority (MARTA)* [24 F.E.P. Cases 1610 (N.D. Ga. 1980)], initially an EPA claim. MARTA had a long-standing practice of hiring employees at 10 percent less than the employee's previous salary. Although this practice appeared to be basically neutral, the court ruled the procedure of using prior salaries had the effect of continuing in perpetuity the lower salary levels paid to females doing the identical work of males.

In the case of *Kouba v. Allstate Insurance Company* [691 F.2d 873 (9th Cir. 1982)], Allstate claimed that it paid its male and female sales agents different wages because it based compensation in part on an individual's prior salary. The Ninth Circuit Court of Appeals held that in order to qualify as a factor other than sex, Allstate's practice of using prior salaries must be business related and that Allstate must use the factor reasonably in light of the employer's stated purpose as well as its other practices. The Court of Appeals sent this issue back to the District Court; however, the case was settled before the lower court decided whether the business reasons set forth by Allstate reasonably explained the company's use of prior salary (Lorber and others, 1985). After remand, in *Kouba* the employer reportedly agreed to change its pay-setting method and to set up a trust fund for the affected female employees (Comptroller General of the United States, 1985).

In the District Court in Eastern Michigan in *Greenspan v. Automobile Club of Michigan* [495 F. Supp. 1300 (E.D. Mich. 1980)], the judge ruled that the company's practices had a disparate impact on females and that women were intentionally underrepresented in professional positions. This court found for both disparate treatment and disparate impact (Majeske, 1985).

Disparate impact, although it may result from seemingly neutral practices, can be rebutted when it results from business necessity or forces beyond the employer's ability to control, such as the labor market. In 1982, in *Briggs v. City of Madison* [536 F. Supp. 435 (W.D. Wisc. 1982)] the District Court accepted a variation of the equal-pay-for-similar-work theory. The plaintiffs in *Briggs* were female public health nurses employed by the city of Madison who claimed that the city engaged in sex discrimination by paying them less than male public health sanitarians. The District Court concluded that the plaintiffs had made a *prima facie* case of sex discrimination. But the plaintiffs did not prevail! The court concluded that the city of Madison rebutted the nurses' *prima facie* case by producing evidence that its wage determinations were made on the basis of the demand in the labor market for nurses and sanitarians. Under the burdens applicable to a disparate treatment analysis, the plaintiffs were then required to show that the reason advanced by the defendant for the wage differential was a pretext for sex discrimination. The court held the nurses failed to do this (Lorber and others, 1985). This "market defense" has since become widely used.

In a similar case in Oregon involving intentional discrimination tried in 1983, *Lanegan-Grimm v. Library Association of Portland* [31 F.E.P. Cases 865 (D. Ore. 1983)], the sex-segregated positions of bookmobile driver/clerk (which was held only by women) and the delivery truck driver (filled solely by men) were involved. The District Court for Oregon compared the two positions for the pertinent skill, effort, responsibility, and working conditions and concluded that the two jobs were substantially equal on each factor. Inasmuch as delivery truck drivers were paid at a higher rate than bookmobile driver/clerks, the court concluded that a female bookmobile driver had established a *prima facie* case of sex discrimination under Title VII. The only defense offered by the Library Association was that the pay differential was established by union contract. But the court rejected this defense on the grounds that unions cannot usurp an employee's statutory right to equal pay for equal work. The court held that bookmobile driver/clerks could recover on a theory of intentional discrimination as well as on a theory of equal pay for equal work. Moreover, the female plaintiff proved that the Library Association's proffered reason for the male-female pay disparity was a pretext by introducing unrebutted evidence that her supervisor had made a derogatory and sexist remark to the effect that a delivery truck driver was paid more because he was a man and the head of a household. In *Lanegan-Grimm* the District Court found intentional discrimination premised on the substantial equality of jobs plus statements that amounted to admission of sex discrimination (Lorber and others, 1985).

A number of cases involving the market defense buttressed by statistical studies to support the legal argumentation need to be reviewed in this passel of lawsuits we are summarizing so that managers can obtain an understanding of the potency of the market defense. Several of these cases concern private and public universities. The first of these is the 1981 Fifth Circuit Court hearing of *Wilkins v. University of Houston* [654 F.2d 388 (5th Cir.), *rehearing denied*, 622 F.2d 1156 (5th Cir. 1981)]. In *Wilkins* female faculty members presented evidence that the university paid male professors more than female professors even when rank, length of service, age, or academic discipline was held constant. The Circuit Court rejected the plaintiffs' claims because their statistical evidence held constant one of these factors at a time and did not take into account the fact that a number of factors operate simultaneously to influence the amount of salary a faculty member receives. The court held that market forces were a legitimate basis for salary disparities between the higher-paid and largely male technical and professional school faculties and the more prevalently female faculties in the humanities, fine arts, and social sciences (Majeske, 1985; Lorber and others, 1985).

A later case in Minnesota turned out to be more receptive toward statistical evidence presented by female faculty members in *Craik v. Minnesota State University Board* [34 F.E.P. Cases 649 (8th Cir. 1984)]. There the Eighth Circuit Court of Appeals considered evidence that was in the form of multiple regression analysis that controlled the factors such as rank, experience, college degree, and degree category. The court held that the statistical evidence, taken together with other evidence showing sex discrimination in appointments and promotions, demonstrated that salary differentials were the result of intentional discrimination. The court also concluded that the university's practice of giving market-related pay increases to traditionally all-male academic disciplines identified as scarce market areas was not a violation of Title VII (Lorber and others, 1985).

A decision in another market defense case with a different fact pattern first held in favor of the male professional plaintiff but was reversed on appeal. In *Winkes v. Brown University* [32 F.E.P. Cases 1041 (D.R.I. 1983) and No. 83-1649 (1st Cir. Oct. 26, 1984)], the university matched a female art history professor's offer from another university but did not raise Winkes' salary commensurately. The District Court rejected the university's defense of market forces because Brown offered no wage survey in evidence except the one offer it had matched. The First Circuit reversed the decision of the lower court and held that Brown could pay the female professor more than the male professor in the same department because she had received a job offer at a higher salary from another university and Brown had to match that offer in order to retain the woman's services (Majeske, 1985; Lorber and others, 1985).

In a related case, the District Court in New York in *Melani v. Board of Higher Education of the City of New York* [31 F.E.P.

Cases 648 (S.D. N.Y. 1983)] concluded on the basis of statistical evidence that the City University of New York had engaged in sex-based discrimination against its female faculty for fifteen years. The university was unable to provide evidence to legitimize its $1,600 pay differential, which the court then found to be discriminatory. The statistical analysis in the case included as many as 98 independent variables, including age, years of service, academic degree, quality of degree, and time elapsed between the completion of successive degrees. Interestingly, the court did not consider whether market demand for instructors in different disciplines might justify paying them different salaries (Lorber and others, 1985).

In view of our discussion in Chaper One of multiple regression, we should pause before proceeding and present some pertinent legal commentary on the *Melani* case from this perspective. The District Court's treatment of the statistical evidence in the case is controversial on at least three counts. First, the court concluded that when similar jobs are being compared, a regression analysis need not control for differences in job title by including variables measuring the additional qualifications specific to a particular job title or a variable for the job title themselves. Second, regression models do not have to include variables measuring post-hire publications, teaching quality, or committee or community work because these variables may be importantly affected by the employer's own actions. Third, statistical analyses do not have to control for academic department since Title VII suits need not account for every factor that conceivably might explain differences in salaries or promotions (Lorber and others, 1985). We might conclude conservatively that the types of statistical analyses and their acceptable handling remain unsettled in the eyes of courts.

Statistical and market defense issues also entered extensively into *Spaulding et al. v. University of Washington* [35 F.E.P. Cases (9th Circ. 1984)]. The nursing faculty in the *Spaulding* case claimed that the University of Washington's reliance on the market to set wages was an apparently neutral policy that had a discriminatory impact on female professors in the School of Nursing. The nursing faculty contended that their jobs were essentially equal to selected male faculty positions because both required teaching of courses, research, publication, the counseling of students, and committee work. The Circuit Court disagreed, stating that different departments placed differing emphasis on these requirements. The court stated that evidence of pay disparity between jobs that are only similar says little about discrimination. Furthermore, the court observed that nursing was considered a discipline distinct from those the plaintiffs chose for comparison. The nursing faculty had also alleged Title VII violations based on disparate treatment *and* disparate impact. In regard to disparate treatment, the court ruled that the nursing faculty had failed to provide evidence for a *prima facie* case. Discrimination was not built into the university's human resource management system. Rejecting the disparate impact claim, the court upheld the university's practice of setting wages according to market prices, stating that every employer constrained by market forces must consider market values in setting labor costs. The court noted that statistics can be exaggerated, oversimplified, or distorted to create support for a position that is not otherwise supported by the evidence. The usefulness of comparative statistics rests directly on their capacity to single out factors that convert merely different treatment into unjustified discriminatory treatment. The court favored the use of sophisticated statistics such as multivariate regression analysis and rejected the nursing faculty's statistics on the basis that they did not control for discipline, job experience, day-to-day responsibilities, and the relative value of different master's degrees (Majeske, 1985; Lorber and others, 1985).

Early Cases on the Market Defense

There have been a number of other early cases (1977–1981) that buttressed the market defense, and these should be mentioned because they were early harbingers (if not clear signs) that many judges would probably have no truck with comparable job worth in the guise of an appeal for pay equity. Four of these are summarized next. In *Christensen v. State of Iowa* [563 F.2d 353 (8th Cir. 1977)], female clerical employees of the University of Northern Iowa brought a class action lawsuit claiming that the university's practice of paying clerical workers (who were predominantly female) less than the amount it paid physical plant workers (who were mainly male) for jobs of equal value to the employer constituted disparate treatment and sex discrimination under Title VII. In 1974 the State Board of Regents had used the Hay Plan of job evaluation to establish internal equity among university jobs. The jobs with similar point values were placed in the same labor grade. The university modified its job evaluation system to provide higher starting wages for physical plant employees because the local labor market paid higher wages for those jobs. UNI thus paid physical plant employees more than clerical employees despite the equal worth of the jobs as determined by the Hay Plan. However, the District Court in Iowa rejected the plaintiffs' claim, and upon appeal the Eighth Circuit affirmed the decision of the lower court, holding that the clerical employees had failed to allege facts showing that they had been the victims of intentional discrimination. The Eighth Circuit also stated it found nothing in the text or history of Title VII suggesting that Congress intended to abrogate the law of supply and demand or requiring an employee to ignore the labor market in setting rates of pay for genuinely different work classifications (Lorber and others, 1985; Reichenberg, 1976).

The second case raising the equal worth issue was the famous *Lemons v. City and County of Denver* [620 F.2d 228 (10th Cir. 1980)], which was also a class action lawsuit by women, only this time by nurses who were employed by the city of Denver. They contended that the city's classification and pay plan discriminated against them in violation of Title VII. Under the plan, the city sought to provide like pay for like work for similar jobs in the surrounding community. The city included key job classes that were selected for use in annual community wage surveys because they could be accurately compared with non-city positions. This survey method supposedly enabled the city to achieve pay parity for its nursing employees vis-à-vis other nurses in the community. The city nurses argued that they should not be compared with other nurses in the community because historically nurses had been underpaid generally since they occupied female-dominated positions in the labor market. In a long-drawn-out and complicated case, the plaintiffs sought to have their positions compared for pay purposes to dissimilar work of equal worth to the city carried out by other municipal employees. The nurses maintained that market rates for nurses reflected a history of sex discrimination and that

Title VII prohibited the perpetuation of that discrimination. However, neither the District Court nor the Circuit Court agreed with the nurses. The latter court articulated perhaps better than in any case reviewed to date what the author labels "the judicial-can-of-worms theory of job evaluation." In brief, the Tenth Circuit stated that *Lemons* brought up a type of pay disparity that could not be remedied by Title VII. The courts cannot require the city to reassess the worth of services in each position in relation to all other jobs and achieve a new set of job relativities in total disregard of pay levels in the labor market and conditions in the community. Moreover, the Circuit Court believed the nurses were not seeking equality of opportunity in their skills as contemplated by Title VII, but instead sought to cross job description lines into areas of entirely different skills. The latter state of affairs would represent a whole new world for the courts, one which the Tenth Circuit was not likely to enter without a better, clearer signal from Congress (Reichenberg, 1986; Lorber and others, 1985; Hutner, 1986; Kurtz and Hocking, 1983).

Third, in *Gerlach v. Michigan Bell Telephone Company* [501 F. Supp. 1300 (E.D. Mich. 1980)], female engineering layout clerks filed a wage discrimination claim in which they alleged that Michigan Bell paid them less than their true value in comparison to male employees in certain field assistant craft classifications. The District Court held that an independent cause of action could not be maintained by the plaintiffs on a theory solely based upon comparable job worth and underevaluation vis-à-vis the male jobs. Also, the court observed that while the relative worth of a job might be relevant evidence under a theory of intentional discrimination, standing alone it will not help the plaintiff in a Title VII sex discrimination case nor is a court in any event authorized to evaluate the worth of jobs (Lorber and others, 1985).

Fourth, in a California case, *Plemer v. Parsons-Gilbane* [32 F.E.P. Cases 808 (D.C. Wash. 1983)], a District Court displayed in another way how the can-of-worms theory is manifest. The court repeated the refusal to interject itself into the value of relative job worth where there was no evidence provided about how the employer evaluated positions. In *Plemer* a female EEOC representative worked alongside a male EEOC officer whose earnings were

$8,700 more than the female plaintiff's. She alleged that there was substantial overlap in the duties performed even though there was no employer job evaluation system. The District Court rejected the plaintiff's claim that the disparity in pay was not justified by the dissimilarities in the jobs, remarking that there was no direct evidence that the employer paid her less because she was female. It is interesting to note that unlike the *Charley Brothers* case (discussed earlier in the chapter), the absence of an employer job evaluation system did not support the inference of disparate treatment in *Plemer* (Majeske, 1985).

Recent Cases Since *Gunther*

The most recent cases since *Gunther* show quite clearly that District and Circuit Courts are hueing closely to rejection of comparable worth claims by female employees unless they can narrowly prove intentional discrimination and establish a discriminatory motive. For example, in *Power v. Barry County, Michigan* [539 F. Supp. 721 (W.D. Mich. 1982)], jail matrons for the Barry County Sheriff's Department filed a lawsuit contending that the county underpaid them in comparison with the male-dominated job of corrections officer. The matrons claimed their jobs were comparable to those of corrections officer and of equal worth to the county. The District Court dismissed this action, concluding that comparable job worth was not a viable legal theory or independent cause of action under Title VII. The court believed the Supreme Court's recognition in *Gunther* of intentional discrimination probably expresses the outer limit of legal theories under Title VII. The court also again got into the judicial-can-of-worms theory that Title VII did not authorize its undertaking evaluation of different jobs and determining their worth to an employer (Reichenberg, 1986).

In *Connecticut State Employees Association v. State of Connecticut* [31 F.E.P. Cases 191 (D. Conn. 1983)], language limiting the viability of the comparable job worth theory was stated once again. In this case four women and the Connecticut State Employees Association contended that the state of Connecticut discriminated against female employees because they were paid at a lower rate than male employees were for comparable or equal work. As in the *Power* case, the District Court noted that in similar cases since *Gunther,* courts have continued to reject wage discrimination claims based solely on a comparable worth theory. The District Court stated that the inclusion of language in the complaint indicating intentional discrimination by the state of Connecticut may well have been the outer limit of legal theories cognizable under Title VII. Again in line with the can-of-worms hypothesis, the District Court cautioned it would not engage in a subjective comparison of the intrinsic worth of various dissimilar jobs. The court ruled that a complaint alleging that the state intentionally discriminated against female employees stated a valid cause of action. Indeed, if the defendants did in fact determine that dissimilar jobs were of equal value and did not provide equal pay because of the sex of the employees, then this would be evidence of intentional discrimination (Reichenberg, 1986).

In yet another case, *American Nurses Association v. State of Illinois* [F.2d (7th Cir. 1986)], the Circuit Court ruled that allegations of sex discrimination based on comparable job worth do not present a cause of action under Title VII. In this class action the plaintiffs allege that the state of Illinois committed sex-based wage discrimination in its classification and compensation of employees. The state had funded a job evaluation study that was conducted by the Illinois Commission on the Status of Women, and the plaintiffs allege that the state had failed to pay employees according to the results of the study. The plaintiffs argued that the state paid female-dominated job classifications lower wages than it paid to employees in historically male-dominated job classifications for jobs that were evaluated as requiring equal or comparable skill, effort, and responsibility. The District Court dismissed the lawsuit because unequal pay for jobs alleged to be of comparable worth based on an evaluative study that the employer commissioned did not constitute a viable legal theory under Title VII (Reichenberg, 1986). However, the Seventh Circuit Court reversed the dismissal of the case because it believed the complaint contained some allegations of intentional discrimination that, if proved, could be actionable under Title VII. The court also noted that an employer does not have an obligation to implement a job evaluation study. Finally, failure to accept the recommendations of a comparable

worth study does not create a cause of action under Title VII and
cannot be used to create an inference that the employer intentionally discriminated (Reichenberg, 1986).

The three most recent cases in the evolving law of comparable job worth and pay equity show the continuing uniqueness of
the issues and standards used by various courts in reviewing the
claims. Although the courts have rejected the notion of comparable
job worth in each case, employees continue to challenge employers'
pay decisions on sex discrimination and equal pay grounds even if
separate job classifications are involved. In the first of these cases,
AFSCME v. County of Nassau [44 F.E.P. Cases 583 (E.D. N.Y.
1987)], male employees working in clerical and secretarial jobs
claimed they were discriminated against because they worked in
predominantly female jobs. The claim was part of a long-standing
pay equity suit filed by AFSCME against Nassau County, New
York. The suit was originally filed by AFSCME in 1984 on behalf
of 5,500 county employees working in mainly female clerical and
secretarial positions. The union charged the county with violating
Title VII and the EPA by maintaining female job classifications and
discriminating in compensation after 1967, when the current
classification system was implemented. The union argued that the
duties performed in these jobs required substantially equal or
greater skill, effort, and responsibility than those performed by
more highly paid employees in historically male jobs. Most
interesting, a group of ten employees (male and female) sought to
be designated as class representatives for all county civil service
employees who worked in jobs with 70 percent or more female
representation in 1967. The male members of the group argued that
they were aggrieved persons because if it were not for the county's
historical discrimination against women, they would be paid more!
Nassau County argued that the men should not be permitted to be
part of the class because they had no legal standing under Title VII
to sue for employment discrimination against women. The District
Court held that Title VII provides remedies only to individuals who
are discriminated against because of who they are. In this case, the
male plaintiffs did not claim that they had been discriminated
against because of their gender. The court determined that the men
not only lacked standing as class representatives but also lacked

standing under Title VII to sue for employment discrimination against women. The court suggested, too, that males who feel mistreated because they are in female-dominated jobs may have to seek a remedy through Congress.

In *Thomas v. Anchorage Telephone Utility* [Alaska Sup. Ct., S-51, July 28, 1987], the Alaska Supreme Court rejected a sex-discrimination challenge to a wage increase for employees in male-dominated electrician jobs that was higher than that received by women in female-dominated clerical positions. The women claimed sex discrimination was evident in a 1975 collective bargaining agreement between the Anchorage Telephone Utility (ATU) and Local 1547 of the International Brotherhood of Electrical Workers. The parties had negotiated a wage increase of 45 percent during a two-year period for skilled trades jobs dominated by men and a 35 percent pay increase for female-dominated commercial and clerical positions. At trial the company and the union presented evidence that competition for skilled electricians was high in Alaska at that time owing to the demand for skilled labor to construct the North Slope oil pipeline. Testimony also showed that the ATU was unable to keep up with the growing demand for telephone installation, that some technicians had been lost directly to pipeline work, and that training electricians could take up to four years. At the same time, the ATU showed that commercial and clerical jobs were easy to fill and that people could be trained for these jobs in four to eight weeks. The Supreme Court of Alaska concluded that the ATU's need to recruit workers constituted a legitimate business reason for negotiating the higher wage increase for the male-dominated classifications than for those dominated by women. The court also found that the union's duty of fair representation of its members did not require that it attain equality of benefits for men and women belonging to it. By its rulings the court affirmed the principle that supply and demand in the labor market can justify an otherwise discriminatory wage system regardless of the comparability of the jobs or the value of the jobs to the employer's operations.

In *Peters v. Shreveport* [770 F.2d 1401 (5th Cir. 1987)], the Court of Appeals in New Orleans gave particular meaning to the awkward and confusing phrase "a differential based on any other factor other than sex" that appears in the Equal Pay Act. In this case the pay differential of interest was between predominantly female police communications officers (PCOs) and predominantly male fire communications officers (FCOs) in Shreveport, Louisiana. The city did not contest the fact that FCOs and PCOs performed equal work. However, it argued that a Louisiana law required it to set a minimum salary for FCOs at a rate of pay that was 25 percent higher than the minimum pay for firefighters. Therefore, the wage differential was caused by a factor other than sex and patently complied with the EPA. The PCOs had argued that for the differential to be valid, gender must provide no part of the basis for it. The Court of Appeals agreed with Shreveport and concerned itself with the correct construction of the phrase "based upon a factor other than sex." The court held that unless an employee's sex was the cause of the wage disparity, there was no violation of the EPA. If the wage differential had existed wholly apart from the consideration of gender, then there was no violation of the EPA. Ultimately, the case was remanded to the District Court for review of the facts in the light of the standards set by the Court of Appeals.

All these cases hue closely to issues of intentional discrimination and establishing a discriminatory motive for sex-based pay inequity. They suggest the courts are still struggling with the language of Title VII and the EPA to settle the complex issues involved in comparable job worth.

State of Washington—One-Half Billion Dollars

In the previous discussion, one of the most important cases was deliberately omitted because it deserves separate treatment. It could have been a landmark case like *Gunther* if it had gone to the Supreme Court. It was a long-drawn-out case stretching from 1978 to 1986 and offers encouragement to exponents of comparable job worth even though it is seen as a victory, in a sense, for opponents of the theory. Some of the issues in the case run backward in the book to matters already touched upon and run forward into issues developed in greater detail in later chapters that focus on collective bargaining and job evaluation methodology. For these reasons we stop and review the case *American Federation of State, County, and*

Municipal Employees v. State of Washington [770 F.2d 1401 (9th Cir. 1985)].

In many respects the comparable job worth and job evaluation challenges that American management presently faces began in the fall of 1973 in the state of Washington. Realizing that many state employees, especially women, were paid less than other working people in private industry and other government units even though their jobs seemed to be equal in value, the Washington Federation of State Employees (AFSCME Council 28) wrote a letter to Governor Dan Evans asking him to take the lead in dealing with the problem. He responded by directing the heads of the two state personnel systems (the Higher Education Personnel Board, covering 15,000 employees, and the Department of Personnel, covering 35,000 classified employees) to initiate a study to identify female-dominated job classifications that had salaries falling below male-dominated classifications but that required comparable skill and responsibilities (Hutner, 1986).

A preliminary study was completed in-house by the directors of personnel in the two state systems previously mentioned by December 1973 and sent to the governor in January 1974. This study confirmed the existence of male-female differences that were not due solely to job worth and that should be corrected. The cost of full implementation of rectifying sex-based pay inequities was estimated at $27-34 million in a two-year period (Hutner, 1986).

This 1973 preliminary study was the first comparable worth study in the United States—the first investigation of discrimination in pay by an employer between male and female jobs with similar job worth, as measured by the jobs' requirements for knowledge, skill, responsibility, and working conditions. The term *comparable worth* was coined here, and the study led to a state-commissioned comparable worth study initiated in April 1974 and completed in September 1974 by Norman D. Willis and Associates, a Seattle consulting firm (Hutner, 1986).

In the 1974 study, 121 job classes were selected for in-depth analysis by a five-member panel. Fifty-nine classes filled with 4,479 employees (70 percent or more of them males) and 62 classes with 9,111 employees (with 70 percent or more of them females) were included in the study. The concept of considering a classification "dominated" by one sex or the other when 70 percent incumbency is reached stems from this study. The evaluation team determined the job worth of these classes using the Willis point factor system of job evaluation, which makes use of knowledge and skills, mental demands, accountability, and working conditions. The study revealed that jobs filled primarily by women were paid about 20 percent lower than jobs held primarily by men with the same job evaluation points, an average gap of $175 per month. An egregious example is a comparison of the pay of Clerk Typist and Warehouse Worker I: both jobs received 94 points under the Willis plan; however, the Clerk Typist was paid in a salary 10 grades below that of the Warehouse Worker I!

At the AFSCME's request the 1974 study was updated in 1976, showing wage discrimination of the same magnitude. Updates in 1979 and 1980 again confirmed that sex-based wage discrimination existed in virtually every female-dominated job. But despite the discrimination documented by the 1975 study, the Washington legislature did nothing to correct the disparities. Outgoing Governor Evans in his last budget proposal requested that the 1977–79 operating budget include $7 million to begin implementing pay equity. Evans' successor, Dixie Lee Ray, deleted the $7 million from her budget proposal, despite her earlier campaign pledges to support pay equity. It was not until the summer of 1983 that any money was provided (a mere $1.5 million), and that was after the AFSCME had started litigation. The AFSCME had filed a formal complaint with the EEOC, charging the state with sex-based wage discrimination in violation of Title VII on Sept. 16, 1981. Then on July 20, 1982, after the EEOC failed to act on the complaint, the AFSCME filed a multimillion dollar lawsuit in Federal District Court against the state of Washington seeking full implementation of the comparable worth increases plus back pay. The trial ran more than a year, and on Sept. 16, 1973, Washington was found guilty of Title VII violations. On Dec. 14, 1983, the court ordered back pay and an end to discrimination (Hutner, 1986).

The District Court had ruled in favor of the plaintiffs, concluding the evidence for sex discrimination was overwhelming historically and had been manifested by direct, overt, and institutionalized discrimination. Discrimination had been found based on both disparate treatment and disparate impact (Hutner, 1986). This was hailed as a judgment worth up to $1 billion.

The state appealed this decision in January 1984 and on Sept. 17, 1984, filed an appeal brief, which was accompanied by *amicus curiae* briefs from several conservative organizations. The AFSCME filed its appeal brief on Nov. 16, 1984, together with amicus briefs from thirty-seven organizations, including NOW, the AFL-CIO, the NAACP Legal Defense and Education Fund, and the National Committee on Pay Equity. Nevertheless, the Ninth Circuit Court reversed the District Court, concluding that since a discriminatory motive had not been shown, the law did not permit the federal courts to interfere in the market-based pay system used by the state. The Circuit Court rejected the belief that an employer must implement a job evaluation study after it had commissioned such a study. The employer should be able to take into account market conditions, bargaining demands, and the possibility that another study might yield different results. The court concluded that the state of Washington's initial reliance on a free market system in which employees in male-dominated jobs are paid higher than individuals in dissimilar female-dominated jobs is not in and of itself a violation of Title VII, even though the Willis study deemed the positions of comparable worth (Reichenberg, 1986).

The Ninth Circuit, as it did in the *Spaulding* case (also, coincidentally, in Washington) rejected once again in the *AFSCME* case the use of the disparate impact theory for sex-based pay discrimination cases. The court believed that basing salaries on the labor market involves the assessment of a number of complex factors not usually ascertainable and too multifaceted to be appropriate for disparate impact analysis. The AFSCME believed that the intent to discriminate could be inferred from the job evaluation study that showed that the state's practice of setting salaries based on the labor market created a sex-based wage disparity for jobs considered to be of comparable worth. In response to this reasoning, the court suggested the state did not create the market disparity and had not been shown to have been motivated by impermissible sex-based considerations in setting salaries (Reichenberg, 1986).

In July 1985, between the time the appeal was heard in April and handed down in September, the Washington state legislature in considering the possible costs for a court-ordered settlement set aside $42 million in its budget, contingent upon an out-of-court agreement, for a settlement of the *AFSCME* pay equity lawsuit. When the Appeals Court overturned the District Court's decision, there was great shock, and the AFSCME announced it would either appeal to the Circuit Court for an *in banc* review or appeal to the U.S. Supreme Court. However, on Dec. 31, 1985, the state entered into a settlement agreement with the AFSCME resolving this prolonged litigation. Under the terms of the settlement, the state agreed to initially spend $46.5 million from April 1, 1986, through June 30, 1987, on pay equity adjustments for about 35,000 employees. Every July 1 thereafter through July 1, 1992, an additional $10 million in pay equity adjustment was to be added to this amount cumulatively, making the total cost of the settlement about $482 million, with about $106 million of this representing pure pay equity increases. Among the various positions that will receive pay equity adjustments as a result of this settlement are licensed practical nurses, hospital attendants, clerk typists, word processor operators, case workers, library technicians, and laundry workers. The settlement has been approved by the Washington state legislature and recently by the District Court (Reichenberg, 1986). The disparity between the $482 million and the $1 billion estimate alluded to above is sizable and is explained by the removal of back pay calculations and the cost of fully funding the pension rights for the employees eligible for pay increases from the computation of the cost of the "front" pay for the female state employees. Also, there was some overestimate caused by the AFSCME's asking for more than the District Court granted (Hutner, 1986).

The significance of the *AFSCME* case and its aftermath for comparable job worth is far reaching. Legal doctrine was not much affected in novel ways because of the truncation of the case at the Court of Appeal level. *Gunther* as a beacon in the sea remains. To that extent knowledgeable management across the entire nation was relieved and viewed *AFSCME* as a victory. On the other hand, a great deal of momentum had been gained by women's groups, unions, civil rights groups, and sympathetic activists and with the public sector to forge ahead. Indeed, the losers (and that is probably not the right term) won almost one-half billion dollars! Quite a winning; hardly a loss in any serious sense. Moreover, the judicial hypothesis about the can of worms was hardly a new one, and the reversal of the District Court's decision amounts only to a ruling that in the particular fact pattern of *AFSCME* no legal violation was established. This conclusion to the case can be turned around to provide guidance for the comparable job worth proponents so that the next time there is litigation a different kind of suit with a better chance of succeeding in court will be put together (Hutner, 1986).

However, before the right case comes along, *AFSCME* signaled to the public sector that there was sufficient moral sentiment, public opinion, employee and interest group pressure, and public employer shrewdness flowing together simultaneously to stir up a maelstrom in state and local government to find out where sex-based pay discrimination existed and to do something about it. In the state of Washington alone the city of Spokane has implemented comparable worth and Seattle, Olympia, Lacey, and Belleview are at various stages of examining the subject (Hutner, 1986). The developments more generally in state and local government around the country are detailed in Chapter Three. Interestingly, American industrial management has failed to pay proper attention to these state and local government activities and assess their implications. An ostrich posture is an inappropriate response to a challenge, but that seems to be the reason management has not dug into the long-run implications of the AFSCME case for strategy and policy change.

Research on Comparable Job Worth Cases

Management and observers of the comparable job worth movement can benefit from an overview of the results of a study of sixty-eight comparable worth cases involving the comparability of two different sex-dominated jobs that have been litigated in the federal court system since 1970. The statistics augment what can be learned from the important cases reviewed in this chapter; they are discussed next.

Eighty-four percent of the cases were filed under Title VII, but 32 percent were filed under the EPA, suggesting that some cases were filed under both laws. Under the Bennett Amendment, exceptions can be made to the EPA requirement that the pay of men and women must be equal in order to have a cause of legal action. Therefore, in the future probably a greater number of Title VII cases will be forthcoming. Sixty-three percent of the cases identified in the research are still at the District Court level, which suggests they are still subject to appeal (Katz, Lavan, and Malloy, 1986).

The private sector accounted for 62 percent of the cases, and the public sector, only 32 percent. Policy-level managers and human resource management specialists in private industry should be alert to this disparity in case loads because they may be in for some surprises that will shake them out of their complacency. Fifty-three percent of the cases involved class actions. Forty-one percent of the cases involved blue-collar workers; 26 percent, white-collar; 22 percent, professional; and the remainder, 11 percent, managerial. Only 34 percent of the cases were in manufacturing, but 66 percent were in the service sector. Where gender could be clearly determined from the case records, 81 percent of the plaintiffs were female and only 12 percent were male. The EEOC was involved in litigation in only 19 percent of the cases (although it could have been involved at lower levels of the dispute resolution process, such as in conciliation). Unions were involved in only 16 percent of the cases and *always* on the side of the defendant company (Katz, Lavan, and Malloy, 1986). Unions have a duty under both the Railway Labor Act [45 U.S.C., Section 151 *et seq.*] and the National Labor Relations Act [29 U.S.C., Section 151 *et seq.*] to represent all members fairly without regard to race, religion, national origin, or sex. (This duty is enforceable by an individual lawsuit or by the administrative processes of the National Labor Relations Board if the discriminatory acts are considered unfair labor practices.)

In these sixty-eight comparable worth–oriented cases, pay was the predominant issue to be settled and was involved in 81 percent of the cases. Promotion was the second most frequent issue (43 percent of the cases). Discharge was the third most frequent issue and was reflected in 24 percent of the cases. Only 4 percent of the cases involved other interested parties, such as government officials or community interest groups. The latter was unexpectedly low, because based upon much of the literature on comparable job worth we would expect that there would commonly be a coalition of women and labor unions involved in comparable job worth lawsuits. Similarly surprising was the data on public pressure. It existed in only 6 percent of the cases studied (Katz, Lavan, and Malloy, 1986).

Turning to the use of job evaluation, in 62 percent of the cases a formal job evaluation was conducted. In fact, in forty-five of the cases job evaluation was an integral part of the case. The most prevalent system of job evaluation used was the classification system; however, in 72 percent of the cases it could not be determined precisely what system was used. But where a system was used by an organization, problems were experienced in implementation because the system was perceived as not fair (43 percent of the problems were here); extra duties were not adequately evaluated (25 percent of the problems); or pay adjustments were not based on job evaluations (also 25 percent of the problems). None of the cases appeared to involve a problem in which the job evaluation system was not up to date (Katz, Lavan, and Malloy, 1986).

Appeals were frequently made to the Bennett Amendment. Seniority was the grounds for appeal 12 percent of the time; merit, 8 percent; productivity, 4 percent; and other grounds not related to gender, 44 percent. These "other" grounds include more experience, more training, or being a participant in a training program (Katz, Lavan, and Malloy, 1986).

Defendant companies won about one-half the cases (49 percent), and the plaintiff(s) won approximately 32 percent of the time. In the remaining 19 percent of the cases, the decision was split, with both sides winning some of their points. The most frequently awarded remedy was back pay (25 percent of the cases). Salary adjustments and reinstatements covered only about 7 percent of the cases in each category. Fifteen percent of the cases at the Court of Appeals level were remanded to the District Court for remedy. But only eleven of the sixty-eight cases involved a financial settlement to the individuals. The average of these settlements was $67,400, with a range from $2,885 to $190,000, which does not include the costs of attorneys' fees on either side and the other costs and expenses associated with defending or moving the lawsuit forward (Katz, Lavan, and Malloy, 1986).

In this study there were a disproportionate number of public-sector cases. This may be due to a higher expectation of fairness on the part of public employees who work in organizations that are highly formalized and who expect their pay to be determined in an equally formalized way. Also, as one of the largest public-sector unions, AFSCME probably has almost 50 percent female membership owing to the traditionally large number of women in civil service work, and has consequently been in the vanguard of the pay equity forces. For example, AFSCME had more than 260 comparable job worth charges backlogged at the EEOC alone. Although job evaluation evidence apparently had little impact on the outcome of the cases, organizations may still find it wise to conduct job evaluations and use them in building their compensation systems (Katz, Lavan, and Malloy, 1986).

Apples, Oranges, and a Can of Worms?*

This chapter has shown that as of today, courts have been very hesitant about endorsing the comparable job worth theory. In the only Supreme Court case pertinent so far, *Gunther,* it was held that a sex-based pay discrimination action could be maintained under Title VII of the Civil Rights Act of 1964 without meeting the equal-pay-for-equal-work standard of the Equal Pay Act of 1963. In *Gunther,* the Supreme Court found intentional discrimination by an employer who paid women less than its job evaluation system indicated their jobs were worth. In this case the Supreme Court did not define the parameters for maintaining lawsuits alleging sex-based pay discrimination and, in fact, emphasized that it was not endorsing the comparable job worth theory.

In the years since the *Gunther* decision, lower courts have given it a narrow interpretation. Looking at the fact pattern of the *Gunther* case, employers have been worried that the failure to implement the findings of a job evaluation study could result in a judgment of intentional discrimination. Courts of Appeals decisions since *Gunther* have reduced that worry. Intentional discrimination will not necessarily be drawn from such failures.

*Comment of former Washington Governor Dixie Lee Ray in defining comparable job worth in 1977.

Courts continue to allow employers to defend against pay discrimination claims by showing that their compensation systems are based on the labor market. Plaintiffs who sue under Title VII must allege *intentional* discrimination, and they face a tough burden of proof because they must establish a *discriminatory motive* on the part of the employer (Reichenberg, 1986). These legal constraints are imposing and would deter weak cases from advancing very far in judicial review. Yet management must be alert to (1) possible cases in the future that might be more broadly interpreted than *Gunther* and (2) possible shifts in Supreme Court philosophy as the current composition of the court changes because of resignations and death. The Warren and Burger courts are history. The Rehnquist court may be conservative in its interpretations of Title VII. At least, many observers of the Supreme Court argue that Rehnquist and the appointments to the court by President Ronald Reagan have set the court in a conservative mold. Others argue that predicting the future course of Supreme Court decisions is hazardous and mostly inaccurate. In closing the chapter we suggest that no one in management underrate Chief Justice Rehnquist and develop the smug attitude that since he strongly dissented in *Gunther,* he will never open his mind again to comparable job worth if a relevant Title VII case was appealed to the Supreme Court with a challenging fact pattern. The challenge of comparable job worth in the 1990s will be further complicated by the settling in of a new U.S. Supreme Court that may surprise American management in many areas of interest by the decisions it hands down.

3

Legislating and Implementing Comparable Job Worth: Lessons for the Private Sector

Many state and local governments are presently realigning the wages they pay by raising the compensation levels in the occupations in which women predominate. The impetus for change may be political pressure from a number of sources, litigation, and self-conscious efforts to role-model pay equity. The next target for change is the federal government (Bergmann, 1986). There is more than a flurry of legislative activity already that will goad the federal government forward. There is, of course, sympathy in Congress for the idea, and already the options for conducting a study of the ways to determine why female federal employees earn less than male federal employees have been laid out (Comptroller General of the United States, 1985).

Wage realignment based on comparable duties when carried out in the public sector will affect pay levels in the private sector. Is this interaction inevitable? If the public sector adopts comparable job worth, will the enactment of comparable worth legislation for the private sector be far behind? How these interconnections might be made are discussed in detail in Chapter Seven. It is important to pause in the present chapter to examine the beehive of activity at the state and local government levels, which is a precursor of the future for both the federal government and private industry. As we have previously seen, once government takes it upon itself to proclaim and remedy a social injustice, it becomes a model employer with respect to human resource management and is then in a position to take the lead and urge private-sector employers to follow suit (Commons and Andrews, 1936).

In the meantime, political action by women's groups, labor unions, and coalitions of the same, plus sympathetic legislators will continue the impetus that began in the watershed years, the early 1960s, when contemporary feminism gained a full head of steam and in the 1970s when it forged ahead. In the last chapter we focused on litigation through the federal courts under Title VII and the EPA. Court decisions obviously set the parameters for sex-based wage discrimination. Therefore, litigation is important in determining what is or is not considered discrimination according to the court's interpretations of the relevant laws. Given the legal framework, the development of compensation systems free of bias is carried out by individual public and private employers with or without some channelized employee or union input. In the United States we do not yet and probably never will have the federal government or any other level of government dictating wage policy, job evaluation rules and criteria, and wage levels (above the socially defined minimum wage). The interplay of statutory law, litigation, union input, and employer actions was most clearly shown in the last chapter, in the AFSCME and state of Washington cases, although the focus in the chapter was on the litigation of leading cases. We turn now to the emphasis by state and local government employers on legislation.

State Governments

As of this writing at least thirty-one states are looking into pay equity, twenty have enacted comparable job worth legislation or pronounced related public policies, and ten states prohibit unequal compensation rates for comparable jobs in state government employment. These figures are changing rapidly, and they are virtually out of date whenever compiled and published.

It appears that Alaska's law, which dates back to 1949 and the FEPC era, well before the EPA and Title VII, was the first. The state's human rights law contains a clause relating to work of comparable character (Perrin, 1985). However, Idaho was the first state to actually implement pay equity for state employees. In 1969, the state legislature passed a comparable worth law by which the discriminatory payment of wages based on sex was prohibited. Then in 1975 Idaho required the state civil service commission to study the internal equity of the state's compensation system using the Hay job evaluation plan. The Hay Group conducted a study for the state, and in 1977 Idaho implemented the internal equity compensation system based on the Hay plan, with some modifications designed principally to meet special market competition in a few job classifications (covering only about 1 percent of the employees). The system covered 8,000 classified employees in 1,100 job classes. It was implemented in a year and increased women's salaries an average 16.2 percent and men's an average 6.8 percent. The salaries of secretaries in Idaho state government rose 20–30 percent. The cost was about 4 percent of the total state budget for the year or about 10 percent of the classified Idaho employee payroll (Hutner, 1986). The details on how the Hay plan was applied to Idaho to achieve pay equity are available (Treiman, 1979).

Idaho and Washington, neighboring Western states, one about one-sixth the size of the other in public employment, make for an interesting study in contrasts. Smaller Idaho led the way to pay equity swiftly, painlessly, and cleanly. The cost for the moral victory inherent in pay equity was cheap. The method employed, the Hay plan, has been used in thousands of private and public organizations throughout the world for building pay systems, and the literature on this proprietary system is readily available (see Burgess, 1984; Rock, 1984).

Idaho could be considered one model. Yet Washington also had the integrity to act and to settle costly problems of pay equity ($482 million worth) even though it had won an appellate decision that relieved it from the pressure of a mandate. Washington, guided by the Willis job evaluation plan and data, may be thought of as a model for the larger states, since it dealt with all the pressures for change that could be expected in a true bellwether situation.

In order to provide a picture of state laws around the nation and remain as general as possible—here we clearly want to see the forest and not the trees or leaves—the data presented in Table 1 are offered. There were three main sources for this table (Lorber and

Table 1. Summary of State Pay Equity Activities.

State	Policy?	Data Collection?	Job Content Study?	Economic Study?
Alabama	—	—	—	—
Alaska	X	X	—	—
Arizona	—	X	X	—
Arkansas	X	—	—	—
California	X	X	—	—
Colorado	—	—	—	—
Connecticut	—	—	—	—
Delaware	—	X	—	—
Florida	—	—	—	—
Georgia	X	—	—	—
Hawaii	X	X	—	X
Idaho	X	X	X	X
Illinois	—	X	X	—
Indiana	—	X	X	—
Iowa	X	X	X	—
Kansas	—	X	—	—
Kentucky	—	X	—	—
Louisiana	—	X	—	—
Maine	X	X	X	—
Maryland	—	X	X	—
Massachusetts	X	X	X	—
Michigan	X	X	X	X
Minnesota	X	X	X	X
Mississippi	—	—	—	—
Missouri	—	—	—	—
Montana	X	X	X	—
Nebraska	X	X	—	—
Nevada	—	—	—	—
New Hampshire	—	—	—	—
New Jersey	—	X	X	—
New Mexico	—	X	—	—
New York	—	—	X	—
North Carolina	—	X	—	X
North Dakota	—	—	—	—
Ohio	X	X	X	—
Oklahoma	X	—	—	—
Oregon	X	X	X	—
Pennsylvania	—	X	—	—
Rhode Island	—	X	X	—
South Carolina	—	—	—	—
South Dakota	X	—	—	—
Tennessee	X	—	—	—
Texas	—	—	—	—

(continued)

Table 1. Summary of State Pay Equity Activities, Cont'd.

State	Policy?	Data Collection?	Job Content Study?	Economic Study?
Utah	—	—	—	—
Vermont	—	X	X	—
Virginia	—	X	—	—
Washington	X	X	X	—
West Virginia	—	X	X	—
Wisconsin	X	X	X	—
Wyoming	—	X	X	X

others, 1985; Perrin, 1985; Comptroller General of the United States, 1985). The states are still feeling their respective ways in the comparable worth area, and commentary is needed to provide as clear a picture as possible. After reviewing salient information about many of the other states, we discuss Minnesota, Michigan, and California in more detail primarily because these large and important industrial states have been more adequately reported on in published sources than the others. The Comptroller General's report was most helpful and revealing in providing a current picture, and the data from it are highlighted because it is based on a survey that was adequately followed up.

As can been seen from Table 1, twenty states have pay equity policies (indicated by x's), which may be defined as any legislation, executive order, administrative policy, or other pronouncement that specifically states a compensation goal of equal pay for work of *comparable worth or value* for state employees. Excluded from this count were pronouncements made by a state that only authorized a pay equity study or evaluation of job classes.

Column 2 in the table indicates by x's how many states (thirty-two) have made or are making *data collection efforts* that identify any sex-based wage differences or occupational segregation by sex among state employees.

Column 3 in Table 2 indicates the number of *job content* pay equity studies by state (twenty-one) that compare the pay of male and female job classes with job evaluation scores.

Column 4 in the same table reflects the states (six) that have

Table 2. Number of States by Size Category
of Total and Classified Positions.

Number of Positions	Number of States*	
	Total Positions	Classified Positions
15,000 or under	7	14
15,001–30,000	11	10
30,001–45,000	9	9
45,001–60,000	11	7
60,001–75,000	2	4
75,001 or more	8	4
Total	48	48

Source: Comptroller General of the United States (1985, p. 6).
*No information supplied by two states.

made pay equity *economic studies* comparing the pay of male and female employees with comparable individual characteristics, such as education or experience.

In Table 2 the states' work force characteristics are compiled. The total number of positions in state government varied greatly, with seven states having 15,000 or fewer positions and eight having more than 75,000. The positions included so-called "classified" and unclassified and full- and part-time. Since similar positions may be considered classified in one state and not classified in another, no single definition for classified position can be used. Generally, classified positions are covered by the states' primary personnel statute and include most positions in the executive branch, but they may also include positions in the judicial or legislative branch depending on the state (Comptroller General of the United States, 1985).

Positions in the survey are equivalent to employment levels in the various states (1 position equals 1 employee). Of course, the number of job classifications or job categories in a state is much lower. It was found that five states had 1,000 jobs or fewer; twenty-two had 1,001 to 1,500 jobs; seventeen had 1,501 to 3,000; four had more than 3,000; and two had more than 7,000. (A job obviously consists of a number of positions filled by a number of incumbents.)

Forty-six of the states used job evaluation to set pay for their classified positions. Of these, thirty-four reported using only one system to set pay for all their classified jobs. (Six other states use two systems, and the remaining six use three or more—up to eleven, as in Michigan at the time of the survey.) Of the thirty-four states using one system of job evaluation, fourteen use the point-factor plan, followed by grading (or the whole-job "classification" technique) in nine states. Ten of the fourteen states using a single point-factor method had been using this method for less than ten years. Eighteen of the twenty states using another method had been doing so for ten years or more.

The types of jobs most commonly covered by job evaluation systems in state governments were administrative, clerical, secretarial, laborers, craftspersons, managerial, professional, and technical. Forty of the forty-six states making use of job evaluation indicated that their primary evaluation system covered the types of positions just mentioned. All thirty-four states with one evaluation system reported that all these positions were covered by that system. Fifteen more indicated that state university employees (except faculties) were also covered, and six included judicial employees in the system.

It is difficult to be general and comprehensive in interpreting the fragmentary statistics selected for discussion in the chapter. A few generalizations can be made, though. There is no question that the states are highly conscious of the equity of their pay systems for state employees. The amount of activity taking place in policy debates, bills introduced, data collection, job content studies, and economic studies is being stepped up. States in the Deep South or close to it seem to be the slowest to take action: Alabama, Florida, Mississippi, Missouri, South Carolina, Texas, and Virginia are not changing. Other states standing pat are Colorado, Nevada, New Hampshire, North Dakota, and Utah. In the remaining states there is action ranging from a little to a great deal. The prevalence of job evaluation systems in the states indicates that these could be used as springboards for action. The apparent rise of point-factor plans of job evaluation by government suggests that the whole-job classification plans of the past, long associated with state government approaches to evaluating job worth (Baruch, 1941), are being supplanted. Job evaluation is certainly not new to state governments, and judging by the numbers of positions and jobs in that employment domain, job evaluation is clearly needed as a tool in human resource management. If there were no job evaluation there, how would it be possible to administer pay free of the possible taints of a spoils system, the very thing merit employment is intended to prevent?

The achievements in public personnel management in the early twentieth century have had a strong impact on human resource management in industry (as, for example, in recruitment, selection, training, and job analysis and evaluation). Industry has copied government in many respects (Ling, 1963). Is it illogical to think at the end of the twentieth century, industry will follow government once again, but this time in the implementation of pay equity? Large companies in particular face the problems of scale in human resource management that states with 15,000 positions face, and they will want to learn everything they can about vanguard activities in tackling the problems of pay equity in the states. Of course, companies with far fewer employees and positions (say, 2,000 employees or more) have managerial challenges day in and day out that cause them to act like public employers who require elaborate systems to administer the bureaucracy. In this sense, the activities of *all* states as employers necessarily interest and should be watched by private industry.

Brief Profiles of Several States

While a report on any specific state's progress in dealing with pay equity is dated upon publication, brief profiles of the various states that are in the process of acting may be suggestive. Let us consider— from one end of the country to the other—such states as Connecticut, Ohio, Iowa, Oregon, and Hawaii.

Connecticut There has been action in Connecticut on several different fronts. A study was conducted by the Permanent Commission on the Status of Women in 1986. The AFSCME has brought suit against the state in the District Court. An employer group, the Special Task Force of the Connecticut Business and Industry Association, has also been looking into comparable job worth (Perrin, 1985). The state itself has been engaged in what is called "Objective Job Evaluation" since 1979. The State Personnel Act requires that Connecticut evaluate all jobs in the classified service utilizing a two-phase approach. The first is reviewing and revising the classification system. The second is evaluating job families by use of objective job-related criteria, such as knowledge and skills, mental and physical effort, and accountability. The resulting ratings may then be a consideration in setting salaries (subject, where appropriate, to collective bargaining). The state was wrapping up its evaluations by 1987. It was committed to striving for equitable pay relationships through the application of job evaluation, labor-market data, and recruitment-retention information. The rates of pay ultimately derived will be set through the collective bargaining process (Reichenberg, 1986). In late 1986, as a consequence of a comparable job worth lawsuit brought on behalf of about 5,000 state clerical employees by their union, Connecticut agreed to pay $5.75 million over two years to achieve pay equity (*Los Angeles Times*, Nov. 19, 1986, p. I-2).

Ohio There has been a flurry of activity in the Ohio legislature. The Bureau of Employment released a report resulting from a two-year study of the state's classification system. The study found that female employees earn 87 percent of what men earn in state agencies. The governor of Ohio announced that the state would spend approximately $4.5 million annually to eliminate gender bias from state job classifications, which would take about two to four years (Reichenberg, 1986).

Iowa In this Corn Belt state the legislature enacted a law in 1983 that provided that the state would not discriminate in compensation for work of comparable value. The law defined comparable worth as the value of work when measured by the composite of skill, effort, responsibility, and working conditions normally required in the performance of work. The law required the state to contract with an independent consultant who would conduct a study for the purpose of establishing an evaluation of jobs under the merit employment system on the basis of their comparable worth, giving particular attention to female-dominated jobs.

The law also established a seven-person steering committee to prepare guidelines for the study, to select a consultant to do the work (Arthur Young and Company was chosen), and to set the completion date for the study. The Iowa Merit Employment Department was required to estimate the cost of comparability adjustments for state employees (Reichenberg, 1986).

Oregon Following the lead set by its northwestern neighbors, Idaho and Washington, Oregon has been in the forefront of the pay equity movement. The state's Equal Pay Act refers to work of comparable character, the performance of which requires comparable skills. A class action suit against the state university system alleging bias was dismissed on a motion by the defendant, citing the *Spaulding* case in Washington, which was similar. The legislature passed a law providing that the state would attempt to achieve equitable relations between the comparability of the value of the work performed by persons in state service and the pay and classification plans with the state system. The law required that a point-factor job evaluation system be applied to all the jobs in state employment. The law also created a seven-member Task Force on State Compensation and Classification Equity appointed by the state legislature and governor. The task force carried out the legally mandated study using the point-factor plan to identify the inequities based on the comparable value of the work (Reichenberg, 1986; Perrin, 1985). Implementation is now underway.

Hawaii In the state most diversified racially and ethnically, comparable job worth has been moving forward. The AFSCME and the Hawaii Government Employees Association filed a Title VII class action against the state. In 1984 the state legislature passed a law that created a temporary commission on comparable worth chaired by the legislative auditor and that included the personnel directors of the state and counties and representatives of the Public Employee Compensation Appeals Board. The commission was required to evaluate state compensation and classification systems; examine job segregation and wage differentials that may exist in state and local government employment; recommend a job evaluation system that would implement comparable worth for all public employees; and examine the compatibility of the recommended job evaluation system with existing civil service, pay, and collective bargaining laws (Reichenberg, 1986; Perrin, 1985). A job evaluation study is now underway.

An In-Depth Story of Three States

As mentioned above, three states have attracted considerable attention for their activities, though for different reasons: Minnesota, Michigan, and California. We turn to each of them now.

Minnesota This state is a harbinger for many others of comparable size with a similar agriculture-industry mix in the economy. In 1979, the State of Minnesota hired the Hay Group to conduct a study of state pay and benefit practices. Point values were assigned to 762 state job classes. In 1981 a legislative body (the Task Force on Pay Equity) issued a report on salary differences between men and women. It had studied Hay's classifications and found documented disparities in the pay scales of male- and female-dominated jobs. The task force recommended a two-step procedure to correct the inequities: legislation to establish a policy of pay equity for jobs of comparable worth and a process to provide the funding. The state legislature adopted some of the recommendations and in 1982 it enacted a law that did three things: (1) set a policy to provide equitable compensation relationships between female-dominated (at least 70 percent women) and male-dominated (at least 80 percent men) classes in the executive branch, (2) defined compensation as equitable when the primary consideration is comparability of the value of the work to other positions in the executive branch, and (3) established a procedure for making comparability adjustments. The implementation procedure included the following four steps: (1) the legislative commission recommended an amount to be appropriated; (2) the legislature appropriated funds, specifying certain underpaid classes; (3) appropriated funds were designated to bargaining units proportional to the total cost of implementing pay equity for persons in job classes for that unit; and (4) the distribution of funds to the specified classes took place through collective bargaining. In 1983 the State Legislature appropriated $21.7 million for the comparability adjustments for underpaid classes over a two-year period covering 1983–85. These pay equity funds were designated separately from funds appropriated for general wage adjustments for state employees. The $21.7 million reflected about 1.25 percent of the payroll budget for each of the years in the biennium. More than three-fourths of the eligible employees were clerical and health care workers. About 8,000 were women; 800 were men. Estimates indicate that the 1985–87 appropriation of a similar amount should complete implementation, and salaries for all underpaid female-dominated jobs would have been brought up to the average pay for male-dominated jobs of comparable value (California Comparable Worth Task Force, 1985). Thus, for under $44 million the state of Minnesota achieved pay equity in the sense of comparable worth adjustments.

In 1984 Minnesota enacted legislation requiring its municipalities to provide employees with equal pay for jobs of comparable worth. The law also required units of local government to develop a job evaluation system and to begin implementation of pay equity plans by Oct. 2, 1985. Under this law an additional 163,000 persons in public-sector employment would be covered for implementation by late 1987. However, police and firefighters were exempt from coverage, based on a belief that comparable job worth would result in lower pay raises for them in the future (or perhaps none) because of their high pay (Perrin, 1985). Implementation has proceeded in the counties, and the decision band method of job evaluation (originally developed by Paterson and Husband, 1970) has been used by Arthur Young and Company to assist the counties in achieving comparable worth.

Michigan   This state has had as many as 57,700 employees in 2,500 classes before downsizing drives in recent years. The comparable job worth experiences are very instructive for all. Michigan has made a triumphant effort in the area of comparable job worth and now seems to be on the way toward full implementation.

As a start, the job evaluation system it had had since 1941 was changed in 1975 when a benchmark factor ranking system of classification was introduced; this was patterned after the design set forth by Philip Oliver in the famous Oliver Report (Job Evaluation and Pay Review Task Force, 1972). The state of Michigan has developed eleven job evaluation plans, each of which is tailored to a separate job family of related occupations. It should be recalled from earlier in the chapter that only one state government in the United States used eleven job evaluation plans (and that was four more than the next highest state). Unlike Minnesota, in which a law would be needed to achieve the result, the Michigan constitution permits the civil service commission to establish pay and personnel authorizations (such as comparable worth machinery) unless the state legislature overturns such authorization within sixty days of their issuance, provided it can attain a two-thirds majority vote.

In October 1983, the civil service commission established a citizens' advisory task force (called the Comparable Worth Task Force) to thoroughly review the disparities between average male and female wages and recommend action to eliminate wage discrimination based on sex to the extent it may have existed in the state classified service (*Report of the Comparable Worth Task Force to the Michigan Civil Service Commission*, 1985).

The appointed task force was charged to direct its attention to two major questions: (1) should the state civil service commission replace labor-market determination of compensation with its own decision making? and (2) are job evaluation techniques sufficiently sophisticated to enable the commission to make decisions competently and objectively, particularly for classifications that are not occupationally related? The findings of the task force were numerous and extensive. The major cause of wage disparities between male and female employees of the state classified system was found to be their unequal distribution among the eleven occupational groups and by skill level, coupled with the weight accorded labor-market rates in establishing wage levels for the various categories. Fifty-three percent of the state's classified employees were female and 80 percent of these women were clustered in two occupational groups: clerical support and human services. In the aggregate, the women in state government employment earned 80 percent of the wages earned by men. However, 99 percent of the females employed in the state classified service earned 90 percent or more of male wages when they were in the same occupational groups and at the same skill level within an occupation. The task force believed that gender-based pay disparities remained in state employment and that they can be removed. It also believed that barriers to equal employment opportunity can be eliminated and that it is only through the eradication of these vestiges of the past that pay equity will become a reality. The task force agreed to a comprehensive program for achieving pay equity that was designed to reduce gender dominance within the eleven occupational groups and to eliminate gender-based disparities within the classified system. It recommended the reduction of the eleven occupational groups to five non-gender-dominated groups within three years through sound job evaluation technology and then that this change be implemented in one additional year. The Department of Civil Service was to develop a wage line for all the existing classes. The female-dominated classes that were below the average line were to receive special pay adjustments of a substantial percentage of the difference between the female-dominated rates and average rates, beginning in the 1985–86 fiscal year. The proration and extent of adjustments was to be addressed through the collective bargaining process and coordinated pay-setting process over a period of four years. The costs of this new approach to pay equity were to be subject to the same labor-market considerations and decision-making considerations and processes, controls, and reviews as any other wage adjustments (*Report of the Comparable Worth Task Force to the Michigan Civil Service Commission*, 1985).

The Michigan task force recognized that at the core of pay equity are the concepts of equal employment opportunity and affirmative action, and it made a number of recommendations in those areas. Referrals to the promotional lists were to include representative numbers of qualified women for previously male-dominated occupations; the posting procedures for vacant positions in state government were to be studied; the Michigan Employment Security Commission referral processes were to be reviewed and changed as appropriate; emphasis was to be placed on career development programs for women in state government, especially for enhancing advancement opportunities for women into supervisory, managerial, and executive positions; career development planning was to be linked with work force planning; and certain

changes were to be made in testing procedures, granting credit for
training as a portion of required experience, refining performance
appraisal techniques, and setting up interdepartmental job
rotations to include experience in administrative and policy
development activities.

Recognizing that the elimination of gender-dominated
classes and the realization of equal employment opportunity are
societal problems that the state of Michigan could role-model
solutions to, the task force recommended two complementary
actions. The existing student intern program should be enhanced as
a means of recruiting and attracting females into technical,
scientific, and professional occupations that were previously male-
dominated. The Civil Service Department should meet with the
Department of Education of the state of Michigan for the purpose of
exploring means by which educational institutions could be
encouraged to minimize societal sex-role stereotyping and enhance
the entry of females into previously male-dominated occupations
(*Report of the Comparable Worth Task Force to the Michigan Civil
Service Commission,* 1985).

The civil service commission adopted the task force report
because it was thought that it could advance pay equity. The eleven
occupational groups are being reduced to five and may ultimately
go to four (nonprofessional occupations, professional, supervisors
and managers, and executives). This would have the effect of
including 33,000 employees' positions in one category, the nonprofessional. Pay equity adjustments were made in early 1986 on the
basis of comparable worth for 21,750 employees (both men and
women) in the female-dominated classes. Almost one-half of these
employees were unionized members of the United Automobile
Workers (UAW), which had organized a large segment of state
administrative support employees. The second largest group of
beneficiaries were in human services work, also represented by the
UAW. The contract as collectively bargained by the Office of the
State Employer and the UAW called for 20 cents per hour retroactive
to Oct. 1, 1985, and another 20 cents per hour effective Oct. 1 as front
money for eligible employees. The two increments of 20 cents were
related to an 80 cent male-female pay gap determined to exist in
state employment for the employees identified. The total of 40 cents

made up for one-half of the differential. The value of the adjustments totaled approximately $21 million, which needs to be viewed against a personnel payroll budget in the 1985–86 fiscal year of about $2.2 billion. This pay equity cost was less than 1 percent of payroll. The contract also established a $2 million "pay inequity fund" to be used in 1986–87 to address pay equity problems not solved by the two hourly increases. Also, the state established a pay equity fund in each of the same two fiscal years for correcting the pay of 3,800 eligible nonunionized employees. The total cost of the pay equity increases for 1986–87 was only $16.5 million (Michigan Department of Civil Service, 1986). Unlike Minnesota, the state of Michigan has no law calling for the implementation of comparable job worth in the other units of government within the borders of the state. The state constitutions in the two states differ with respect to the role of the state civil service authority and, as a result, Minnesota took one lawful path to achieve comparable job worth for its state employees while Michigan took another. Every state and governmental jurisdiction will have its own road to travel, if it embarks on a comparable job worth effort.

California Comparable job worth activity in our largest state, which has about 122,000 full-time state civil service employees, has been diverse and is well worth examining, but California has not made the same progress in implementation as either Minnesota or Michigan, nor does it have the history of promulgation reflected in Idaho, Washington, Iowa, or the other states previously discussed. Each state is unique, of course, as we have seen.

In 1983 a bill was introduced in the California State Assembly to create a Comparable Worth Task Force, which reported in August 1985 on the existence of a wage gap between male and female employees in both the public and private sectors of the state's economy, on wage discrimination, and on previous state action involving comparable job worth. The task force functioned in a role similar to those in Minnesota and Michigan, but it appears to have been more comprehensive in its search for data. For example, it conducted surveys to obtain information from the 100 largest employers in California; 40 employer associations; 1,000 members of the Small Business Association; 1,200 employee organizations such as those belonging to the California Federation of Labor, the AFL-CIO, and the UAW; and every city, county, and school district. All this covered fifteen months and resulted in nine volumes of testimony and supporting documentation (California Comparable Worth Task Force, 1985). In addition, there were two minority reports containing important points of view that were privately published by members of the task force. In this book, unless noted to the contrary, we review materials from the longer report issued by the task force as a whole.

In California as a whole (in the private and public sectors), the male-female pay gap is 60 cents for every male dollar. However, in state employment, primarily because of collective bargaining, the average female salary has increased to 74.3 percent of the male employee's pay. Women in the state generally tend to have less work experience and less technical training than men and work in the less productive industries. Yet statistical studies have failed to explain more than one-half the pay gap, typically leaving at least a 20 percent differential unaccounted for. Also, studies that have examined the characteristics of jobs, rather than workers, have consistently shown that the jobs performed chiefly by women tend to pay less than jobs requiring similar skill, effort, responsibility, and working conditions held mainly by men. The differential is about 20 percent in this instance also.

The task force considered whether factors such as intermittent employment, less education, shorter job tenure, and limited career choices are the primary causes of lower earnings. It rejected the arguments that women choose low-paying jobs and that intermittent nature of work patterns account for the male-female pay gap. On the other hand, it acknowledged that these factors appear to be additional consequences of discrimination against women.

The task force found that the labor force of California, as in other parts of the country, is highly segregated on the basis of sex. Thus, if it is to be successful, any effort to reduce the pay gap must begin by changing the pay relationships between jobs. More effective enforcement of the California Equal Pay act would have only a small effect.

The findings of the task force were far reaching and deserve attention, although by now the reader should have reliable expectations of what the findings are likely to be on account of what other state studies and socioeconomic research have already disclosed on sex-based pay discrimination. Sex discrimination has depressed the pay of women in female-dominated jobs, and existing laws are insufficient to eliminate the differentials. Women become trapped in such jobs because there is inadequate child care, uneven enforcement of current laws, only nominal affirmative action efforts, insufficient educational opportunities, and much traditional sex-, race-, and ethnic-based discrimination. The California Fair Employment and Housing Act should be amended so that the words "substantially equal" would be interpreted to mean comparable and would be applicable to state employees. Maximum opportunity and encouragement should be given women to move into traditionally male jobs and steps taken to increase the salaries for female-dominated jobs (which have been undervalued) to be paid what they are worth. No job classes should be downgraded or reduced in compensation in order to accomplish the purposes of implementing comparable worth. No employer's argument that the prevailing or labor-market-conforming wage system is being followed in paying employees will be accepted if it perpetuates discriminatory pay practices.

The task force found that minority women are additionally discriminated against in the workplace and thus suffer from both sex- and race-based discrimination. All pay remedies addressed to sex are also to be addressed to race and ethnicity so that minority women can achieve equity with other women and men. Job evaluation systems should be improved to reduce or eliminate the use of gender as a factor in pay. Public and private employers should have the flexibility to determine the type of job evaluation system to be used lawfully to achieve pay equity. Since only 20 percent of the employed women in California belong to labor organizations, collective bargaining cannot be expected to be relied on as the sole means to achieve comparable worth. But where workers have bargaining representation, collective negotiations can be a useful means to achieve pay equity. Workers should not be asked to forfeit an existing job benefit in order to obtain nondiscriminatory compensation. When the California legislature requires employers to achieve pay equity, it should require that the employees (or when unionized, their representatives) have a voice equal to their employer's in evaluating job components, assigning wages, determining the type of study or job evaluation methodology to be used, determining the nature of the remedial plan, and implementing the study and the plan.

The task force also turned its attention to the enforcement of protective labor legislation, particularly under the California Equal Pay Act and the California Fair Employment and Housing Act. Enforcement of the former suffered because of a lack of public knowledge about the law and the high turnover among intake officers, which led to the improper handling of claims. As for the latter, FEHA lacked funds to create a pay equity program that included technical assistance and enforcement. These California problems could partly be solved if Congress funded federal labor law administration agencies at increased levels and thereby more vigorously enforced pay equity claims under Title VII. The other part is motivating employers in both the public and private sectors to post more explicit notices about remedies for equal pay, partly because current notices do not give sufficiently specific notice of employee rights.

The task force reviewed in great detail the problems of the state government employers, which included the state of California, the judiciary, the legislature, the University of California, and California State University, all of which have been confronted with the comparable worth issue, generally through collective bargaining and legislative directive. The state's job classification and pay system for its own work force was created in the 1940s and had not been meaningfully reviewed or changed since then. In 1981 the legislature enacted a law that directed the State Department of Personnel Administration to consider the comparable worth of jobs when establishing state salaries and to submit annual reports to the legislature analyzing salaries for female-dominated positions. The State Department of Personnel Administration did submit reports for 1981 through 1984. In the latter year, the legislature, after reviewing the reports, determined that salaries for the state's female workers were not equitable and approved a $77 million budget appropriation to begin remedial salary adjustments. That appropriation was intended to be the first of five earmarked for pay equity adjustments. The scope of the future appropriations was to be determined after the completion of a comprehensive state job classification evaluation. However, Governor George Deukmejian vetoed both the appropriation and the money to fund the job evaluations, and the plan was not implemented. As a result, the California State Employees Association, an 80,000-member organization, filed a lawsuit against the state executive branch, alleging discriminatory pay practices and a failure to implement the law. The 1984 lawsuit accuses the state of violating Title VII and seeks back pay for 37,000 women in female-dominated jobs. After much delay, the case is scheduled for trial in San Francisco in the U.S. District Court during early 1988.

In 1985, the legislature again approved a comparable worth adjustment appropriation of $31.5 million in the state's 1985–86 budget. Governor Deukmejian again vetoed it. The same scenario was repeated in 1986 and 1987. The governor has consistently expressed the view that comparable worth in the sense of pay equity is an issue that should be exclusively addressed by the collective bargaining process. For example, in 1984 some female employees of the state received raises in addition to across-the-board increases of 8 percent given to all state workers. These additional raises (ranging from 2 to 5 percent) were awarded to some workers in female-dominated classifications. However, the Deukmejian administration identified these raises as salary adjustments, specifically disclaiming that they were part of a comparable worth plan that could be phased in over time (California Comparable Worth Task Force, 1985). There are other forces at work in the state (interested legislators, feminist groups, unions, civil rights activists, and coalitions) that may change the current approach in California. Moreover, pressures for pay equity are coming from other government units in the state.

Among other things, the task force considered the University of California (which may be America's best research university, given the reputation of the institution and the number of Nobel laureates on the faculty of 18,000), with 68,000 employees, and the California State University (which is undoubtedly America's largest

teaching-oriented state university, with 19 campuses, 25,000 full-
and part-time faculty members, 36,000 full- and part-time staff, and
350,000 students). The task force found that both universities needed
to carry out more analyses of their work forces and report in greater
detail on the extent to which they might have sex-based wage
discrimination and where remedial salary adjustments and desegregation were needed. The analytical work and subsequent changes
made in the UC and CSU systems to implement comparable worth
are important for all American private and public colleges to watch
because these are large, well-managed university systems that could
be models for other universities (or businesses that operate on a
large scale and have a similar skill mix in their work forces, not, of
course, including professorial jobs). Considering the large number
of comparable worth lawsuits involving university personnel
discussed in Chapter Two, any improvements in the human
resource management and pay systems innovated by the UC or CSU
system and made known to other institutions of higher learning
could be helpful in reducing and resolving potential litigation as
well as improving university administration throughout the nation.

    As for the task force's recommendations on other units in the
government of the state of California, the task force recommended
that all state employers, including the judiciary, and the legislature
for its own employees, ought to conduct comprehensive job
classification studies for the purpose of proposing specific plans to
remedy pay inequities. These plans should be implemented by 1990.
Each state employer should be granted the flexibility to utilize its
own process for reviewing its pay system and remedying sex-based
wage discrimination. All state employers should be required to
conduct annual reviews of their pay systems and of the status of
workers in female-dominated occupations within their agency.
Also, all state employers should be required to consider the
comparability of the value of jobs when setting salaries. Lastly, the
state legislature should appropriate the funds necessary to implement pay remedy plans for state employees.

    Turning to the counties, cities, and school districts in
California, the task force observed that local governments have not
been subject to any legislation requiring them to examine their pay
systems for evidence of sex-based pay discrimination. However, the

legislature did enact a law [Cal. Gov. Code, Sections 53247.8] that essentially prohibited local governments from refusing to negotiate salaries on the basis of comparable worth, although the application of this law to all governmentally chartered entities in the state has been questioned. The task force found that many local government employers were inadequately informed about comparable job worth, frequently confusing it with equal pay and affirmative action. At the same time such employers assert that their pay systems are free from sex-based pay discrimination, although they have not conducted a comparative review of job classifications dominated by women. On the other hand, many local public employers have begun to assess salaries on the basis of comparable job worth through collective bargaining, and these reassessments have resulted in significant pay adjustments for women in female-dominated jobs and have not produced economic hardships for cities and counties.

The task force's recommendations on what local government entities should do to bring about comparable job worth paralleled its proposals for state employers. All local public employers should be subject to an affirmative obligation to review their existing salary-setting mechanisms to ensure that by 1990 they provide for equal pay for work of substantially equal value and to modify them if they do not. The review should examine sex, race, and ethnicity. Each local government employer should be granted the flexibility to utilize its own process for reviewing its pay system and remedying sex-based pay discrimination. Upon enactment of laws requiring local government employers to review and/or modify their pay systems, there should be a two-year "safe harbor" period during which the employer's review and/or modification would not be admissible in state courts relating to wage discrimination claims. However, the fact that a local government is reviewing or modifying its pay system should not preclude collective bargaining negotiations over comparable worth nor should it preclude litigation. Also, local governments should have a satisfactory pay equity plan, including an implementation schedule, to qualify for state funding.

The private sector in California presented real problems for the task force. With few exceptions, specific information was not readily available from private employers on their efforts, if any, to review and modify their compensation systems to eliminate sex-based wage discrimination. The task force recognized that private employers should comply with the pay equity principle mandated in Title VII and the California FEHA by reviewing their own compensation and classification systems. However, the task force also recognized that every employer has unique concerns and necessarily requires flexibility to determine both the type of review it will utilize and the types of systems it will use to classify employees and pay them.

California is a state having population clusters outside of manufacturing, the service industry, and governments that are not heavily unionized. In Southern California, particularly, employers have had a strong interest in maintaining a union-free ambience (Taft, 1965; McWilliams, 1983). As a result, the remaining industries that have large concentrations of female workers are less intensively unionized. Where there are unions, they tend not to be those in the forefront of the movement for eliminating sex-based wage discrimination (California Department of Finance, 1987).

The task force believed that it would be unrealistic to rely on collective bargaining as a means to achieve comparable worth for all private-sector employees because a large majority of workers are simply not represented by labor unions. At the same time it rejected the argument consistently raised by California employers that implementation of the comparable worth principle is unnecessary because vigorous efforts to bring women into traditionally male jobs will eventually lead to pay equity. Private employers are concerned about the possible impact of the cost of implementing comparable worth, especially to the degree it may affect their ability to compete effectively with out-of-state and non-U.S. businesses.

California private employers of 500 or more employees constitute less than 1 percent of the state's private employers but employ almost 30 percent of the state's private-sector workers. However, the task force believed that the legislature should require *all* employers to review their compensation systems to ensure that they pay equally for work of substantially equal value, regardless of sex. Large employers (with 500 or more employees) should complete the review and be in compliance by 1990. Small employers (with less than 500 employees) should complete the review and be in compliance by 1992, but need not keep records. The task force recognized that salary reviews and modifications might be made in a variety of ways and recommended that legislation retain the maximum flexibility for each employer to accomplish equal pay for work of substantially equal value by whatever means is reasonable for the employer. Upon enactment of any laws requiring private employers to review and/or modify their compensation systems, there would be a two-year "safe harbor" period during which the employer's review and/or modification would not be admissible in pay discrimination claims in litigation in state courts. The fact that a private employer is reviewing or modifying its pay system would not preclude collective bargaining over comparable job worth nor would it preclude litigation. Finally, private-sector employers should have a satisfactory pay equity plan, including an implementation schedule, to qualify for state contracts.

The task force recognized that there were a number of factors that added to (or played a part in) the sex-based pay differential. These included the lack of education about comparable worth in the work force and in small business, pressure for women to enter traditional education and career programs, lack of adequate child care, lack of vigorous affirmative action efforts, and the special problems facing minority women. These were symptoms of discrimination but not the cause. In California, as stated, the Department of Personnel Administration does not in fact set salaries for employees subject to collective bargaining, and it cannot unilaterally put salary or benefit changes into effect. Furthermore, it does not use comparable job worth methodology in negotiating salaries for state employees. Thus, comparable job worth in California has been thoroughly explored and analyzed. Yet it lags behind Minnesota and Michigan in practical implementation. If the task force recommendations discussed above are ever translated into action, the state could forge ahead rapidly and lead the parade.

Local Governments

We have already alluded to the comparable job worth activities in local government and noted that there is a paucity of data on how far these have advanced. By 1984 ten cities and counties in the state of Washington were undertaking pay equity activity (Hutner, 1986). Minnesota has had a very strong flurry of activity owing to the requirements of state law, as discussed above. Local governments were protected from legal action until Aug. 1, 1987, in proceeding with job evaluation studies and comparable job worth implementation in 855 cities, 87 counties, and 436 school districts—an estimated 163,000 individuals, of whom 56 percent were women (California Comparable Worth Task Force, 1985). The completion of this work will be very important for the government employees affected but will also have spillover effects in the private sector all over Minnesota. If and when all fifty states adopt legislation similar to Minnesota's, the effect nationwide on business would be electric. This is the reason comparable job worth is such a challenge to management and such a source of fear—fear of the unknown implications.

The California picture is Minnesota's on a greatly magnified scale. There are almost 7,000 local government units in California, reflecting 439 cities, 58 counties, 1,029 school districts, and 5,200 special districts (such as water, lighting, fire protection, and the like), as well as 70 community college districts. Different types of local governments provide widely varying services and are likely to have quite different work forces. Cities tend to have more male-dominated classifications than do counties, owing to the historical sex segregation of jobs. For example, police, fire, and public works maintenance jobs loom large in cities. Health and welfare workers, which tend to be female-dominated, are important in counties. Also, local governments tend to have a large number of bargaining units because of the strong organizational drives of such public-sector unions as the AFSCME and the Service Employees International Union, two of America's largest unions (California Comparable Worth Task Force, 1985). We need to be alert to the fact, however, that the vast majority of local government units have not yet begun to act on comparable job worth.

But several local governments have implemented (or are in the course of installing) the principle of comparable job worth, and they have used various mechanisms. Some jurisdictions have contracted for technical job evaluation studies and changed their compensation practices according to the results. Some have piggybacked on other jurisdictions' studies or reevaluated jobs entirely through collective bargaining. Many local governments have simply awarded increases for women in female-dominated jobs as a result of negotiations with the union. In general, the number of classifications that receive increases depends on the number of bargaining units involved unless the public-sector entity voluntarily undertakes a study of all classifications and implements the results. For the most part, the impetus to implement comparable worth in local government originated with employees or unions. It also appears that success in implementing comparable worth principles there can be attributed to strong union leadership and cooperation among the particular unions involved, a supportive attitude by the particular local government employer, the cooperation of male employees, and the strength of local women's groups.

A brief summary of selected cases of comparable job worth implementation in California follows. With 4,000 employees, the city of San Jose became a focal point for the entire nation in 1981 when the first comparable worth strike took place. This singular event (which is explained in depth in the next chapter) grew out of employees' appeals to the city council and lack of results as early as 1978. The AFSCME focused in 1978 on the pay of clerical and library employees and asked San Jose not to use market rates when sex stereotyping was a factor in pay. A task force of nine city workers and city personnel department representatives made a study of nonmanagement jobs with the assistance of a Hay-plan consultant. This study showed that female-dominated jobs paid 2–10 percent on the average below the overall wage trend pay administration line, whereas male-dominated jobs paid 8–15 percent above the pay line. Of forty-six classes paid more 15 percent below the pay line, thirty were female-dominated. The results of the study became an issue in collective bargaining and a strike for nine days by AFSCME workers. After the strike, the city of San Jose agreed to pay $1.4 million over two years in addition to the across-the-board increases granted all city employees. In 1984 all underpaid female-dominated classes were brought to within 10 percent of the pay line (California Comparable Worth Task Force, 1985).

In 1981 in the city of Berkeley (with 1,000 employees), a contract between the city and the SEIU provided for a joint committee to review wage rates for 13 clerical classifications and the award of back pay beginning in 1982. The job evaluation factors to be considered included internal and external comparisons and comparable job worth. The review was completed without using an outside consultant. About 150 clerical workers received a 10–15 percent pay increase over a one and one-half year period; the increase totaled $1.1 million including the back pay.

In the City and County of San Francisco, with 25,000 employees—12,000 of whom were represented by the SEIU—and a total annual budget of $1.5 billion, ad hoc studies as early as 1978 by local women's groups and unions pointed out race- and sex-based pay inequities. A joint city–SEIU committee established in collective bargaining submitted a report in December 1984 recommending that the city act to remedy the inequities. Then the joint committee negotiated an agreement that created a Pay Equity Fund, which would accrue beginning July 1, 1985. Adjustments were made to the pay of 7,000 city employees with an across-the-board average increase for 1985–86 and 1986–87. The exact amounts of pay for each classification were to be determined jointly. The cost was estimated to be 2.3 percent of the city's total personnel budget. There was considerable conflict in City Hall between the City Board of Supervisors, the City Attorney, and former Mayor Dianne Feinstein over comparable job worth before the matter was finally resolved.

The picture in the City, County, and School District of Los Angeles is a difficult one to summarize, but it is an important one, because it is an exemplar for large urban areas. The Los Angeles Unified School District, with 78,000 employees and an annual budget of $2.5 billion, has taken significant action. In 1983 and 1984 the Board of Education adopted resolutions to study the relevant options, to identify female-dominated jobs, and to seek pay adjustments. A union, to which the clerical workers in the LAUSD belonged, the California State Employees' Association, proposed in negotiations that the LAUSD undertake a job evaluation study that examined the various types of systems. Through collective bargaining, 14,000 classified employees received pay equity increases of .55–1.5 percent beyond across-the-board increases for 1983–84 and slightly greater increases for 1984–85. The cost was $1.5 million for 1983–84 and $3.0 million for 1984–85.

With about 65,000 employees (and 38,000 of these represented by the SEIU), the County of Los Angeles has been engaged in a controversy and lawsuit with the SEIU, which has so far unsuccessfully proposed in negotiations a study involving comparable job worth. The SEIU undertook its own study, which was completed in April 1985 and piggybacks on the Minnesota county studies, to document sex, race, and ethnic discrimination in wages and promotion practices and to compare entry-level requirements for male- and female-dominated jobs. At the same time, employees filed a sex- and race-based wage discrimination claim against Los Angeles County with the EEOC that is still in litigation at this writing. In the city of Los Angeles a landmark comparable job worth settlement was reached in May of 1985 that resolved a complex but fairly obvious problem of sex-based pay discrimination. The AFSCME represented 5,000 employees in clerical and library worker jobs. Women occupied 70 percent of these jobs, and they were inequitably paid in comparison to men in such male-dominated positions as maintenance workers, garage attendants, gardeners, warehouse workers, and delivery drivers. AFSCME employees had filed a complaint in 1983 with the EEOC, contending that the city's pay structure discriminated against female employees. Mayor Tom Bradley and the city council urged a settlement through collective bargaining with the AFSCME. The result was the achievement of an agreement for a three-year period to phase in 10–15 percent special salary increases for 3,900 city clerks and librarians. The cost of the salary increases was estimated to be $12 million or about one-half of 1 percent of the city's $2.1 billion general fund budget. The AFSCME then dropped its charges filed with the EEOC (*Los Angeles Times,* May 9, 1985, p. I-34). It should be recalled that this settlement was reached after the *AFSCME v. State of Washington* case was resolved in favor of the AFSCME and before the reversal on appeal and subsequent negotiated settlement in 1985–86. The reasons for the settlement could be endlessly speculated on and were probably affected by politics as well as the simple justice of pay equity. This writer views the decisions as a landmark that in the perspective of the next two decades will prove to have set an important precedent.

Other localities in California that have taken one type of action or another include Santa Clara County, Sacramento Unified School District, and Pasadena. In general, throughout California, and probably the nation as a whole, public-sector studies of their job structures will show that women dominate the lowest-paying jobs, and men, the higher-paying but not necessarily more valuable, hard-to-fill, or difficult jobs. The research and documentation that is going on around the country will probably never be compiled in one place to show fully how much sex-based pay discrimination exists nationally. Such a compilation is hardly necessary and may be redundant, though, because in the field of comparable job worth we are experiencing the spread of a phenomenon that is moving faster than management's awareness of it. The factual materials described in this chapter should be viewed as landmarks for tomorrow.

How costly are the types of economic adjustments that have been made by the states and local government bodies? We turn to estimates of these next.

Costs of Comparable Job Worth Pay Adjustments

Hildebrand (1980) and Perrin (1985) represent the school of thought in economics that comparable job worth is economically unsupportable. Their calculations and speculations when funneled into the popular press and read by corporate managers are very frightening to prudent people. Bergmann (1986) and Cook (1985) approach the issue of costs more like institutional economists whose views are tempered by a can-do attitude toward the formulation and implementation of public policy. Institutionalists tend to be problem solvers (Witte, 1957). Admittedly, the economical costs of implementation represent a hot issue that has generated unceasing controversy (Lindsay, 1984; Killingsworth, 1985; O'Neill, 1984).

Yet the data that are available from estimates given in publications concerning state and local government implementation of comparable job worth are not draconian or depletive of the public treasury. Indeed, they are reassuring and suggest that the costs of implementation for affected female employees are neither large nor necessarily protracted before pay equity is achieved. These observations are important to keep in the forefront because government employers are not small and they do employ many women. The constraints on state and local government spending by tightfisted taxpayers are legendary. Also, the male-female pay gap in government employment may be closer to 80 cents than the 64 cents applicable throughout the economy. This fact may make it easier to narrow the male-female pay gap in government employment, although the large size of government work forces tends to make the task of achieving equity more difficult. On pure numbers alone the hundreds of thousands of small businesses in the United States should find it relatively easier to fight internal sex-based pay discrimination than does government, because the size of small business necessarily means fewer people are involved and the costs would be correspondingly more limited.

The costs for attaining comparable job worth in the states, cities, and other jurisdictions referred to earlier in the chapter seem moderate, if not modest. In one review of such costs, the researcher's estimates as percentages of payroll were as follows: Minnesota, 1 percent of payroll for each of four years; Ohio, 1.5 percent of the general fund's state payroll (but this may be needed for several years); Oregon, 1.1 percent of the state payroll; the city of Los Angeles, .5 percent of a budget of $2.1 billion (Hutner, 1986). The National Committee on Pay Equity in late 1987 announced that most states phase in pay equity adjustments over a two- to four-year period at an overall cost of 2 to 5 percent of the payroll budget. Minnesota had actually spent only 3.7 percent of its payroll budget over a four-year period and completed its pay equity effort. The state was next planning to implement adjustments for city, county, and school employees, a project for 1988 and thereafter that was expected to take two and one-half years at a cost of 2.6 percent of local payroll budgets (National Committee on Pay Equity, 1987). Other figures mentioned in this chapter (such as the 1 percent discussed regarding Michigan) are in line with these. Obviously, many millions of dollars are involved in small percentages of very large payrolls. Cost is also obviously a function of the rapidity of the timetable for implementation as well as the decimal involved in the male-female wage gap in a public- or private-sector organization. If the wage gap is 64 cents, parity achievement will cost more than if it were 81 cents. An employer with the lower figure would be advised to stretch out the time period for achieving comparability, unless there is a reason to accelerate the process. For many organizations, about 1–2 percent of payroll for up to five years should go a long way toward resolving the matter and would in most instances be sufficient. Realistically, though, a higher percentage might be required, depending on the organizational profile and sex composition of the work force and success of efforts to eliminate inequities that presently exist.

These percentages of payroll should look to many companies as monetary allocations that are far less than the 4–6 percent of annual payroll commonly earmarked for merit increases for employees in a calendar or fiscal year. These amounts are manageable for many companies even if added to the usual percent of payroll to be increased annually (about 4–6 percent per year) for funding merit, promotional, and general increases. If the equity adjustments were funded by deducting 1–2 percent of payroll from the merit increase budget for 1–5 years, that approach might be very acceptable to employees, considering how much perceptions of equity and the morale of female employees might increase. Male employees probably will not altruistically stand by, but we have not been shown by public-sector experiences to date that men become less productive or more antagonistic toward women as a result of efforts made to implement comparable job worth.

Conclusion

The state and local government activity in comparable job worth is pioneering. All such endeavors contain trial and error, inefficiencies, and mistakes, however. Management needs to draw positive lessons from these curves and turns in the road as well as from the straightaway that leads in more certain directions. Unfortunately, no one knows what this is in the field of comparable job worth. Litigation and legislation have brought about change. Collective bargaining has been an important part of both. We turn next to a more in-depth consideration of collective bargaining, because many believe that the negotiatory processes and give-and-take of bargaining can adapt to the challenge of comparable job worth and provide an innovative means for applying the techniques of job evaluation.

4

Negotiating
Comparable Job Worth
in Organizations

Unions have already proved that the institution of collective bargaining can be used to deal decisively with comparable job worth. This newly found capability of what some perceive as an obsolescent institution utilized by a moribund labor movement in an era when trade unionism seems no longer to have great numerical strength and ideological support may seem surprising. But the resiliency of collective bargaining should not come as a shock to anyone. It is too early to plan its funeral. Comparable job worth is a great rallying point for trade unionism, the women's movement, civil rights advocates, and others who seek economic justice and fair play. This cry is also not likely to wane.

Management can reap great benefits from the doctrine too if it so desires and interprets the challenge of comparable job worth not as a threat to its status, but as a problem of pay equity that it can and must solve. Actually, whenever management sits down with the union to negotiate pay adjustments, it is plunged into policy change decisions (some major but most minor) and will end up as a party to the problem solving needed to address sex-based pay discrimination if that is the pay adjustment concern of the union.

In dealing with the AFSCME and the SEIU, which have substantial female memberships, not to mention the American Nurses Association (which is almost all female), management can expect to find an adversary on the other side of the table with formidable knowledge and experience. Public-sector managers, policy-level executives, and human resource managers need to do much prior thinking and preparation before confronting the AFSCME's challenges in the pay equity arena. Management needs to do research and study where it stands on comparable job worth before it can bargain on the topic. Male employees in the bargaining unit are likely not to be altruistic about moderating bargaining demands that potentially benefit them or to give up what they might otherwise demand and win for the sake of giving pay equity to female employees. Unions will feel this nonsupportive type of male pressure at the table, and management might even be looked to by male unionized employees as the last bastion of their protection against a crusading union leadership and disgruntled inequitably paid female employees in the union. Put another way, collective bargaining can become more complicated than ever for management when there is a comparable job worth overlay.

Moreover, management needs to consider how much it can trust adversaries in solving a problem such as comparable job worth. We must remember that the framework for management-union relations in the United States was set in 1926 under the Railway Labor Act, in 1935 under the Wagner Act (National Labor Relations Act), and in 1947 under the Taft-Hartley Act (Labor-Management Relations Act) forty to sixty years ago—on the quasi-Marxian theory that labor and management were natural adversaries with virtually irreconcilable conflicting economic interests. In recent years we have found that adversarial behavior and conflict set the wrong tone for management-union relations in an internationally competitive world. Cooperation is needed. Also, new challenges, such as comparable job worth, were never conceived of forty to sixty years ago when the American framework for management-union relations was initially put together.

Today we find that unfair pay lawsuits by women are and should be made against both management that discriminates against them and unions that unlawfully and unfairly represent them. Of course, all collective bargaining agreements that disadvantaged the economic life of women and were in force before the EPA and Title VII were enacted were lawful prior to 1963 because sex discrimination was not prohibited by statute. However, the point is that standing alone, collective bargaining was not able for decades to extirpate sex discrimination. Residual male trade unionists' antipathy toward equal opportunity for women in industry still functions as a barrier to making full use of collective bargaining for the implementation of comparable job worth, as suggested above. This can be clearly seen in the building trades and construction industry.

There is still another facet of the problem of an adversarial stance when it is lawfully built in and emphasized in management-union relations and the theoretical foundation for interaction between the two parties. When relations are bitterly conflicted, unions can express their antipathy toward management by filing an inordinate number of grievances against management in a concentrated time period. Clogging the grievance procedure to clobber management with meritorious and unmeritorious grievances is a commonly found form of trade union behavior. Since the enactment of the EPA and Title VII, unions that have been antipathetic toward management have also had another channel open to them. They could encourage disgruntled female employees who were also, of course, union members to file charges against management for sex-based discrimination, including pay discrimination, even, paradoxically, in situations where the union negotiated the collective bargaining agreement with its provisions on wages, hours, and terms and conditions of employment! Looked at another way, individual or class action lawsuits could be instigated (or at least encouraged) by the union as a further blow to an already clogged up grievance procedure in an effort to fight management. How commonly this happens is not known. But the lesson to be learned is that the outmoded conflict we must still live with in management-union relations today is hardly a solid rock on which to build a foundation generally capable of handling the implementation of comparable job worth. A problem-solving outlook on the part of both management and union negotiatiors is needed.

In this chapter we proceed by taking a closer look at union involvement in dealing with the male-female pay gap problem. We then look at the pertinent strikes in the city of San Jose and at Yale University, which were, respectively, public- and private-sector work stoppages that shocked management across the country and were clear signs of the new challenge. The San Jose strike, as we saw in the last chapter, was the first pay equity event to obtain widespread attention, although the *AFSCME v. Washington State* decision stirred up pay equity opponents more thoroughly than San Jose, *Gunther*, or anything else had done before (Hutner, 1986). However, the comparable job worth strike drama that caught the public's eye was at San Jose. Last, we conclude the chapter with a characterization of how management can adapt to and develop a posture for negotiations on comparable job worth. This has great pertinence for policy-level executives but should be of particular interest for line and staff managers and human resource managers who sit at the bargaining table and must negotiate wages, hours, and terms and conditions of employment.

Union Involvement

From prior chapters, we have learned that unions have been responsible for some of the most important pay equity successes achieved to date. However, only 14 percent of women workers belong to unions, and they are in two categories. One is government, where, of course, there are hundreds of thousands of unionized teachers in the American Federation of Teachers and National Education Association affiliates. The second is manufacturing, especially in electrical appliances and products (such as in companies like Westinghouse and General Electric) and in textiles (such as in the innumerable women's and men's garment-making companies organized by the International Ladies Garment Workers Union and the Amalgamated Clothing and Textile Workers Union). Also, about one-third of the women workers in the transportation, communication, and public utilities sector belong to unions; hence, we see sizable memberships in the Communications Workers of America (which has organized many telephone companies), the Newspaper Guild (which has had major impact on newspaper publishers), and the SEIU (which has very broad jurisdictional boundaries encompassing a wide variety of service workers in the public and private sectors). The percentage of unionized women is about as high in these industries as in government, but the absolute number is small. On the other hand, in the finance, insurance, and real estate industries, only 2.2 percent of the female employees are organized. Of the service industries category, 6.3 percent of women workers belong to unions. In wholesale and retail trade, 6.4 percent are union workers (Hutner, 1986).

The service sector of the American economy has produced the largest growth in jobs in recent years. For example, there was an increase of five million jobs in service occupations alone while employment in the manufacturing sector fell during the same period. We all know that the majority of women work in the service sector. The largest percentage of women workers—about 35 percent—are clerical workers. The next largest group—about 20 percent—are service workers. Professional and technical occupations provide 18 percent of the jobs in which women are employed. Most of the women workers in the service-producing sector are not union members, and the common perception is that they are difficult to organize. The continuing influx of women into this growth area of the economy (which is resistant to unionization and likely to remain so) means that reliance on collective bargaining as their road to comparable job worth would be unrealistic (Hutner, 1986).

The AFL-CIO as the American trade union center (or point of coordination for organizing and lobbying activity on behalf of the national unions) has taken an interest in comparable job worth. The severe declines in union membership in the traditional union strongholds of manufacturing, construction, mining, and transportation have caused unions to seek members in the service industries. Thus, we find such oddities as the United Automobile Workers organizing state government employees in Michigan, the SEIU organizing a branch of the Equitable Life Assurance Society, or the Teamsters (associated in the public mind with truck drivers and warehouse workers) going after hospital employees! In the process of this organizing at the boundary of or clearly beyond their designated and/or traditional jurisdictions, unions have discovered that eliminating sex-based pay discrimination is an issue with great appeal for women (Hutner, 1986).

Actually with the decline of blue-collar workers, the target areas for union organizers for the past three decades have been white-collar workers, the South, and the service sector. The white-collar area has a very large pink-collar segment in it consisting of women in clerical jobs. However, people in white-collar male-dominated managerial, professional, and technical jobs in private industry are resistant to unionism. Similarly, perhaps taking their cue from them, pink-collar females are uninterested or indifferent. The area of the United States with the greatest number of unorganized employees, namely the Southern states, retain union-busting right-to-work laws. And the service sector of the economy—another potential growth area—has already experienced some increase in unionism among workers (such as school teachers, social welfare workers, custodians, and others) who were most discontent and exploited in pay. Therefore, the labor movement has no choice today but to think of how it can become more attractive to women and to revise its organization strategy accordingly if it wants to get back on the growth trail.

International Business and Competition

To this point we have sketched the broad picture of collective bargaining and the problems of union growth. There are several specific problems affecting American trade unionism today that have an important impact on comparable job worth: the foreign competition faced by American firms engaged in international business, concession bargaining and two-tier wage structures, and union attitudes toward job evaluation and seniority. Each of these problems requires some discussion.

American firms and multinational corporations face great competition today from overseas producers, particularly in the Pacific Basin, that usually have lower labor costs. Acting on the theory that the implementation of comparable job worth would raise its labor costs by increasing the wages and salaries of women to the levels of men in comparable male-dominated jobs with the costs generated then passed on in the product market, the American business firm often argues that it cannot afford the costs of pay equity. Unions that perceive their own destinies, the job security of their members (and probably have few women members), and the survival and growth of the union as threatened by offshore competitors may very well adopt the theory of the managers they deal with about the economic unfeasibility of comparable job worth. The same might hold true for unions that have felt pressed to agree to such concession bargaining gimmicks as pay cuts, the postponement or stretchout of pay increases, or accepting low pay increases; givebacks in benefits (such as consenting to the renewal of employee contributions to the cost of health insurance in instances where this was previously noncontributory—the employer paid all); or the creation of two-tier pay structures. In the latter, newly hired employees accept jobs at lower rates of pay than senior employees occupying the same types of jobs *and* continue to be paid inferior rates because their jobs are permanently paid on a lower schedule, a lower wage line, as it were. In any of these instances, where the application of concession bargaining has an adverse impact on a sex-dominated (or, of course, a race-dominated) class of employees, the concessions could be a cause of action for a lawsuit grounded on discrimination. The fear of such lawsuits and the union's appearance of unfairly representing members might prevent widespread application of two-tier wage structures, although we see many in operation today in airlines, retail grocery stores, and transportation companies. To date pay cuts for public-sector employees and proposals for economic retrenchment in the form of two-tier wage structures have not caught the imagination of human resource management and compensation specialists in government. The vigor of the comparable job worth movement in the public sector might meet its severest test in some state or municipal fiscal crisis yet to come, which would stiffen administrators' resistance to implementation of the concept as much as perceptions of labor costs in international business competition have affected private-sector management (Lorber and others, 1985).

Union attitudes toward job evaluation are also important when we think about comparable job worth. There is no uniform or consistent union view on the subject. Traditional craft unions that are still male-dominated have railed against job evaluation for many years. In fact, the most detailed and carefully reasoned attack on job evaluation prepared by the Machinists' Union is a well-known gem in the literature of compensation (International Association of Machinists, 1954). The skilled tradesperson considers pay simplistically as a very direct function of the labor market: he (or possibly but rarely she) charges what the customer will bear and wields bargaining power in this context. Industrial unions that have organized workers not along craft lines but by company or establishment unit have typically favored the use of job evaluation. Typically, these unions have such diversified jobs encompassed in the bargaining unit and such widespread membership desires for variations in pay that reflect minute differences in the work performed that they have supported managerial use of job evaluation. The differences in paychecks that reflect the small differences in work appease (and perhaps also please) the membership that works in electrical product manufacturing plants, automobile factories, tire companies, steel mills, and the like. Hence, job evaluation fits well, and if and when rates of pay on new jobs set by management are not to the employee's or union's liking, grievances can be filed in protest and will usually culminate in job restudy and establishing a new rate that is made acceptable to the protesters. In many collective bargaining agreements, rates on new jobs are a strikable issue during the life of a contract. This means employees may walk off the job lawfully, and it would not be a wildcat strike, because in their contract they had negotiated a clause permitting rates on new jobs to be strikable. By extension of meaning, it can be seen that the product of job evaluation ultimately comes under the control of the worker and the union.

In the type of union that functions as a professional association, such as the National Education Association or the American Nurses Association, use is made of job descriptions and job evaluations as in an industrial union, except the local union would have far fewer jobs with which to concern itself and the sophistication in job evaluation would in all likelihood fall short of that found in traditional mass-production industry. Where the AFSCME and the SEIU prevail, they interface with administrators of merit systems in public employment that often have had decades of experience with job evaluation. As we noted earlier, all the states reported on have job evaluation systems; some, such as Indiana, have seven, and Michigan had eleven.

When unions bargain in the public sector, they are pioneering in negotiations over comparable job worth. We can benefit by examining how the city of San Jose, California, and Yale University in New Haven, Connecticut, muddled their ways through strikes and negotiations in what was virgin territory at the time.

The San Jose Strike and Aftermath

San Jose represents for the first time in the history of the challenge of comparable job worth a case where (1) the issue was placed on the bargaining table through a formal collective bargaining process and where (2) the workers struck over the issue when the negotiations reached an impasse. The settlement, reached after nine days of striking, allocated $1.4 million over a period of two years for extra "internal equity adjustments" to "predominantly female-dominated positions" over and above agreed-upon general pay increases. Under the settlement, the city of San Jose acknowledged comparable worth as a legitimate issue but stopped short of adopting it as a salary policy (Farnquist, Armstrong, and Strausbaugh, 1983). The city administration prefers to look upon the experience as dealing with the pay gap between female- and male-dominated jobs and with internal equity (Hutner, 1986). Yet if we look at the San Jose case in some detail, it is hard *not* to conclude that it is an exemplar in comparable job worth and a clarifier of what is at stake in the challenge to management. Let us consider the richness of San Jose as a case study.

In the period since 1960, San Jose has moved from being one of the world's largest agricultural centers to being considered the high-tech capital of the world, ensconced in Silicon Valley, one of the most affluent metropolitan centers in the United States. Less well known is that San Jose had gained a reputation as a feminist power center. Some have even gone as far as to call it the "feminist capital of the world" (Hutner, 1986). At the time comparable job worth was introduced locally, seven of the eleven city council members, including the mayor, and three of the five members of the County Board of Supervisors were women. Fourteen of the fifteen cities in Santa Clara County have had women on their city councils in recent years. Women have also been employed in great numbers in well-paying professional occupations in the San Jose area for some time. The city of San Jose put a major effort into affirmative action during this period. The first phase of the city's affirmative action plan focused on "work force parity," the matching of the sex and race compositions of the city's work force with those of the local labor market. The concept of work force parity dominated the direction of San Jose's efforts for seven years, and as it was gradually achieved in many segments of city government, other issues began to arise (Farnquist, Armstrong, and Strausbaugh, 1983).

In 1977, a group of women employed by the city who had banded together to develop a proposal for affirmative action for all women employees submitted a report to the city council. Among other ideas, this report introduced the concept of compensating women's classifications on a basis different from market rates of pay. No formal action was taken. The next year the women successfully influenced Local 101 of the AFSCME, the bargaining agent representing most city employees. The AFSCME included in its 1978 contract proposal a request for a study of the relationships between men's and women's pay in city employment. The city did not want to explore the comparable job worth concept at that time. Also, with the passage of Proposition 13, attention in the city of San Jose was directed toward the wage freeze required by the state of California as a condition for receiving state bailout funds. The latter were vital because Proposition 13 had radically reduced the city's use of property taxes as a revenue source and immediately put local governments in California into a financial crisis. Therefore, the increased use of the state's surplus funds was essential for fiscal survival. Eventually, the California State Supreme Court ruled that the state-imposed wage freeze was an unlawful limitation on receipt of the bailout funds, thereby relieving some of the financial pressures (Farnquist, Armstrong, and Strausbaugh, 1983).

When negotiations between San Jose and the AFSCME resumed, comparable worth again became a major issue, though the city administration reaffirmed that it was not interested in studying the relationships between male and female employee salaries. In April 1979, eighty women employees staged a one-day sick-out designed to impress on the city council the fact that they felt the city was not being responsive to their needs. Coincidentally and simultaneously, the new city manager had been attempting to resolve the problems involved with *management salaries,* especially in regard to how they were determined. The city manager's previous experience with the Hay plan of job evaluation (formally known as the *Hay Guide Chart–Profile Method of Job Evaluation)* led him to recommend the Hay Group to the city council for establishing an equitable management compensation system. The AFSCME then requested that the city contract with Hay to conduct its proposed study of male-female salaries in *nonmanagement* positions. The city manager advised the city council that he thought the Hay plan was not appropriate for setting salaries in nonmanagement positions and that the pay of unionized employees should be negotiated through collective bargaining. But the AFSCME prevailed, and the city council authorized the study, stipulating that there was no commitment to do anything but review the results (Farnquist, Armstrong, and Strausbaugh, 1983).

The San Jose job study was designed to *go beyond* the comparisons of pay rates for female and male employees by including the concept of a job's *internal value to the organization.* This internal value was to be established by evaluating every city job on some common, quantitative criteria. Comparisons could then be made between male- and female-dominated jobs having the same internal value to the organization. Under the theory of comparable job worth, the female-dominated jobs in San Jose would be shown to be underpaid in relation to the male-dominated jobs with the same value, and adjustments could be made to achieve parity in the compensation of similarly valued classes. The Hay plan, one of the oldest and most widely used methods of job evaluation, was applied to the city of San Jose's job structure without being tailored in any way to focus on the comparable job worth issue. However, three large groups of city employees were exluded from the internal value study: members of the police officer and firefighter bargaining units, for whom the relationships among city jobs was relatively unimportant, and the 366 employees in management work, which had been studied and evaluated a year earlier using the Hay plan. The results of the management study were used to revise the pay structure for management based on internal equity but without a comparison of the male- and female-dominated jobs (Farnquist, Armstrong, and Strausbaugh, 1983).

The job evaluation study started with a review, update, and

revision of the city's job classification plan. New specifications were written, positions were reallocated, and the approximately 540 job classes were consolidated into about 300 accurately described and current classes (or jobs). The evaluations were conducted by nine city nonmanagement employees, selected to maximize their representativeness across departments and employee groups. In addition, one manager participated in the committee evaluation process to ensure consistency with the management job evaluations previously conducted. After being trained in the Hay-plan technique and job evaluation process by the Hay consultant, the committee did its work and evaluated each nonmanagement job in the city. To avoid going off on a long tangent explaining how the Hay plan is carried out and how well it worked in San Jose, we move on to the results obtained, presenting in Chapter Six the Hay-plan mechanics together with a comprehensive view of the contemporary challenge of job evaluation for management. Suffice it to say here that the results of the Hay-plan application in San Jose and the employee involvement process used were regarded from the standpoint of employee acceptability as fair, systematic, and credible (Farnquist, Armstrong, and Strausbaugh, 1983).

The final set of values for each job in San Jose was initially treated as it would be in a routine compensation analysis. A scattergram was plotted to illustrate the existing relationships between current pay rates and job evaluation values. Each plotted point represented a single job class, and a regression line was then calculated and drawn to indicate the average trend for this relationship, as shown in Figure 3. In this case, as can be seen, the regression line of best fit has a break in the slope with a bent pattern down because the city's pay patterns indicated lower rates of pay increments for the higher point values. Also, as can be seen in Figure 3, considerable dispersion existed around the general pay trend line. More than one-third of all the classes studied were at least 15 percent above or below the overall trend. In the Hay plan, the band formed by the area within 15 percent of either side of the trend line is referred to as the "error factor" zone and represents the margin of error expected from the rating process. Jobs outside the band were earmarked as needing special pay adjustments if internal

**Figure 3. Scattergram: City of San Jose Job Evaluation
Points by Pay.**

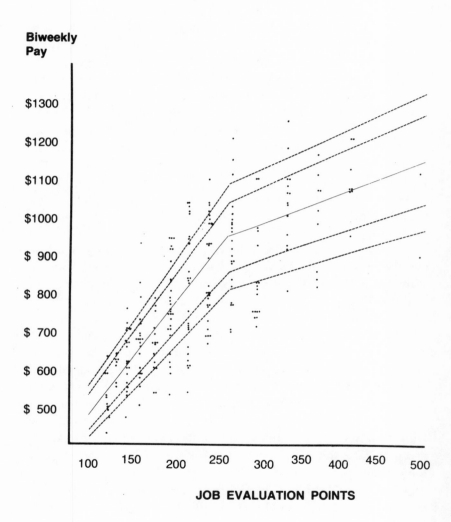

Source: Farnquist, Armstrong, and Strausbaugh (1983, p. 368).
Used by permission.

equity was to be achieved. The classes located within the band were considered to be paid sufficiently close to their organizational value.

The next step was an external comparison of San Jose salaries with those of the fourteen largest California local governments on twenty-eight selected benchmark classes using a standard set of public agencies in the labor-market area to establish comparability. This analysis showed that San Jose's nonmanagement pay practices were slightly above average overall, compared to other jurisdictions (Hutner, 1986).

Lastly, several special analyses were made of the city's pay practices, including compensation level by type of job or occupational group, by extent of working conditions, and by the predominant sex of jobholders. This last analysis was obviously the key to the comparable job worth issue because it compared the pay practices of female- and male-dominated jobs having the same Hay point values. Ideally, jobs having the same internal worth to the city should have turned out as compensated about the same regardless of which sex had traditionally occupied them. In fact, it was found that female-dominated classes were paid an average of 2 to 10 percent *below* the overall trend. Male-dominated classes were paid on the average 8 to 15 percent *above* the trend line. Still more dramatic sex differences in pay were revealed when the undercompensated classes (those at least 15 percent below the trend) and the overcompensated classes (those at least 15 percent above the trend) were examined. We can see from Table 3 that of forty-six classes in the study paid significantly below the trend line, thirty were female-dominated (which amounted to 45 percent of all the female-dominated classes), whereas only seven were male-dominated (representing only 6 percent of all male-dominated classes). The picture by gender domination is reversed when we look at overcompensation. Of a total of thirty-two classes that were overcompensated, twenty-seven of these were male-dominated (21 percent of all male-dominated classes). Only one female dominated class (1.5 percent of all female-dominated classes) was overcompensated.

The results of San Jose's study were made public in the collective bargaining process, and much media and other attention was given to male-female pay differences, raising questions about pay equity in city employment. Should, for example, a female-

Table 3. Class Composition.

	Male-Dominated	Mixed	Female-Dominated	Total
Overcompensated classes	27	4	1	32
Classes within ±15% of trend	92	25	36	153
Undercompensated classes	7	9	30	46
Total	126	38	67	231

Source: Farnquist, Armstrong, and Strausbaugh (1983, p. 367). Used by permission.

dominated class, such as senior librarian (represented in Figure 3 by the intersection of 493 points and $900), be paid the same as a mixed class (not gender-dominated), such as senior chemist (493 and $1,100), with the same rating value? Should the female-dominated typist clerk II (140 points, $550) also be paid the same as the equally valued but male-dominated aircraft refueler (140 points, $729) or automotive equipment inspector (140, $827)? The challenge of comparable job worth is brought home with great clarity in considering the parity of such jobs as appraised by the same job evaluation plan according to sound and acceptable procedures within the same employing organization.

It should be pointed out that some male classes in San Jose that had the same number of points under the Hay plan as female-dominated classes were not only paid 15 percent *above* the wage trend line. They also related comparatively to point-equal female jobs that were 15 percent *below* the wage trend line, resulting in these instances of an inequity of 30 percent! (Hutner, 1986).

But the city of San Jose can in no sense be considered an egregious example in these types of disparities. The city paid at a higher level than did a number of similar public-sector employers in its comparison group. The peer group agencies paid female-dominated classes 5 to 15 percent on the average below the wage trend line, or about 3 percent lower than the San Jose level. Also, comparing itself to ten years previously, San Jose had been 8 to 18 percent under the trend line for female-dominated classes but had subsequently moved up to 7 percent in relation to the trend line. However, male-dominated classes had moved up a similar amount, which had the effect of not reducing the male-female pay gap appreciably.

When the results of the Hay-plan job evaluation study were released, both the city and the AFSCME agreed that job segregation by sex had occurred and that men were more likely to be in the higher-paying and women in the lower-paying jobs. To the business agent for the AFSCME, the major reason for wage disparities in San Jose was sex discrimination. The union thought that a woman should be able to make a *prima facie* case of discrimination if she was a member of an occupational class filled mostly by females. The AFSCME argued that there would be no pay equity unless women's wages were raised to accord with the study. The city administration believed many other factors entered into the male-female pay gap. The political leaders of the city acknowledged that the labor market works imperfectly and that wages may reflect discrimination, but they argued that the city's pay levels had to be in line with the market in order to maintain citizen support. Negotiations got underway, with the city and the AFSCME having quite different views. The city wanted to take action to reduce the wage gap between the male- and female-dominated classes, and the question became how much the increases for women should be. At the same time, the city did not want to cut anyone's pay, because it believed that if it did so, it would become seriously noncompetitive in the market, unable to attract and retain workers in the skilled trades. The AFSCME demanded that San Jose meet the market wage for skilled trades employees at the top end of the city pay scale and demanded equity adjustments for secretaries and clerk typists at the bottom end. The city also took the position that it would not raise the pay of male-dominated classes falling below the trend line. These classes would be paid labor-market rates. Finally, the city was interested in special salary equity adjustments for female-dominated classes that would narrow the male-female wage gap (Farnquist, Armstrong, and Strausbaugh, 1983).

Money issues loomed large for San Jose in 1981. Inflation was 13.5 percent in 1980 and 10.4 percent in 1981. Proposition 13 meant that money from the state of California was in heavy demand by municipal governments. The AFSCME wanted COLA money plus considerable front pay. And in the midst of this came the *Gunther* decision from the U.S. Supreme Court (Hutner, 1986).

In the San Jose conflict during June 1981 the *Gunther* decision as seen by the AFSCME clearly meant that women had the right to bring comparable worth suits based on sex discrimination under Title VII, which was viewed as much broader in scope than the EPA. Although the Supreme Court stressed that it was not passing judgment on the theory of comparable worth, union officials believed that *Gunther* made it possible for women to use the principle of comparable value to show that they had been discriminated against. As a consequence, the AFSCME immediately filed an action against the city with the EEOC alleging nonimplementation of a job evaluation study that showed sex-based wage discrimination. The lawsuit was interpreted by the city as an act of bad faith negotiations, and the AFSCME and San Jose became stalemated. The result was a nine-day strike during July 5–14, 1981, with an estimated 350–400 of the city's 2,000 union-represented employees participating—and most of these strikers were solid-performing, long-service employees who felt strongly about their equity (Hutner, 1986).

While the strike was underway, parties on both sides continued to negotiate. Impasse came with the AFSCME demanding the pay for all classes be moved to the trend line over a period of four years and San Jose indicating a willingness only to move the pay for all classes to the band within 10 percent of the trend line (as shown in Figure 3). This adjustment would move the settlement to a level that would result in several more classes receiving special adjustments than with the original 15 percent band.

The largest hurdle to the final agreement was caused by the uneven distribution over the scattergram of jobs filled by union members. Employees in many of the jobs in the Hay job evaluation study, although represented by the union, were not dues-paying members because of the union security clause in the collective bargaining agreement that permitted this arrangement. This situation was true for several of the most severely underrepresented jobs, the ones that would have received 20 to 30 percent raises if they were moved to the 10 percent band. Conversely, the majority of the female-dominated classes, including most of those composed of active union members, were located close to the 10 percent band and were eligible for only small increases of 1 to 2 percent. This overall state of affairs created circumstances whereby a negotiated compromise that might depart sharply from an objective job evaluation could be salable.

When the strike ended and the agreement was signed, San Jose marched down the road to greater pay equity. The two-year contract authorized a general salary increase of 7.5 percent the first year and 8 percent the second year for all classes and set aside $1.4 million for "special equity adjustments" to female-dominated classes below the 10 percent band. Instead of moving the female-dominated classes up only to the 10 percent band, all female-dominated classes below the band would receive fixed adjustments of 5 to 15 percent over the two years so that some would move within the band to end up only 5 to 6 percent from the trend line. Those classes closest to the 10 percent band would receive the minimum 5 percent over two years, and those farthest would receive 15 percent. Thus, for example, the account clerk II job was 12.44 percent under the trend line (or 2.44 percent below the 10 percent band), entitling it to receive an adjustment of 5 percent in yearly adjustments of 2.5 percent. Accounting technician, which was 31.25 percent under the trend line, would receive the maximum 15 percent adjustment at the rate of 7.5 percent each year. The effect of the agreement was to place a limit on the special adjustments over 15 percent and use the money saved to move the classes less than 5 percent below the band closer to the trend line. Special adjustments were given to some of the female-dominated classes. Adjustments were distributed for female-dominated classes that were not below the 10 percent band, and some mixed classes continued to receive special adjustments so that consistent pay relationships with certain job series could be maintained (Farnquist, Armstrong, and Strausbaugh, 1983).

Both city management and union representatives agreed that the 1981 pay equity settlement improved clerical wages in the private sector in Silicon Valley and that it made it easier for the city to hire help, resulting in the rippling effect that other employers feared and for which women workers hoped. In August 1983, the city and AFSCME negotiated a new one-year contract. In it, they continued with the third year of the four-year pay equity program taking all classes with 50 percent or more women workers to within 7.5 percent of the trend line, adjusted for the 15.5 percent general increase after 1981. The policy also affected classes within the 10 percent zone for the first time—about fifteen more classes in all than in 1981 (Hutner, 1986). Since 1984 San Jose has once again negotiated a pay equity contract and gone as far as it intends to resolve the issues of comparable job worth that arose about a decade ago. It is perhaps time for a researcher to examine the totality of the experience from the perspective of elapsed time.

Some observers believe that the San Jose strike helped the women's movement and caused working women generally to think about collective bargaining as a device that they too should use to better their economic condition, much as working men have been doing for decades (Hutner, 1986). Other observers regard the San Jose conflict as perhaps not centered on comparable job worth at all but an event that circumstantially was given such a direction by a union and city that were seeking the resolution of pay inequities (Lorber and others, 1985). It seems hard to dismiss San Jose cavalierly as not being a major salvo in the comparable job worth struggle. All the ingredients of collective bargaining, the use of job evaluation, power politics, action from the women's movements, sex-based pay disparities, the labor-market defense, and ideological clashes were there and interacted prototypically.

The Yale University Strike and Aftermath

Not too long after the San Jose conflict was resolved, on Sept. 26, 1984, 1,600 clerical and technical employees at Yale University, thousands of miles from San Jose, engaged in a major private-sector pay equity strike. Unlike the short strike and one-day sick-out in the city of San Jose, the strike at Yale went on for ten weeks and seriously disrupted the academic and social life of New Haven, a kind of "company town" dominated by having in its midst such a prestigious university. To avoid having to cross picket lines, many professors moved classes to rooms off campus in church basements, movie theaters, nursery schools, or wherever rooms could be found for instruction. Maintenance and dining room workers in a separate local of the same national union at Yale, most of whom were male, honored the picket lines too, so that the residential college dining rooms, centers of student life, were effectively closed. Many university functions were shut down during the strike. Disagreements among the faculty, the students, and the Yale administration about settling the strike significantly divided the campus (Hutner, 1986).

The San Jose and Yale strike and pay equity situations taken together might portend that comparable job worth can be a strike issue in the public sector as well as in private-sector settings involving services of a public-sector type, such as education, health care, environmental concerns, utilities, and white-collar clerical and technical jobs. This may not mean, of course, that comparable job worth will be struck over in mines, mills, highways, or on the docks (Lorber and others, 1985). But since the American economy has swung toward the service industries, it may not matter greatly whether male workers in some industries do not want to put their personal energy and commitment into striking for comparable job worth. The honoring of picket lines by male-dominated unions and locals may be sufficient support for a while. This fraternal display of solidarity was certainly helpful to the striking women at Yale.

Institutions of higher learning can be as tough and immovable as private business firms in opposing affirmative action policies for themselves and in resisting the challenge of unionization of their employees. Local 34 of the Federation of Union Employees won the right to represent the 2,650 clerical and technical employees at Yale in 1983 after three years of organizing work by its parent union, the International Union of Hotel and Restaurant Employees. Women made up 82 percent of the group; 83 percent were white, 14 percent were black, and 3 percent belonged to other minority groups. The "C and Ts" (as the group was known at Yale) worked at 257 different jobs: secretaries, computer programmers, departmental administrative assistants, psychiatric aides, laboratory technicians, editorial assistants, telephone operators, athletic trainers, and the like, covering the gamut of service and support positions so prevalent in large-scale organizations today and that enable them to carry out their mission and objectives. Efforts to organize the C and Ts at Yale had been underway since the 1960s and had been vigorously and successfully opposed by Yale until 1983. The conventional wisdom is that female clerical workers are difficult for a union to organize. This difficulty is also supposedly magnified in an all-in-the-family company-town ambience, which would appear to be an accurate portrayal of Yale in New Haven (Hutner, 1986). Finally, the unionization of nonacademic staffs (not to mention the unionization of faculties) is not wanted by most universities and is opposed with the plethora of tools available to modern management desirous of keeping its environment "union-free" (the popular euphemism for nonunion).

The pay equity situation at Yale was quite dismal. The statistics provided by the university to the local union showed that women workers in the C and T group earned $13,290 on average and had worked at Yale an average of 6 years. Male workers earned $14,056 and had worked an average of 5.6 years. Black workers had worked 6.8 years and earned $13,563 (Hutner, 1986).

The pay policy of Yale for C and Ts (which may have been more implicit than explicit and thus should be viewed more as "captured" policy than overtly admitted) was to hire employees at rates of pay low in the salary grade range and then to move them slowly up. The practical effect of this, according to the union, was that the majority of employees in every salary grade were clustered in the bottom 15 percent of the range for a particular grade. Throughout the campus only 3 percent of the C and T group were at the maximum in their particular grades. Yale apparently believed that its pay policies and turnover levels were tolerable, however.

The union did not suggest that a job evaluation study be conducted primarily because it judged the C and Ts were so obviously underpaid that any increases likely to be gained would not result in overpaying employees. Also, the union thought that if a study was proposed to Yale and agreed on, Yale could argue that pending knowledge of the results of the study, it would settle for a two- or three-year agreement with only the usual increases. The union wanted "more" (Hutner, 1986).

The negotiations between Yale and the union were further complicated by a concerned group of Yale faculty and graduate students who made various studies of the dispute, hoping that agreement on the basic facts might help to resolve the issues. One of these studies, following a regression analysis methodology used by the National Research Council in its studies, found that after adjusting for age, time at Yale, time in grade, and education, women were on the average paid approximately $700 per year less than men and minorities about $1,000 less than whites within the C and T work force. The concerned faculty–graduate student group suggested that a complete study of sex-based pay discrimination for Yale University as a whole could show even greater discrimination than had already been found.

In April 1984, after many months without progress in bargaining, the union and Yale settled a number of noneconomic issues in an effort to avert a strike. The parties continued to bargain over economic issues but got nowhere. Students, faculty, and local and state leaders urged submitting the remaining dispute issues to binding arbitration. The union was willing to do this, but Yale balked. The university did not want an outsider, such as an arbitrator, to decide such an important matter. (Few private employers want such interference and justifiably do not want a quasi-judge whose own financial resources are not at stake to function in an inappropriate *paterfamilias* role.) Yale argued that the union's demands were too costly. Moreover, Yale asserted that it did not discriminate, and therefore pay equity was not an issue. Yale followed the principle of equal pay for the same work and perceived the dispute as a typical union gambit for higher wages (Hutner, 1986).

The strike began in September 1984 and lasted, as mentioned, ten weeks. During the holiday vacation break in December when most students return home, the C and T strikers went back to work, believing that there was no sense in picketing empty buildings. In late January 1985, Yale and the union reached an agreement on the disputed issues and signed a three and one-half year contract that was retroactive to July 1984. The agreement provided an average increase of about 35 percent over the duration of the contract. A salary administration plan with steps based on years of service was established, and the salaries of current employees were adjusted to the steps where they belonged by virtue of their seniority. The settlement also improved the pensions and health care benefits for the C and T employees. In addition, the agreement provided for a joint management-union committee to study job descriptions and classifications and make recommendations on revisions. The committee was empowered to review employee appeals from the Yale personnel department's decisions on the correctness of an employee's job classification. Overall, even without resort to the usual technique of a joint job evaluation study conducted at an early state of the dispute that compares the point values of jobs and publicizes egregious pay differences between female- and male-dominated jobs, the Yale case should be considered a milestone. It involved comparable job worth and resulted in a victory for pay equity (Hutner, 1986). The management of Yale (or "administration," as management is usually designated in institutions of higher learning) was forced to mend its ways by strike pressure. Would management have met the moral and economic challenge of comparable job worth more adequately by being proactive and bringing about change on its own, guided by unilateral or bilateral job evaluation studies and a responsive policy?

The Potential of Collective Negotiations

With the experiences of Yale and San Jose fresh in mind, the reader should also think back on the early stages of comparable job worth implementation in California, Michigan, Minnesota, and Washington State. To date, there has been a great deal of energy for change and the accomplishment of pay equity generated by collective bargaining. The driving forces within the latter have been unions, management, and government (in the sense of passing enabling legislation or encouraging civil service mandates). The hoary tools of job evaluation have been dusted off and introduced at either an early or late stage (or both) during the struggle for comparable job worth. In some instances collective bargaining was set forth as the best and only dynamic solution, as seems to be the case today in California, given the governor's predilections. In other cases, the comparable worth issue was seen as a public policy problem needing study. This realization was due to pressures from various groups in society and perhaps to a nagging feeling as well on the part of management that sex-based pay discrimination probably existed in the jurisdiction, which appears to have been true for San

Jose, Michigan, Minnesota, and the state of Washington. Unions also became involved in these cases, where public policy was a large part of the impetus. Altogether momentum for change built up and was released in action to implement change.

Negotiations over economic issues are the central core of collective bargaining. For the past three decades, pioneering efforts in collective bargaining have focused on welfare issues, such as changing or adding to benefit plans, dealing with plant closings and employee placement and retraining programs, and helping the union and its members survive adverse circumstances in various ways. We reviewed some of these labor affairs earlier in the chapter, and they do not need repeating here. The institution of collective bargaining appears to have the resiliency and flexibility to assist in the implementation of comparable job worth. But the question as to whether an employer should want to bargain over comparable job worth is a profound one that cannot be answered casually.

In collective bargaining, compensation normally is the strike issue, ratification issue, and financial issue that has an impact on an employer's profitability. Wages are a mandatory topic in collective bargaining, which means that when this issue is raised by management or the union, the other side must bargain over it in good faith. Otherwise, the party refusing to bargain engages in an unfair labor practice under the National Labor Relations Act, Section 8(d), which is unlawful (Lorber and others, 1985). The bargaining table is therefore a natural and logical place for handling comparable worth and a mere continuation of negotiations concerning the relative worth of certain jobs as part of a general effort to achieve pay equity. By bargaining over comparable worth, management can locally control (if only in part) the results and avoid the uncertainty and expense of litigation when it is resorted to by plaintiffs for a remedy. Because labor costs are a major expense in business management or a significant budgetary concern for government employers dealing with the issue of comparable job worth at the bargaining table, collective negotiation helps to identify the possible size of those costs and offers an avenue for controlling them. The affected parties at the table, management and the union, decide what to do—not some *paterfamilias* in the form of an arbitrator or government bureaucrat from a newly established wage-control agency (Mulcahy and Anderson, 1986).

Collective bargaining over comparable job worth also has a negative side. If bargaining reaches an impasse, the employer may be sued in a court or by an administrative agency. In these cases, the union could advance waiver arguments based on management's acknowledgement of comparable job worth or pay inequities at the table. To protect itself, management should insist that the parties agree in writing that when they are negotiating comparable worth they are doing so without the intention of setting a precedent. This understanding should ensure a free flow of information. Management should also require that all bargaining on comparable job worth be premised on the resolution of all related issues in the negotiations (Mulcahy and Anderson, 1986).

The risk of litigation is likely to increase when the employer bargains over the issue of comparable worth but does reach agreement. This will become an immediate concern if the employer acknowledges sex-based pay inequities and fails to correct them. The union may then argue that the employer has acknowledged an inequity problem and, through bargaining, has waived any argument it may have to deny that an inequity problem exists. Moreover, if no agreement is reached, any dispute resolution mechanisms that may exist and are recognized under law or by the agreement of the parties may come into play. Mediation or arbitration could thus enter in and may further compound the problem. By bargaining, the entire bargaining unit and all other employees may also be rallied to present a united front on the issue, and this solidarity could place the union in a very strong position at the table (Mulcahy and Anderson, 1986).

The approach to bargaining comparable job worth may vary from one union to another. For example, a union request may include a general pay increase for a group of employees (to the detriment of other employees) or general language that is intended to commit the employer and union not to discriminate on the basis of many factors, including sex. Ultimately, a determination of whether a particular comparable job worth proposal fits in the category of being a mandatory subject of bargaining requires an examination of the particular language at issue. Since comparable job worth adjustments are wage related on their face, they are mandatory subjects of bargaining. But if the bargaining demand is stated in general language or the union proposes a study, the employer may be in a position to lawfully refuse to bargain on that topic. For mandatory subjects the employer has a lawful duty to bargain. However, the latter does not compel either party to agree to a proposal or make a concession. The law requires only negotiation in good faith and reasonableness in terms of where and when (Mulcahy and Anderson, 1986).

If the decision is made to bargain over comparable job worth, management must first realize it has a duty to bargain but not a duty to agree. Agreements in management-union relations usually are the product of compromise. Second, management must not agree to make comparable worth adjustments until the possible impact of the adjustments from a variety of vantage points is assessed: financial, legal, political, social, and moral. If a comparable job worth study is agreed on, management should have carefully considered its legal and political consequences and concluded that they are acceptable. Third, management must have definite objectives in bargaining over comparable job worth. Specifically, it should identify what the parties are willing to trade off in a world of scarce resources in order to achieve comparable job worth. Finally, management must know the limits of its authority. If the policy-level executives have indicated that comparable job worth is desirable, then the negotiations should not waste time debating the merits of the issue. Instead they should concentrate on ways to implement comparable job worth from the most responsible economic perspective (Mulcahy and Anderson, 1986).

Before bargaining on comparable job worth, management must consider the logistics of negotiating on the topic. A decision is needed on how bargaining will be conducted. If comparable job worth is treated as part of the regular negotiations between the parties, the issue may get lost among more pressing and immediate demands. Moreover, if agreement is not reached on the issue of comparable job worth, it may be the stumbling block that creates an impasse in the total negotiations. An impasse on the issue of comparable worth would probably frustrate a financial agreement for *all* members of the bargaining unit, not merely those affected by comparable job worth. Quite possibly, the best way to avoid such frustration is to take comparable job worth away from the main bargaining table and assign work on it to a comparable job worth task force. This group could concentrate its energies on the issue without diffusing energy over all the other issues being negotiated. Working within clear parameters, the task force could do its work and report its progress back to the bargaining committees at the big table, which would be required to negotiate the ultimate details of the comparable job worth settlement as well as all the other economic and noneconomic demands (Mulcahy and Anderson, 1986).

In terms of management strategy, the options involved with respect to comparable job worth are three: enthusiastically supporting it, approaching it with cautious reservation, or expressly rejecting it. Each option is worth elaboration, beginning with the last, which so far seems to have been the most common one in the United States. Line and staff managers share in solving the problem of how "their" employees are paid and need guidance in how to do this. Top management must sort out its concerns and choose policies and a time frame for addressing *what* to do about pay equity and *how* to implement its choices. The human resource manager and staff must act as a source of in-house expertise, technical skill, collective bargaining sophistication, and administrative capability while being an agent of planned social change.

Whenever management chooses to reject the issue of comparable job worth, it should make clear that it is only saying no to the issue and not engaging in refusal to bargain, which is an unfair labor practice. Management should offer substantive reasons why comparable worth is not necessary or desirable in a particular organization. This approach should preserve managerial flexibility in the event that it is later embroiled in litigation over comparable job worth. Another approach is to reject comparable job worth pay adjustments as a remedy to the male-female pay gap, arguing that the organization's pay rates are labor-market-driven and are based on well-conducted, up-to-date surveys, and pointing out all the efforts that are being made by management to provide equal opportunity and upward mobility for female employees consistent with federal and state laws.

Still another approach—traditional in arms-length bargaining—places management in a more hard-nosed, adversarial posture. In this instance, management requires the union to provide convincing evidence of the reasons for comparable job worth pay adjustments substantiated by objective and verifiable evidence indicating that an adjustment is necessary. The union would be expected to share any evidence it has of intentional sex-based pay discrimination. Under this approach the union would be expected to take the initiative and conduct a pay study. Management would defend its bargaining position by providing wage survey data reflecting the labor market. If the union asserts that the labor-market data merely reflect gender discrimination, then management asks the union to prove its assertions (Mulcahy and Anderson, 1986).

The ultimate in the hard-nosed approach is to back the crusading union into a corner and protect management to the maximum. This posture is not recommended for building a foundation of trust and cooperation with the union because it polarizes management and the union on the comparable job worth issue. Nevertheless, if a bellicose management decides on this approach, it does not cooperate with the union in a pay equity study. Management prepares itself to attack the union's study once it is completed and reluctantly provides the union with very little information. Management at this stage should be guided by the advice of its attorneys about its duty to provide information and its bargaining strategy because critical, irreversible mistakes need to be avoided. Management may to its surprise find that the union demand for information and a study is built on sand and is only a policy made to be in vogue with the bargaining goals of more visible, headline-seeking unions. Management can call the union's bluff in these cases. It can also pierce the facade of insincerity more thoroughly by talking directly to its employees about comparable job worth to find out why employees may not be seeking higher-paid sex-dominated jobs and feed this information back to the union, causing it to be defensive. In an effort to put still more pressure on the union, an aggressive management can force the union itself to deal with the pay equity issue internally. A shrewd tactic in this regard is to negotiate the union into still another corner by causing it to accept the funding of any pay adjustments to address comparable job worth directly from the money pool available for other wage adjustments. A wise union will, of course, try to avoid this onus and politically unappealing tactic. However, if management can cope with it, the union will be faced with the difficult duty of fair representation of all members of the bargaining unit, because in the strategy described, the union is compelled to reward certain employees with larger wage increases and others with lesser ones in order to narrow the male-female pay gap. The members who think they lose out may have a legal cause of action.

Turning from this lexicon of dirty tricks in collective bargaining over comparable job worth, we have a middle-ground strategy whereby management agrees to a study, which brings up a number of considerations. Although a proposal to conduct a study may not be a mandatory subject that *must be* negotiated in collective bargaining, it is clear that an employer and a union *may agree* to negotiate over the commission of a study, the methodology of a study, and what will be done with the results of a study. The union will probably want a study conducted that is based on the internal comparison of jobs, using a quantitative method of job evaluation for determining the value of jobs according to points. Management will want a study that focuses on the external labor market and the going rates of pay found there. Actually, internal and external data are needed for any meaningful study even if they show contradictions in possible job values.

These contradictions, as well as decisions about who will determine job comparability, will need to be resolved by the parties (management and/or the union), a joint committee, or possibly a competent, experienced, objective outside consultant. There would also have to be agreement in the selection of an outsider (if indeed one is to be retained) and how to share the costs of the study (which, incidentally, could easily top $100,000 if 200 or more jobs were involved and much spadework research were needed). Sometimes management takes the position that it alone should pay for the study so that the union does not have a vested interest in or any influence on the results. Shared costs could, however, force implementation when management does not feel ownership of the results.

After the parties have chosen a mutually acceptable definition of comparable job worth and have agreed on an overall methodology for the study and on a formula for bearing the costs of the study, they must decide on how comparability will be concretely determined. This usually means agreeing on the use of a job evaluation plan that contains the factors, definitions, weights, and other specifications desired. The plan chosen should enable the gathering of data that cover skill, effort, responsibility, and working conditions pertaining to the job.

The scope of the study needs to be defined at any early stage of the planning. The crucial concern here is whether all jobs will be evaluated or only male- and female-dominated jobs and no mixed jobs. If the convention of 70 percent is used to define domination by gender and only such jobs are studied, the costs of the study could be reduced and the completion time accelerated. However, an overall study provides knowledge of context and the total structure and may turn up some surprises about how discrimination finds its way into pay plans and causes indefinite and unlawful pay practices management never knew about or has long since forgotten about.

The final results of a well-conducted study can be as much of a problem as the issue of comparable job worth that caused the need to look into pay equity. If sex-based wage discrimination is found, how will the costs of dealing with it be funded? What will be the timetable in years for bringing pay levels into line? Will the results of the study be binding or advisory? Have the parties agreed to bargain over implementation of the results of the study? What is management's pay policy going to be for managerial and non-unionized employees in light of implementing comparable job worth pay adjustments for members of the bargaining unit? The economic pie for annual pay adjustments is rarely large enough to provide an ample slice for everyone. Management needs to explain how and why employees who are not union members obtain pie slices that may not be up to their expectations while not signaling at the same time that their slices might be enlarged by a militant, effective union. An open, honest explanation of the consequences of a pay study may be the best course of action.

A study can provide the greatest amount of control for management when the employer is desirous of eliminating pay inequities or establishing a compensation system based on comparable job worth and the union is committed to a resolution through the collective bargaining process. It is theoretically possible for management and the union to change an adversarial battle into a win-win situation by resolving the comparable job worth issues voluntarily, appropriating the funds for equity adjustments when needed, preventing lawsuits, avoiding EEOC interference, and continuing the political skirmishing that seems inevitable but can also be made controllable. Responsible negotiations between the parties working together to resolve the sticky bargaining issues presented by comparable job worth can produce responsible results that management and the union can probably live with (Mulcahy and Anderson, 1986).

There is plenty of evidence to date from the cases mentioned in this book that collective bargaining accompanied by job evaluation studies offers a solution to the challenge of comparable job worth for unionized employees. We turn in the next two chapers to a close look at job evaluation and in the last chapter to a consideration of the policies and procedures that can be applied to achieve pay equity and close the male-female wage gap in organizations and for employees that are nonunion.

5

Job Evaluation
as a Management Tool

To do or not to do job evaluations; that is the question! We need
to know whether they are potentially useful or a petard to avoid.
Generally, job evaluations can be very helpful in making judgments, in coping with problems arising from charges of discrimination, and in deciding whether two jobs appear to be substantially
equal or comparable. If this generalization is true, then why is there
such an unceasing debate on the subject? The answer is not simple
and is at the core of the comparable job worth challenge to
contemporary management in the United States. We need to know
a great deal about the nature of job evaluation, which is the
substance of this and the next chapter, before settling on an answer
as to whether improvements in the techniques of job evaluation can
solve the problem of implementing pay equity. Even when we
thoroughly explore job evaluation, we may not come up with a firm
answer; however, we will end up with a rationale and a firm
position that management should uphold.

Exploring the Roots

No policy-level executive, line or staff manager, or human resource
specialist in today's highly regulated world of personnel management would deny that one of the most important technical aspects
of planning and administering compensation for employers is

describing, analyzing, and evaluating jobs. Job evaluation and pay administration are clearly the central subject matter of compensation from operational and managerial standpoints. It is a maxim of human resource management that unless pay matters are under control, personnel experts have little time for other important activities such as training, career planning, making the workplace nontoxic and safe, and the like (Patten, 1977).

Job evaluation originated in the form we know it today in the 1920s. During the 1940s the National War Labor Board (NWLB) strongly endorsed the concept and encouraged companies to install systems of job evaluation as the best available means for bringing order out of the chaotic and inequitable job structures that existed at that time (Belcher, 1974). The NWLB was created under a presidential executive order during World War II to serve as a final arbiter of salary disputes between labor and management. In 1942 the board issued an order calling for salary adjustments to equalize the wage or salary rate paid to females with rates paid to males for *comparable* quality and quantity of work on the same or similar operations. However, in its application of this standard to specific cases, the board emphasized that the standard did not require it to evaluate the worth of work that was different in nature. Instead it examined the wages paid to men and women who did *similar* work and required that their wages be equal if the quality and quantity of their output was *comparable* (Lorber and others, 1985). But despite the board's guidelines, companies—of which General Electric and Westinghouse are examples—having studied the jobs in their plants to determine the degree of skill, effort, responsibility, and pertinent working conditions involved, reduced wage rates if jobs were being performed by women by 18 to 30 percent. Sex-based downward adjustments were a general practice in those years, and the NWLB remarked in some of its deliberations that as a rule of thumb, any female job rate below the rate paid male common laborers was probably discriminatory (Cook, 1985).

The roots of modern job evaluation and a rising consciousness of sex-based pay discrimination crossed fifty years ago, and the two are intertwined today. The practice of setting rates of pay for women in female-dominated jobs below the pay of men in male-dominated jobs continued into the 1960s, when many union contracts still contained separate male and female pay scales in which the highest pay for women fell below the lowest for men (Cook, 1985). Judging by the amount of litigation still in the American court system, there is ample evidence that pay equity problems are broadcast today, a quarter of a century after remedial legislation was enacted. It is common in this litigation for plaintiffs and defendants to retain expert witnesses who have conducted job evaluation studies to assist them in pretrial discovery, analyzing depositions, making job evaluation studies, preparing reports, and giving testimony.

To return to a more fundamental plane, job evaluation can be seen implicitly in the pay differentials of apprentices, journeymen, and masters in the guilds of medieval Europe. Adam Smith, the Scottish philosopher and founder of political economy, discussed job evaluation in the 1790s (Heilbroner, 1953). Job evaluation of some type, informal or formal, well conducted and systematic or casual and inadeqate, would thus seem to be inevitable. The basic concern is how to carry out job evaluation in the best way. Specific guidance from the past is not very helpful.

As a field, job evaluation has not been notable for innovation in technique or theoretical advancement. Innovation beyond the four basic types of job evaluation that have been in existence for many years (the ranking, classification, factor comparison, and point plans) have been relatively few. The innovations that have been made in recent years are essentially in the area of job analysis and the study of tasks and duties rather than job evaluation per se.

It is essential that a lawful and thorough job analysis be conducted before a job description can be written. An adequate and accurate job description is needed for each job to be reviewed by a corporate job evaluation committee, compensation specialist, or consultant. In recent years job analysis (the process of empirically gathering the facts about job duties and tasks) has become a focal point in employee selection, owing to Title VII of the Civil Rights Act. Many Title VII lawsuits have been concerned with the role of discrimination in *selection* for employment, and job analysis has consequently emerged as critical to the prosecution or defense of a discrimination case. In this way job analysis and its associated methodologies have become very intertwined with the law.

The adoption of the *Uniform Guidelines on Employee Selection Procedures* by the federal government has since 1978 further elevated job analysis to prominence in the processes and systems of human resource management, and the adoption of these guidelines has been given great credence by the EEOC and courts. The result has been the creation and/or slow popularization of relatively new techniques in job analysis, such as the Position Analysis Questionnaire (PAQ), the Comprehensive Occupational Data Analysis Program (CODAP), Guidelines Oriented Job Analysis (GOJA), the Iowa Merit Employment Systems (IMES), Functional Job Analysis (FJA), and the Job Element Method (JEM), all of which are worth serious consideration (Gatewood and Feild, 1987). Other new and important techniques include the Occupational Analysis Inventory (OAI), which is similar to the PAQ; the Management Position Description Questionnaire (MPDQ); the Work Performance Survey System (of Gael, 1983); the Job Information Matrix System (JIMS); the Critical Incident Technique (CIT); the Behavior Consistency Method (BCM); the Work Elements Inventory (WEI); and the Versatile Job Analysis System (VERJAS) (see Belcher and Atchison, 1987, for further discussion of these approaches). However, except perhaps for the PAQ and FJA, which have also been used in compensation forensics centered on comparable job worth, the other methods of job analysis listed (which are rarely recognized outside of academia by the acronyms shown) are more important as data-collection tools in employee selection decisions than for making judgments in job evaluation. Therefore, we simply acknowledge their existence and their theoretical importance and note where further information about them can be obtained. They play *almost no part* in practical day-to-day job evaluations carried out by businesses and public employers today. In reality, most versions of job evaluation analyze jobs in terms of specific factors and scales for each factor. Despite the proliferation of the relatively new job analysis questionnaire methods, the use of a job analysis interview is still the major method of obtaining job information. The flexibility provided in interviewing apparently outweighs the advantages of consistency and possible analytical power in the more structured techniques (Belcher and Atchison, 1987).

After being in operation for a number of years, all job evaluation systems eventually tend to become classification systems wherein rewards reflect job and hierarchical levels. This is an important point to bear in mind, because it means that in companies or agencies with well-established job structures, the jobs that exist have been slotted in the structure through one means or another and constitute a system at a given point in time. The system may be orderly, equitable, and lawful, or it may be the opposite. A proper type of audit would reveal its real operational characteristics. However, the inclination of many organizations is to obtain the facts on a new job and simply refer to the existing structure in attempting to evaluate the subject job. It would be possible to utilize the "old" job evaluation system and reevaluate the job in question according to the criteria of the old system. But it is more likely in cases like this to "eyeball" the new job and determine where it might best fit in the structure relative to all the existing jobs. This is what is meant by the statement that all job evaluation systems tend in time to become reward systems based on the job classification method and its concepts of level (Patten, 1977). Lethargy, smugness, or a sense of satisfaction based on the philosophy of "if it ain't broken, don't fix it" probably causes many organizations that are not sensitized to pay equity to leave their pay structures intact and unchallenged. For them, job evaluation is not a problem. It may turn out to be a tinderbox in the litigious ambience of human resource management today, though.

Some Basics

To obtain a clear concept of the meaning of job evaluation, we must begin with some basics. For any organization, private or public, the objective in building and designing a pay structure (or several structures) is to relate all the jobs in the company or agency to one another and fix the dollar amount of their worth in an acceptable manner. In any organization moving for the first time toward a rational system(s) of compensation and planning, job evaluation and job pricing are extremely important. On the other hand, in an establishment that has an ongoing compensation system, maintaining the structure over time is of primary concern (Patten, 1977).

Structure building and maintenance are, therefore, very fundamental.

As we already know, and has been explained elsewhere
(Patten, 1977), the labor market does not tell the compensation
administrator exactly what to do about building the job structure.
Instead, building a job structure becomes a complex problem of
administration, judgment, and power (if a union is involved in the
situation). Nevertheless, the market is something that must be
studied in order to test the validity and acceptability of the structure
that is built. There are also other values in the culture that must be
considered and assessed insofar as we are able to do so. We measure
these job-related values by a method called job evaluation.

Job evaluation may be defined as a systematic method of
appraising the value of each job in relation to other jobs in an
organization. In common practice, we refer to *jobs* as work done by
employees paid by the hour, and we refer to *positions* as work
carried out by employees paid by monthly or annual salary.
However, jobs and positions are often used synonymously in day-
to-day managerial parlance. But in a technical sense, the term *job*
includes a number of positions. Also, in common practice, position
evaluation is considered the same as job evaluation.

At its best, job evaluation is systematic, methodical, and
consistent. At its worst, it can be an ineffectual way of ordering
information that is quasi-scientific. There is a great deal about job
evaluation that is subjective, but, by and large, it involves an
attempt to be objective when passing judgment on a body of data
related to the job.

Job evaluation is concerned with jobs, not with individuals.
People fill jobs, and ordinarily their compensation reflects how well
they perform in them. But the job is a separate consideration from
the person and is a grouping of tasks or duties in an arbitrary way.
Job evaluation places a relative value on the job regardless of the
incumbent.

In taking a broad view of job evaluation, we should note that
organizational planning builds organizational structure from the
top down by dividing the total tasks to be performed into manageable and efficient units and by providing for their proper integration through management. Industrial engineering builds

organizational structure from the bottom up, giving its main attention to technology, operations, systems, machines, and equipment. Job design fits between this process of building down and building up. Jobs are designed mainly through the development of job descriptions, job specifications, performance standards, and work rules. The tools of job design structure the nature of industrial jobs and help to identify behavior and worker qualifications required for the conduct of work.

Traditionally, five steps have been used to establish the relative value of jobs. The first step is to conduct a job study, or, as it is commonly termed, to conduct a job analysis to obtain job facts. The job analyst tries to obtain facts regarding the duties and responsibilities of the job. He or she also seeks information about the work requirements for successful performance in the job. In identifying worker requirements, the analyst must refer to public policy such as the EPA or Title VII. The data ultimately obtained in job studies are recorded in as succinct and precise language as possible.

Second, a decision must be made on the criteria or factors that make one job worth more than another to management. The analyst must decide what the organization is paying for and work together with top management to obtain confirmation that it agrees on these. The factors chosen are then used to determine the relative value of jobs. Sometimes these factors are determined a priori; in other cases they are identified a posteriori, after an exhaustive study of an organization and the type of work performed in it.

The third step is to choose a job evaluation system for relating the jobs to one another according to the compensable factors selected. The system chosen can be a traditional one (and probably will be) or one that has more recently been created (which almost never happens). The system can be ready-made or it can be custom-built for an organization (and usually should be).

The fourth step is to apply the system, which commonly means having a job evaluation committee meet, reach and record decisions, and set up the structure. Sometimes an outside consulting firm may do this. Occasionally, an insider (such as someone from the human resource department or an internal consultant) will do the evaluations. The latter approach is almost always unwise, because organizational ownership of the resulting structure will be low and many subtleties in the job evaluations may never be considered. The use of a competent outside consultant may be the best, fastest, and cheapest alternative for a small organization with no expertise in job evaluation. However, for most organizations the model of a job evaluation committee of diversified persons in management (always constructed to include women and minorities) knowledgeable as a group about the jobs and work being evaluated is the best approach to use. Inside or outside consultants and compensation specialists would work with the committee to help solve any problems during the committee's work.

The fifth step is to price the job structure in order to arrive at the organization's proposed wage structure. Here wages and salaries are assigned to jobs depending on their location in the job family or hierarchy. The way this is done depends on whether we are considering a ranking, point, classification, factor comparison, or newly created system of job evaluation. Unions, if involved, will want to inject their judgments. In this way, the organization's jobs are priced, and the average of the prices equals approximately the wage level determined by survey data tempered by the judgments and policies made by management and the union.

Comparable job worth issues become especially critical at this fifth or pricing stage because it is at this step that the discrimination that exists in the labor market is imported into the company or agency. The importation is implicit for those organizations that do not question why rates of pay in the labor market(s) are at the level they appear to be as indicated in the survey. The importation is explicit for organizations that accept them uncritically, or deny that they reflect discrimination, and argue naively that market rates are a dynamic reflection of pure (or almost pure) competitive supply and demand.

Surveys of the labor market(s) can be done before, after, or during the time the job evaluation committee is performing its work on internal considerations. Obviously, it is always best to have current external market data to which the internal data can be tied. The survey will usually provide information only on a relatively small number of "benchmark" jobs (those that are well known, stable in content, populated by enough employees to have labor-cost importance, and representative of jobs at various organizational levels). From the information on benchmark jobs extrapolations are made to other jobs in an organization for the purpose of rate setting. The internal relativities of all the jobs in the structure are thus set in reference to the benchmark jobs at the top, middle, and bottom of the structure. This is why any sex discrimination encapsulated in a benchmark job insidiously spreads throughout the rest of the structure and infects all the jobs with sex discrimination in a typhoid Mary fashion. Any management concerned with pay equity must self-consciously face up to the typhoid Mary phenomenon, as well as to all other evidence of sex discrimination entering the job evaluation process, and put in place the proper policies and procedures for pay rates that reflect with certainty internal job worth as registered by the judgments made in the job evaluation process. Labor-market data should be examined only as a guide.

There is a way around the job evaluation steps discussed above; this is called direct market pricing. A version of it is sometimes called the guideline method (Sibson, 1981). It can be used for a quick-and-dirty type of structure building or the opposite, a careful comparison of selected jobs of interest based on high-quality data collected in a well-designed manner. Since many firms use direct market pricing, a few words are in order.

Some organizations believe that they must be (or want to be) responsive to the labor market over the total range of jobs in the company or agency. These organizations tend to have jobs that are commonly found in labor markets (much like benchmark jobs are), and they choose to recruit at all levels in the relevant labor markets. In these circumstances, the organization usually designs its pay structure so that it can respond to the market first or, in the extreme, not use the internal procedures of job evaluation at all (Belcher and Atchison, 1987). A good example of a sound direct market pricing system is EVALUCOMP, developed by the Executive Compensation Service of the American Compensation Association (ECS) in 1975. The ECS conducts an annual survey using model job descriptions of a large number of occupations in top, middle, and supervisory management; in the professional, scientific, and technician fields; and among a number of sales and office jobs. The

organization using the system prepares a description of each of its
jobs, usually by matching its positions to those surveyed and
adapting the model job descriptions. Once the jobs have thus been
matched, each job can then be priced by reference to the survey data,
and the price can be updated each year based upon the annual
survey. The resulting array of jobs and salary ranges can then be
compared internally and adjustments made to reflect internal equity
considerations (Treiman, 1979).

Traditional job evaluation takes much of the guesswork out
of building a job structure, and there is always the hope that the
resulting structure will be substantially acceptable to both management and the employees. In general, there is widespread acceptance
largely because no better alternative to job evaluation is presently
known! However, there remains considerable disenchantment with
the product of job evaluation from the measurement standpoint
among compensation specialists both in academia and in the world
of work because it represents less than the ideal toward which they
strive. Policy-level executives and line and staff managers also have
their reservations about job evaluation. Except for those who
advocate direct market pricing, no one in management seriously
argues about discarding job evaluation and going it alone. In
reality, such a strategy is, as we have argued, a contradiction: jobs
will be evaluated willy-nilly. The only issue is one of the quality
of what is done!

Compensable Factors and Discrimination

After obtaining the job facts and preparing job descriptions, we
indicated that an organization that is going through the traditional
job evaluation process with the professional and technical help of
a compensation specialist makes several important decisions
involving management in order to determine what the company or
agency is paying for. The first of these decisions involves choosing
relevant compensable factors for the pay plan. These factors should
be present in different amounts in the various jobs. They should
ideally be few in number, perhaps no more than fifteen. They
should be sharply differentiated in type and not overlap. However,
the factors often are vague (such as initiative, hazards, mental and/

or visual effort, and physical effort) and are selected because they are thought to be relevant or are used by other work organizations. They should be capable of being tied one way or another to skill, effort, responsibility, and working conditions as those terms are treated under the Equal Pay Act and Title VII litigation.

Second, consideration should be given to whether we should select clusters of jobs or all jobs in an organization for the purpose of applying one or more job evaluation systems. It may be decided that two or three factors are being paid for throughout the organization and that all jobs in the organization should be included in "one big tent," or, in other words, one system of job evaluation should be used to encompass all extant jobs. However, it may be decided that more than one system is needed. For example, maybe the compensable factors that are important in compensating production employees are indeed different from those used in paying sales or engineering employees. Of course, there are likely to be different compensable factors applicable to executive jobs and clerical jobs. Jobs in the same tent or cluster (for example, production, sales, or engineering) may appear to require their own set of compensable factors, but perhaps they could be made susceptible to evaluation under the same job evaluation plan. At the very least it may be necessary in most organizations to have two job evaluation plans: one for exempt and one for nonexempt employees.

Third, key or benchmark jobs should be identified because they are the best starting points as sources of data for ultimately evaluating all existing jobs. Benchmark jobs are ones that affect wage levels the most. They can be meaningfully related to other key jobs and to nonkey jobs and, as we have indicated, serve as a focal point in the entire job evaluation process.

Fourth, a decision must be made on whether to use a ready-made job evaluation plan or to develop a new plan. There are reasons, of course, for not reinventing the wheel, but an organization should never use a ready-made plan that does not fit its own circumstances or use apparently irrelevant factors that lack face validity.

The factor or factors chosen by an organization need not explain why a certain job is paid a particular amount of money but only why one job receives or should receive higher pay than another. Also, since jobs and organizations change, we should expect that what the organization is paying for, that is, the factors, may also change in time—and probably should change.

From our discussion of the process of how compensable factors are derived, it should be obvious that the process is rational but quite subjective. In today's litigious environment with extreme government regulation of pay and human resource management, we need to have a meaningful and lawful answer to the question: Why are the compensable factors chosen by an organization for its use in a job evaluation plan *the* compensable factors?

Job evaluation is a management prerogative, as we argued in Chapter One; we have suggested at the same time that this is not a naive sweeping view of the subject. Management commonly conceptualizes what it is paying for in job evaluation by specifying scales on such matters as extent of job-related knowledge, work experience, responsibility for product, complexity of the work, and the like, up to perhaps about fifteen variables in traditional job evaluation plans. The important issue today within job evaluation is how to pay employees in such a manner that there is an absence of a pay differential that could be based upon sex or minority status (in the context of this book, especially sex). Management has and should have the right to choose the compensable factors that have meaning for it as long as no law is violated and discrimination is averted.

Treiman and Cheng (1985) have shown how this can be done by the use of multiple regression analysis, to capture the implicit policy underlying an organization's pay system by predicting the existing pay rates for all jobs within a company or agency from a set of characteristics thought to legitimately affect pay rates. Ordinarily these would be the factors in an existing job evaluation system, plus one other factor, percent female. If the resulting regression coefficient or weight associated with percent female is substantially different from zero, "femaleness" would be said to be a compensable factor that has entered into an employer's de facto pay plan. This coefficient means that an expected, or average, difference in pay between two jobs that are identical with respect to all of the other measured compensable factors in the job evaluation plan differ by one unit in their percentage female, which is thus interpreted as a measure of the extent of gender discrimination in pay in the organization. We can say that pay differences arise *because of* the sex composition of jobs if and to the extent that sex is found to be a compensable factor in a compensation system. Put another way, if and to the extent that the sex composition of jobs predicts pay differences among jobs that are equal with respect to their evaluated levels in compensable factors in the job evaluation plan, we have discrimination operative. To remove this discriminatory effect, the organization would need to adjust its pay rates so that the coefficient associated with percent female goes to zero. This in effect would remove gender as a compensable factor from its compensation system after the internal job evaluations have been carried out.

Under these definitions, women's jobs could, of course, pay less on average than men's jobs without pay rates *depending on* sex or race or arising *because of* the sex composition of jobs. For example, in many organizations most managers are men, and most clerical employees are women. We would expect the men's jobs to pay better not because they are male-dominated, but because they require managerial skills and responsibilities. Discrimination would be inferred only among jobs requiring substantially equal levels of skill, effort, responsibility, and working conditions for their performance where male incumbents were paid more than women jobholders.

This statistical strategy for identifying and correcting pay discrimination has four major advantages, as Treiman and Cheng (1985) have indicated. First, it resolves a major dispute concerning the appropriate interpretation of pay prediction equations. Critics of the regression approach to discovering discrimination point out that unless *all* legitimate compensable factors are measured, regression equations that include percent female as a variable will overstate the effect of gender as a predictor of pay rates. This criticism is well taken. But by placing the burden on the employer to show that observed differences in the pay rates of male- and female-dominated jobs are based on factors other than sex, we create a powerful incentive for the employer to do a very good job of measuring whatever it is he or she is paying for. Given the historical pattern of pay differentials based on sex and race, it is not unreasonable to argue that if an employer cannot demonstrate that a pay differential correlated with the sex or race composition of jobs is actually due to some legitimate difference between jobs, it probably *is* gender that is being paid for, which is discriminatory and must be corrected.

This point speaks directly to criticisms of the adequacy of job evaluation procedures as a method for discovering pay discrimination. When job evaluation is used as a tool for defending against an accusation of pay discrimination, the arguments made about the subjectivity of the tool are irrelevant. In these instances the point is not to use job evaluation to arrive at any particular basis for deciding on the relative worth of jobs but simply to discover whether sex is an implicit basis of compensation in an organization and to correct this condition when it is found.

Second, the policy-capturing approach proposed by Treiman and Cheng (1985) is minimally disruptive of the status quo, because it permits the retention of the existing wage structure in an organization except insofar as it contains discriminatory elements.

Third, this approach permits the incorporation into the pay prediction equation of differences between individual workers in seniority, merit, the quantity and quality of production, and any other lawful consideration.

Fourth, it provides a way of taking account of legitimate problems of employee recruitment and retention. Certain jobs may be in particularly short supply and, hence, command higher pay rates than other jobs requiring similar levels of skill, effort, and responsibility as reflected in job evaluations. Such pay differentials should be permitted, even when correlated with the sex composition of jobs, if, but only if, the employer can demonstrate that the organization's ability to recruit or retain workers would be seriously compromised if the jobs in question were paid less. It would be up to the employer to mount a business necessity defense in these cases.

The weighting of job evaluation factors is a final matter of choice, rather subjective, and undoubtedly a management prerogative. In fact, the selection of factors and the decision of how heavily to weight each factor's contribution to the total job evaluation score (as in point systems) are central considerations in the design of a job evaluation plan. Indeed, the choice of factors and factor weights actually dictates the ordering of jobs on the scales of job worth, which are the crucial parts of the job evaluation plan. Specifically, one set of factors and factor weights may produce a particular ordering of jobs while a different set or a different weighting of factors may produce a radically different ordering of the jobs being evaluated (Treiman, 1979). For example, let us consider a job family of occupations in manufacturing work that was female-dominated and a similar family that was male-dominated. The application of factors and weights that would best fit the male-dominated array of jobs might poorly fit the female-dominated job family. A built-in bias would thus operate. This bias could be deliberate or unintentional depending on management's awareness of the subjectivity inherent in choosing and weighting the factors used. For this reason, in exercising its prerogative in evaluating jobs and constructing the job evaluation plan, management should be particularly sensitive to how factor choice and weighting might work out in practice, possibly to the great advantage or disadvantage of either gender. Control against bias should be a paramount concern.

Union Attitudes Toward Job Evaluation

To this point, we have been discussing unilateralism (management's acting on its own) in job evaluation. Bilateralism (management-union collaboration) in job evaluation is not unknown. There have been some important but quite old studies of bilateralism in the past involving an automobile company (Gilmour, 1956) and the steel industry as a whole (Stieber, 1959). The cooperative wage study method of job evaluation (CWS) has been an important but somewhat neglected technique that has, however, recently been reviewed, brought back to the attention of management and human resource specialists, and described in detail (Treiman, 1979).

In a national survey of 39 unions with a total of 7.2 million workers comparing members' views in 1971 and 1978 (Janes, 1979), job evaluation was approved in more than 50 percent of the comments made. The unions' responses indicated they reserved the right to challenge the job evaluation systems at any point and at any time. The 1978 survey reported a decrease in resistance to job

evaluation practices. Over the 1971–1978 period there was a sharp
decline in the number of unions reporting job evaluation plans that
were company-designed but union-modified and an increase in
plans that had greater union participation in their design. Unions
reported that they had difficulty in implementing job evaluation.
Among factory workers the main problem was a lack of understanding of the plan. Among office, professional, and technical employees, there were complaints that management, instead of using
job evaluation as a guide, used it as the sole criterion in setting pay.

There has been a very recent return to bilateral approaches
in which parts of the AT&T colossus and the Communications
Workers Union have cooperated to create a method of job evaluation that would explicitly deal with the remaining pay equity
problems in a major section of the communications services
provided in the United States today (Hutner, 1986). This effort in
the telephone business may contain important ingredients that can
be adapted by other companies seeking to deal with the challenge
of comparable job worth.

The broad issue of union attitudes toward job evaluation
also needs to be addressed more fully than has been done so far in
the book.

These attitudes have ranged from outright rejection of job
evaluation (the International Association of Machinists asserts that
it is a serious threat to collective bargaining), to participation (the
International Ladies Garment Workers Union actively conducts
independent job studies), to indifference and toleration, and to joint
union-management involvement. Sometimes management wants a
joint approach to job evaluation, and sometimes unions want it.
The need for a job evaluation scheme may be initiated by either
management or the union (Slichter, Livernash, and Healey, 1960).

To reach agreement on the location of jobs along a scale of
worth is the basic consideration in any job evaluation effort.
Agreement is customarily a process involving the working through
of issues by job analysts and an executive job evaluation committee,
giving due attention to supervisory opinions and criticisms and
employee views. Employee criticisms may be handled through
various forms of union participation on either a formal or an
informal basis. The extent to which consensus is achieved marks the

degree of success of the job evaluation effort. Again, acceptability is the governing variable here. If we view the evaluation process realistically, we see few differences between a bargained and an evaluated scale of pay. Give-and-take is inherent in both methods.

If management constructs the job evaluation plan and insists the union accept it without revision, the plan will probably fail. The union may pretend to assent but retaliate by formally registering complaints through the grievance procedure at every opportunity. The net result is that the grievance pot would boil more vigorously than ever with controversial ingredients such as points and factors thrown into the already volatile brew.

If management seeks union approval of the plan before installing it, the results could be quite different. This does not mean that every employee will be happy with his or her job's ultimate location in the structure. Nor does it mean that management will like revisions that have been made in the plan as a result of employee and union criticism. Yet both union and management will have had their say, and the process at least narrows the range of bargaining and separates generalized free-floating discontent from a desire for specific changes.

In developing a job evaluation plan, union and management should consider matters not strictly in the area of job content analysis, such as what to do about paying for dead-end jobs, what changes should be made if particular market rates seem too high or too low owing to labor shortages or surplus, what to do about craft rivalry and competition for top rates, and how to share technological gains. These matters transcend the traditional procedures of job evaluation and suggest that an improved understanding and administration of the collective bargaining agreement can come about through the use of organizational development methods applied to working through a system of job evaluation. A consensus may be reached on the important matter of rewards in the work setting, and this result should buttress the job evaluation program as a technical system. For these reasons it is important to see job evaluation as an organizational problem-solving process and not merely a species of measurement problems. On the other hand, we must remember that the job evaluation barnacles of the 1940s are very thickly encrusted on the installation of many job evaluation plans and are not easily scraped away. This means that job evaluation is perceived by many people even today as a mere measurement problem.

More recent efforts at joint management-union job evaluation that appear to be carried out in an organizational development and planned change mode are highlighted in the effort being put into this approach by AT&T and the Bell group of operating companies, which are among the largest employers of women in the country outside of government. In 1980, AT&T (before the divestiture) and its three unions agreed to cooperate in developing and testing a job evaluation plan (known as the OJE plan, for Organizational Job Evaluation Plan) that would be free of gender bias and applicable companywide for about 1,400 job titles (many of which were thought to be duplicative). AT&T wanted to be able to update changes in job descriptions continuously during the three-year life of the contract as new technology changed job content. AT&T and the Communications Workers of America (CWA), AFL-CIO, examined the existing job evaluation plans in the company and took the best from them to jointly develop a new plan that was tested in a pilot study for a year at the Chesapeake and Potomac Telephone Company in Maryland. In the 1983 strike following the collective bargaining in the industry, wages and the job evaluation plan were problems. As a result, the twenty-two operating companies set up their own joint committees to study the plan and asked for help from AT&T and the CWA to learn about what they needed to know for installation of the plan. The twenty-two companies are grouped into seven regions, and progress toward implementation has been slow. The system can be used to evaluate both clerical and nonclerical jobs and still has AT&T managerial and union support. When the company and union negotiated a new three-year contract in 1986, some new provisions for the OJE system were made. There are some problems in implementation that stem from the politics of control—who runs the plan—and from reported indications that some companies or regions may not be interested in the bias-free OJE system (Hutner, 1986).

Types of Job Evaluation Plans

There are two major types of job evaluation plans (or four—two subtypes of the two major types—if we make certain conceptual assumptions). There are the qualitative, or the nonquantitative, types of job evaluation comprising the ranking and the classification methods. There are also the quantitative methods composed of the point plans (also called point-factor plans) and the factor comparison plan. There is no reason to think that quantitative plans are inherently any better than the nonquantitative plans (or vice versa). Which type is better depends on the goals of a particular application and the jobs to be evaluated. Point-factor plans are probably the most popular and seem to have the widest applicability.

There are a few new types and special types of plans. Some of the special types really could be fitted under the categories previously mentioned because they amount to ranking and pinpointing one factor that can be applied to all levels of jobs in the work organization. The federal General Schedule (GS) of jobs and the way the GS jobs are classified are examples of special types of the classification method that have endured with some modification for many decades and have had worldwide application.

The Hay plan is a special factor comparison plan that has been widely installed in the United States. Indeed, newspaper advertisements listing job opportunities for compensation administrators may state that "knowledge of the Hay plan is helpful," which suggests its popularity.

A type of job evaluation that has been used in Britain and on the continent makes use of Elliott Jaques' *time span of discretion*. Jaques (1956, 1961, 1964) has some very different ideas about how to evaluate jobs. He regards all the contemporary methods of job evaluation as subjective exercises in using judgment and believes that none engages in the meaningful measurement of tasks, duties, and human qualifications related to job performance. Instead he recommends that differences in jobs be measured by a single factor, the time span of discretion. This is defined as the time inherent in a job during which an employee carries out work without checking back with an organizational superior for guidance, direction, clearances, and approvals in problem solving and decision making. Time spans are longer the higher one's position in the company or agency hierarchy. Plans such as this one that focus on one factor have arisen in the last two or three decades but are almost never used and remain decidedly unpopular today.

There are any number of special types of job evaluation plans, such as the cooperative wage study (CWS) plan of the American steel industry, which has been described in several books. The American Association of Industrial Management, formerly the National Metal Trades Association, has a point-factor job evaluation plan that is well known. The National Electrical Manufacturers Association has still another popular type of point-factor plan.

Ranking Method

Let us turn to a more detailed review of the most popular types of plans, beginning with ranking. We should note that these plans are probably the most numerous in the United States, although there is little solid quantitative evidence to support that remark. The reason for this is that typically when someone conducts a survey asking, in effect, "Do you have a job evaluation plan and, if so, what kind?", many employers utilizing gross ranking simply either do not respond to the survey or state that they do not have any job evaluation plan. But the truth is that if they do have their jobs set up in an array, they (in effect) have them ranked and they are making pay distinctions.

Ranking is the oldest method of job evaluation and goes back to one of the earliest types of employee performance appraisal. During World War I officers were rated person to person like a totem pole to obtain a rank order of ability. After the war, in the 1920s, the concept of ranking was carried over into ranking jobs in private industry and used both in performance appraisal and job evaluation.

In a very small organization it is possible to rank grossly the jobs in it and obtain quite acceptable results. If a work organization has thirty or forty employees and six to eight different jobs, it is fairly easy to rank them. How helpful this ranking is becomes another question. If the ranking brings acceptable order out of chaos, then we could argue that it is useful.

It is also possible to rank jobs functionally, and a well-known contemporary practice in evaluating middle-management and top-management jobs involves functional ranking of those jobs. This refinement of gross ranking by breaking the jobs into different functional fields of business may be described as follows. We take, for example, all the jobs in industrial relations and rank them in relation to one another. We next take all the jobs in accounting and the controller field and rank them in relation to one another. We repeat this ranking for marketing, public relations, engineering, and all the other functional fields in the organization. Once all jobs are ranked by business function, the ranks are related to one another, and a job structure is built by the resultant ranking. In other words, by taking a functional approach first and evaluating all jobs by function, we solve the compensation problem of building an overall job structure.

If there are a large number of jobs to rank, ranking becomes very difficult. There are ways to simplify the task, and often the paired comparison technique is used in ranking. Using this method, the job evaluation committee considers a job and ranks it in relation to all other jobs. A second job is taken and related to all other remaining jobs. A third, fourth, and nth job are subsequently compared until the ranking task is done. There is a formula that indicates what is required overall in order to compare one job to every other job in an organization.

$$\text{Ranking task} = \frac{n(n-1)}{2}$$

For example, if there are 10 jobs to be ranked (substituting 10 for n in the formula), 45 comparisons are made.

$$RT = \frac{10(10-1)}{2} = 45$$

If there are 20 jobs, comparing them one to another results in 190 comparisons, a formidable choice.

$$RT = \frac{20(20-1)}{2} = 190$$

The method obviously becomes quite unfeasible if a large number of jobs need to be ranked, because the human mind does not seem able to make a huge number of meaningful comparisons. But even in these cases, there are means for carrying it out (Burgess, 1984).

Classification Method

The classification method has a number of unique characteristics. The method can best be described and analyzed generally or by illustration. The latter is preferable in some respects, especially if we use as an example the GS (or General Schedule) of classified jobs in the federal government. This system was formalized under the Classification Act of 1949, which has been amended but still provides for eighteen predetermined grade levels into which literally thousands of jobs are slotted.

In the ranking method the whole job is scrutinized, ideally by a group of knowledgeable managers who have an up-to-date job description to read for guidance. They go about their evaluative work without specific guidance as to where the jobs fit into a structure of predetermined grades. In the classification method the quantum improvement is the guidance made available by the carefully worded grade-descriptor language. The process can be likened to placing a book on a bookshelf. The classificatory scheme of labor grades provides by analogy the shelves from the floor to the ceiling. The language of the job description enables the reader of it to judge where the job (which is analogically a book) should go horizontally or vertically on the bookshelves. Unfortunately, not all books are readily shelved because the job description may suggest that two (or sometimes three) shelves might be logical spots to place the book. Jobs may contain peripheral tasks that make them not fit neatly into the shelves. Naturally, we struggle to write unambiguous grade-level descriptors, but to do this we rely on the use of positive, comparative, and superlative forms of English adjectives. This introduces subjectivity, but it seems unavoidable if we want to try to make meaningful distinctions.

The classification method should be viewed as a refinement of ranking. As far back as 1838 the federal government had rudimentary ways of classifying "clerks," but there was no overall system per se. Until the beginning of the twentieth century there were few people who worked for the federal government, perhaps between 100,000 and 200,000, according to a leading expert (Van Riper, 1958). The federal job evaluation methods of the times apparently worked adequately until employment levels rose. Finally, in 1923 the federal government created a formal system of classifying jobs. It has been amended several times, most notably in 1949 and 1977.

In the 1920s, a number of municipalities also adapted the classification method of job evaluation and used it for city employees, including such large employee groups as clerks, sanitation workers, firefighters, police officers, and sometimes teachers, although public school teachers tended to be clustered in a separate group compensated by millages levied on behalf of school districts. In recent years there has been a movement away from the classification method in government employment toward the point-factor plans.

As the classification system of job evaluation has evolved in the federal sector, it has become the duty of the U.S. Civil Service Commission (now the Office of Personnel Management) to establish standards for jobs. Jobs are then placed in different classes. The largest group includes more than two million employees who are covered by the General Schedule; their jobs are divided among eighteen grades. Most of them are in fifteen grades, and the three grades on top are called the supergrades, constituting a senior executive service. Written standards provide guidance as to why a particular job should be placed in one of these grades. Thus, a job is written up, it is carefully studied and examined, and it is slotted in the structure at the appropriate point, GS-14, GS-15, GS-12, or whatever it happens to be, like a book on a shelf.

A very large part of the staff of the Office of Personnel Management is concerned with writing these standards. There are many volumes that detail the standards. The decentralized agencies of the federal government—such as the Department of Agriculture, the Department of Labor, and the Department of Defense—have personnel administrators who classify the jobs in these departments, place jobs in the structure, and administer the ultimate classification or reclassification of employees, subject to a periodic postaudit by pay experts employed by the Office of Personnel Management. These auditors travel throughout the nation. Using questionnaires

and information on how employees are classified, they decide
whether employees are improperly classified and whether, for
example, such persons should be reduced from a GS-15 to a GS-14,
or from a GS-9 to a GS-8. The auditors have a postaudit and
correction function that for salary administration purposes is
actually implemented by the particular agency where the employee
works. Employees can appeal classification changes through an
appellate mechanism. Unionized employees also have representatives who can help them in these matters.

Many studies have indicated that the federal government has
an excellent and workable classification system that is widely
accepted by federal employees at all levels. For example, a job that
is classified a GS-15 in Washington is likely to be graded the same
as a GS-15 in Alaska, or in Germany, or, in fact, in any other part
of the world where there are federal employees. This assumption is
not entirely correct, however. The preponderance of federal
employees probably are properly classified, but there is enough
vagueness in the way in which the grades are specified and there is
sufficient possibility for aggrandizing the language in the job
description so that jobs can be pushed up or down in the structure
by skilled wordsmiths. The extent of this chicanery is difficult to
assess. However, on balance, the modernized classification system as
used by the federal government probably has done a fairly good job
of keeping employees properly placed in the structure.

A few more words on the use of federal job standards are in
order because they have led to important changes in the federal
classification system to make it more workable. There was no
requirement that these standards follow any particular format,
although a guideline set of eight factors to be considered in
developing each standard was made available:

- nature and variety of the work
- nature of supervision received by the incumbent
- nature of available guidelines for the performance of work
- degree of originality required
- purpose and nature of person-to-person work relationships
- nature and scope of recommendations, decisions, commitments, and conclusions

Job Evaluation as a Management Tool

- nature and extent of supervision exercised over work of other employees
- qualifications required

The federal government was not interested in having all the agencies fall into lockstep in using standards and encouraged flexibility instead. It recognized that the same factors or pattern of factors may not be applicable to all jobs and also that standards written in language that has meaning within an occupational community were preferable to standards written in highly abstract terminology that could conceivably cover all occupations. As a result, some classification standards were written in narrative form, some used factor comparison concepts, and some used point-factor methods.

Complaints began to develop that the classification process was too complex and not easily understood by most federal employees, that grade level was not clearly defined, and that many classification inequities existed. This led to the Job Evaluation Policy Act of 1970, which gave rise to a benchmark factor ranking system. The details of this system need not concern us except to note that the end result was to make the classification standards consistent through the use of a point-factor method. The eighteen GS grades were left intact, as were the administrative procedures for making GS grade assignments (Treiman, 1979). Table 4 shows how the two different systems were bridged in a conversion chart. Much more thought should be given to imaginative bridging techniques in job evaluation, because other applications of them could be made to implement comparable job worth. (We illustrate another one subsequently in the next chapter.)

The pay administration methods used in conjunction with the GS classification system are worth brief review. The president of the United States recommends changes in pay levels in the GS system to Congress. The PATC—professional, administrative, technical, and clerical—survey is used annually to obtain pay data. These data are collected by the Bureau of Labor Statistics in the U.S. Department of Labor, an agency with a reputation for expertise in quantitative analyses. The data from the survey are then supplied to the executive heads of the Office of Personnel Management and

Table 4. Conversion Chart Relating Federal System Points
to General Schedule (GS) Grades.

GS Grade	Point Range
1	190–250
2	255–450
3	455–650
4	655–850
5	855–1100
6	1105–1350
7	1355–1600
8	1605–1850
9	1855–2100
10	2105–2350
11	2355–2750
12	2755–3150
13	3155–3600
14	3605–4050
15	4055–up

Source: Treiman (1979, p. 159). From U.S. Civil Service Commission, *Instructions for the Factor Evaluation System, Section VII. General Introduction, Background, and Instructions* (Washington, D.C.: U.S. Government Printing Office, 1977).

the Office of Management and Budget. The president considers their proposals before acting on pay changes. He may recommend or withhold adjustments for all or some of the positions in federal employment. Congress, of course, has the sole role of appropriating funds and controls the purse strings. It may decide on a higher or a lower pay increase than that proposed by the president. It has committees that review the Office of Personnel Management's proposals and often place ceilings on the pay of higher GS and political appointees. By the use of ceilings, Congress has, in effect, refused to maintain comparability in pay between top federal and top industrial executives in the private sector. At the lower GS levels, pay between the federal and private sectors probably favors public employees slightly. However, to the extent that the PATC survey conducted by the BLS taps into labor-market data and these are used in determining the pay of federal employees on the General Schedule, sex-based wage discrimination is introduced into federal pay levels. This is implicit but nevertheless insidious and a contradiction of the concept of government as the model lawful employer.

The GS system is based on predetermined grading worked out in such a way that the pay specialist can use shadings between one grade and another and also between one job and another to fit jobs into a proper grade. Because of the aggrandizing descriptions of duties and the averaging out of duties, sometimes a job is not properly placed in the structure. One important criterion that federal job analysts have used for slotting a job is, "He or she would be willing to do my work but I would not want to do his or hers," which serves as a reference point in determining job content of more important and less weighty jobs. Also, because heads of federal departments and agencies may want to move a job up or down in value, and because they have the authority to assign duties and responsibilities, these shufflings of books in the bookcase result in distortions of the structure. There has been grade escalation or structural creep, too. However, when one considers the number of employees encompassed by the contemporary modernized GS system, despite its imperfections, it probably deserves more praise than criticism from the standpoint of such goals in compensation as equity, acceptability, and control. But it has survived only through modifications. The tendency is for classifications of the pure type to either meld with point-factor concepts in some way (as did the GS system) or leave themselves open to being replaced by point-factor plans (as has happened in many state civil service systems).

Conclusion

In this chapter, we have been examining nonquantitative methods of job evaluation, which are usually administered by management unilaterally. They are the older methods that have stood the test of time. In the next chapter we move closer to the cutting edge in job evaluation and take up methods and ideas that have currency and are more in the melee of the comparable job worth controversy.

Job evaluation has indeed been impressive over the years as an evolving tool to serve management in rationalizing the internal pay structure. Its greatest success lies not in its claims to scientific accuracy but in the fact that it requires management to describe and classify positions and to analyze their interrelationships for the purposes of recognizing and correcting anomalies and bringing about order where there was, or could otherwise be, chaos and inequity. However, weaknesses in the application of job evaluation principles and systems may retard complete acceptance of job evaluation as a management tool. Understanding some of the factors that impair the acceptance of job evaluation by employees should help to define the conditions under which sound internal job relationships can be developed and maintained.

6

New Methods
for Evaluating Jobs

In building a structure of jobs, we will usually find that there are two or more equally good solutions to a particular job evaluation problem. The lack of complete agreement with regard to any one solution does not invalidate it or make the results of using it less valuable. The most effective method utilized depends mainly on the purpose and needs of the business or agency, the training of the job evaluation committee, and the professional skills of the evaluator. Very broadly, we can assert that job evaluation is an organizational development intervention for improvement in the reward system of an organization itself. It is so basic and durable that over time we are likely to forget that job evaluation is an intervention and is changeable rather than being a closed system that is impervious to change (Patten, 1977).

Competent job evaluation demands a very broad perspective and keen insight into the management process and into the nature of a wide variety of jobs in a work organization. Wage and salary administrators who supervise job evaluation must be able to devise, maintain, and improve job evaluation systems. Managers and employees must thoroughly understand and accept the objectives of job evaluation. They must learn about the financial reward system of the employer and be able to develop acceptance and ownership feelings about it. Job evaluation and its installation must be approached so that ultimate ownership is made possible. For this

165

reason, we all become uneasy about existing systems of job evaluation and their judgmental nature. We should seek a better product that should eventually become available as the behavioral sciences mature.

The quantitative methods of job evaluation may hold greater promise than the nonquantitative ones in terms of employee acceptance and well conceived efforts aimed at organizational development and planned change. Therefore, in this chapter we examine the new face (or faces) of job evaluation, recognizing that some of the visage is more cosmetic than basic, and that much of it is rooted in the past, too.

Point-Factor Plans

The point plan of job evaluation is a very old method, one about as old as the federal classification system. It goes back at least to the 1920s. Merrill Lott is considered the originator of the method (Lott, 1926). He wrote the first book on the point-factor method, and over the past sixty years this has become the most widely used quantitative job evaluation method. It has cloned a wide variety of prototype variants and remains popular in our growing service sector as well as in other parts of the economy.

Point plans are very helpful devices in making judgments about jobs because they allow a job evaluation committee to look at jobs, the factors against which the jobs are to be evaluated, and then the specific points in terms of which the factors are divided. A point plan is thus like measuring with a yardstick or ruler. From the standpoint of exercising consistent judgments in a methodical way, a point plan is much easier to use than ranking: it provides instruments with which to measure jobs.

Often, unions will accept point plans, particularly industrial unions like the United Automobile Workers or the International Union of Electrical, Electronic, Salaried, and Technical Workers (IUE), which see value in a tool that allows acceptable differentiation in the work of myriad semiskilled jobs. Also, point plans have been popularized by various employers' associations and consultants. These groups prefer plans that are composed of scales of factors, with points representing the various degrees of each factor pertaining to a job. They recognize nevertheless that they are measuring grossly with a yardstick and not minutely as with a micrometer.

The ranking method and the classification method are called nonquantitative, or qualitative, because they evaluate the whole job. This evaluation can be done grossly (or functionally, then grossly), as is the case with the ranking method. Or evaluation can be done in a more refined way by grading, that is, by taking the whole job and placing it in a predefined structure of grades, as under the federal GS classification approach. Under the pure classification approach the grades are identified and the analyst, guided by position classification rules and standards, simply takes the job and puts it in a grade structure. But the point method is opposite in technique to such whole-job ranking. We start by breaking the job down into logical parts and then we evaluate it. The breaking down of the job is the key to the greater ease in job evaluation attributed to point plans.

The factors that are to be used in a point plan can vary up to fifteen or sometimes more. Some pay specialists have insisted that one factor is enough, such as "problem solving." Few, however, subscribe to this radical view. The weights of the factors may vary also. Usually a factor like physical effort or unavoidable hazards has lesser maximum point value than a factor such as experience required or responsibility for supervising others. Naturally, the predetermination of total points assigned to the various factors has a serious effect on the important compensable factors in the design of the jobs under study. This observation should again remind us of the importance of the ultimate acceptability of a job evaluation plan and the need for inclusion in it of the values weighted in a desired manner by the ultimate users of the system.

The degrees in a point plan may increase arithmetically or geometrically. If they increase geometrically (8, 16, 32, 64, and so on), they can go up in value much more rapidly than they could if they were arithmetic (10, 20, 30, 40). The average employee cannot understand the logic of a geometric progression; an arithmetic progression is more easily understood. But often from an evaluation standpoint, a geometric progression is preferable because human judgment can perhaps be assisted technically by concentrating on larger intervals. A job evaluation scale can be built either way, or both scale types can be used in the same plan, depending on the factor being evaluated.

The factors that would be used in a point plan customarily differ between office and factory, and exempt and nonexempt jobs. There are some compensation specialists today who use point plans for exempt jobs. However, other experts believe that point plans really are not sufficiently potent for evaluating high-level exempt jobs. Nonexempt factory and office jobs can be evaluated easily with point plans, but different factors are normally used for the plant and office. For example, the working conditions factor is very important for evaluating skilled, unskilled, and semiskilled jobs in a plant but of less importance in a sanitary, air-conditioned office. The meaning of "responsibility" differs of course from a plant to an office job and among the various levels of jobs in each. Physical and mental skills scales would obviously differ with education and experience and again between office and plant jobs.

As part of the process of installing a job evaluation system using the point-factor method, the developers ultimately devise a manual that contains all the jobs as described, that is, job descriptions. The manual must be kept up to date and maintained if it is to be a useful tool. The manual defines and names the specific factors and points and what the differences between the points mean. Benchmark jobs that illustrate the different degrees on the factors may also be shown. Some examples of these procedures and concepts are provided in this book, beginning next in reference to a very viable specific point-factor plan. We pause to consider it before returning to our general discussion of quantitative job evaluation plans (specifically the factor comparison method).

A Modern Point-Factor Job Evaluation Plan

The discussion so far in the chapter has not examined a specific job evaluation plan in detail. To this point our purpose has been to describe job evaluation plans quite generally in order to portray how they can be distinguished. No opinions were offered as to which plan was "best" or the strengths or weaknesses of each. In a universal sense no job evaluation plan can be said to be "best" or ideal. If we argue that job evaluation is primarily a problem-solving technique that is most effectively introduced and used as an organizational development intervention, then the validation of the usefulness of the technique to lawfully solve an organization's problems in building an equitable job structure is sufficient. Considering the great popularity of the point-factor type of plan and methods such as the Hay plan, which is also built on the use of points and factors, we should probably conclude that point-factor plans are rightly perceived by many users as the best for them. Moreover, in the public sector there was a long history of using the classification method dating from the 1920s, which has been substantially reversed in state governments by the widespread use of point-factor plans. Therefore, if the author were to choose one method for discussion to illustrate traditional but solid thinking, he would select point-factor plans. If he were to pick a prototype point-factor plan, he would choose for didactic and other purposes the Bank Administration Institute's (BAI) plan. This is a well-designed plan with clearly stated factors and degree points. It is applicable to the very important service sector of the economy and the financial institutions there. From an explanation of the BAI plan we can also advance our discussion of how job evaluation can be used to bridge across job families or occupations by means of conversion charts. While the technique of bridging is not free of the pitfalls inherent in job evaluation, it does have some potential for dealing with ways in which different job evaluation plans placed into use in a large establishment can be interrelated.

We have already seen that attempting to evaluate all the jobs in diverse job families together under one plan for a large establishment is often quite futile, except for applications of the Hay plan or of the federal government's GS system. For example, in an organization with several thousand employees and several hundred jobs ranging from the chief executive officer down to a data entry clerical job in the office or packer in a warehouse, it is not feasible to have one job evaluation plan covering every job. A purist in the measurement field might justifiably think that the use of the same measurement rod for everyone's job would provide an opportunity for application of a common and equitable metric. However, job evaluation is not measurement and fails to purely meet the requirements that must be fulfilled for measuring the phenomena to which it is addressed. On the other hand, it has practical value as a problem-solving technique, which is indispensable for organizational development and management in an environment where executives must be able to explain the bases for their decisions. The bases must be lawful but do not need to satisfy the canons of psychometricians or other measurers of human and social phenomena.

Persons who evaluate jobs need guides to carry out appraisals of the value of the work that can be used and will register a belief afterwards in the minds of the evaluators that the relevant dimensions of the jobs have been examined in the cultural context in which they exist. Evaluators need to control their biases when they appraise jobs with which they are familiar in the real world of work they experience daily. The process of job evaluation can be made relatively bias-free if the biases and subjectivity in the minds of the evaluators can be controlled and not be made to enter in the actual evaluation process. How? The author's belief is that a group of work-experienced managers and employees in, for example, a bank should be appointed and normally serve as a job evaluation committee. It should include knowledgeable women and minorities. It should be guided by a competent job analyst or compensation specialist who thoroughly understands the BAI job evaluation plan and has trained the job evaluation committee in a particular banking establishment in how to use it. Such an approach stands an excellent chance of producing job evaluations that are useful, realistic, and "valid" for that establishment. ("Valid" inferences are inferences about the value of the job drawn from the job description evidence that seem justified by the job evaluation committee's consensus and are not unlawful.)

Figures 4 to 18 reflect the points and factors in the BAI plan. A few comments are made on each factor and about the plan as a whole. The skill, effort, responsibilities, and working conditions that the EPA encompasses are reflected carefully in the plan, although they are grouped a bit differently in the BAI plan:

I.   Skill
     1.   Basic knowledge and experience
     2.   Judgment
     3.   Developing and maintaining customer (and public) relationships
     4.   Relationships inside the bank
     5.   Accuracy
     6.   Manual dexterity
II.   Responsibilities
     7A. Supervisory and advisory or line control
     7B. Management advisory or staff capacity
     8.   Policy formulation and interpretation
     9.   Investment of funds
     10. Care of bank assets
III.   Effort
     11. Physical demand
     12. Concentration demand
         a.   Visual effort required
         b.   Mental effort required
IV.   Working conditions
     13. Physical surroundings
     14. Personal hazards

Turning to the plan itself, it can be seen that the skill requirements of the job are evaluated by six factors (basic knowledge and experience, judgment, developing and maintaining customer (and public) relationships, relationships inside the bank, accuracy, and manual dexterity). These compensable factors were chosen by management as its prerogative, and they have considerable face validity. Each factor is explained and defined clearly in good English. Each factor is subdivided in degrees, which, in turn are clearly defined and stated to represent separate levels on a scale. A careful reading of the language under each degree shows that the scale levels are as carefully differentiated as possible, using adjectives and/or additional duties and tasks of increasing importance. The point values ascend from the lowest to the highest degree and are approximately arithmetically differentiated. The differences between degrees, however, have not slavishly followed arithmetic or geometric scales.

In some instances, such as Factor 2 (judgment) and Factor 5 (accuracy), matrices are used to assist in the process of making judgments. Zero points may be awarded where a particular job may not contain elements of the work that deserve points. Factors 2, 3, and 4 permit this. However, Factors 1 and 5 do not. Yet would one argue that an organization could logically have jobs that contain less than what is called for in the first degree of Factor 1 (basic knowledge and experience)? Also, would we want to have a possibility of zero in Factor 5 concerning accuracy, particularly in a bank where most of the detail work is founded on accuracy? Maybe a guard or custodian need not be accurate in the same sense that a bank clerk or administrator should be, but those would be jobs employing relatively few people in a bank.

Factor 6 (manual dexterity) would apply to keyboarding in general and word processing. The factor is worded in the job evaluation plan as it would apply to older office equipment.

Factors 7 through 10 are aimed at responsibilities of importance in financial institutions. Thus the supervisory and advisory factor is split into two separate matrices, shown as 7A and 7B.

A split is found in policy formulation and interpretation in Factor 8, which permits a maximum award of 100 points for certain jobs involving policy formulation, but only 50 points as a maximum for policy interpretation. The distinction in point-value maxima for policy formulation and policy interpretation obviously conforms with managerial views of the job worth of the two.

Factor 9, investment of funds (loans, etc.), and Factor 10, care of bank assets, represent scaling and matrix approaches respectively on job evaluation for these two responsibility areas, which are important for banks.

Effort is evaluated under Factor 11, physical demand, and Factor 12, concentration, with a subdivision into visual and mental

(*opposite*) **Figure 4. Skill Requirements—Factor No. 1, Basic Knowledge and Experience.** *Source:* McCurry (1979, p. 135). Used by permission.

This factor appraises the degree of knowledge, skill and adaptability required to overcome the problems and difficulties of the job.

"Basic knowledge and experience" may be interpreted to mean *ability,* acquired through formal or self-education, job training and experience acquired *inside* or *outside* the bank. In using this factor, consider the basic *requirements* of the *job itself* and avoid rating the person on the job.

Degree	Point Value
1. Requires only the ability to *understand and carry out simple verbal or written instructions,* performing simple and closely supervised duties.	20
2. Requires the ability to *understand a variety of routine procedures* and methods, or to demonstrate *aptitude* for and *some proficiency* in the performance of *routine clerical functions* which might include the operation of such office equipment as: typewriter, bookkeeping machine, etc.	60
3. Requires the ability to *master and employ a variety of somewhat complex* procedures and methods, involving the *use* of *semi-skills* (such as shorthand, or *proficient* operation of such office equipment as: Vari-typer, comptometer, etc.) in the performance of *advanced clerical* or *advanced stenographic* or *secretarial* duties, etc.	100
4. Requires the ability to *use expertly* and/or *supervise* others in the correct employment of a *variety* of *complex* methods and procedures, involving, for example, advanced business arithmetic, cost accounting techniques, etc., or *expert skill* in the performance of *top clerical* or *top secretarial* duties.	140
5. Requires the ability, through extensive *education and training, to comprehend, interpret and apply the techniques of a specialized field*—for example, accounting, business administration, finance, etc. and/or Requires the *ability to organize, control and evaluate* work of others (a large and important section or a minor division), *correlate* information, set up detailed procedures from general requirements, make explanations or reports of a complex nature, employing technical oral or written expression, etc.	180
6. Requires the ability to apply *broad training and experience,* in a specialized field, such as general banking, trusts, statistics, accounting, finance, etc. and/or Ability to *organize, direct, and administer a division* of importance to bank operations, profits, or prestige.	210
7. Requires the ability to apply advanced training and experience in a specialized field, such as banking or finance; and/or Ability to organize, direct and administer a minor department or a division of considerable importance to bank operations, profits, or prestige.	240
8. Requires the ability to *apply exhaustive training and experience* in a highly specialized field *and general comprehension of fundamentals* of the bank's operation as applied to the organization, direction, and administration of *several important divisions* or a principal department.	250

173

Figure 5. Skill Requirements—Factor No. 2, Judgment.

This factor measures the degree of judgment required by the job. Judgment may be defined as the operation of the mind involving comparisons and discrimination by which knowledge or values and relations are mentally formulated.

In using this factor, consider only the kinds of decisions customarily required to be *made solely and independently by the incumbent in the job,* taking into account the relative importance of decisions for the bank as a whole.

Consider first the relative importance of decisions that must be made, and, second, the difficulty in reaching independent decisions.

Difficulty in Reaching Independent Decisions	Relative Importance of Decisions			
	A	**B**	**C**	**D**
	Small consequence; decisions subject to close follow-up	Some significance; subject to review by supervision before serious consequence	Important to bank; adverse effects accrue before ordinarily reviewed by supervision	Major importance to bank; serious economic benefits or losses only proved by experience
Degree	**Point Value**			
1. No independent decisions required, or of negligible importance.	0	0	5	10
2. Most facts available; one course indicated or rely on specific precedents.	10	20	35	55
3. Most facts available, alternate courses open.	30	50	85	105
4. Limited facts obtainable; alternate courses open.	50	75	105	155
5. Base decisions principally on broad policy interpretation.	80	110	155	220

Source: McCurry (1979, p. 136). Used by permission.

Figure 6. Skill Requirements—Factor No. 3, Developing and Maintaining Customer (and Public) Relationships.

Consider the extent to which the job requires the development and mainte- nance of good customer and public relations. This would include strengthening of existing accounts and developing new ones; enhancing the reputation of the bank through securing customer satisfaction; handling of complaints and adjust- ments; developing and improving public relations. Credit should be given for public contacts only in cases where such contacts are a requirement of the job (i.e., essential to proper performance of job) .

Degree	Point Value
0. No customer or public contacts of any consequence required.	0
1. Requires some ability in maintaining good customer and/or public relationships. No special customer service required.	10
2. Requires the ability to handle mildly irritating or embarrassing *situations where good manners are sufficient.*	25
3. Requires the ability to handle irritating and embarrassing situa- tions involving use of some *tact and diplomacy.* Make a limited interpretation of customer's needs.	45
4. Requires the ability to handle *frequent situations involving tact and diplomacy* to meet and adjust unpleasant attitudes, some of which may cause personal embarrassment. Required to make sig- nificant interpretations of customer or potential customer's needs.	70
5. Requires the making of decisions as to customer's requirements necessitating a *high degree of observation and interpretation,* toward building up and maintaining the reputation of the bank. Ability to handle difficult customer relationships.	110
6. Ability to make major decisions requiring the *highest degree of observation and interpretation* to mold and influence the reputa- tion of the bank through developing and giving special customer service.	150

Source: McCurry (1979, p. 137). Used by permission.

effort using matrices. These scales are reminiscent in structure and design of those that we have already discussed in the BAI plan. The physical demand scale contains a zero degree, which recognizes that some very sedentary jobs in a bank simply do not deserve point

Figure 7. Skill Requirements—Factor No. 4, Relationships Inside the Bank (Job Relations).

This factor appraises *the extent to which the ability to obtain the attention, respect, support, and concurrence of fellow employees (NOT under the same supervisor) is an actual requirement* of the job. Credit should be based on the significance of contacts with individuals in other *departments, divisions, or sections* on overall efficiency of the bank. (Branch jobs will usually be rated on this factor primarily in regard to required relationships with the home office, except in the larger branches where relationships with persons in other sections or divisions of the same branch are important.)

The success of relationships with others is *largely dependent on ability to achieve objectives through the use of poise, dignity, tact, diplomacy, confidence, and decisiveness.* In using this factor consider the *levels of* authority dealt with and *the scope of effect* of poor relationships on overall bank efficiency or effective operations.

Degree	Point Value
1. No contacts required outside of own section or division, or if so, of negligible importance.	0
2. A few contacts required of *minor importance.*	10
3. Requires the ability to make *pleasing impression* and work *harmoniously* with others on *routine* matters involving some give and take.	20
4. Requires the ability to *secure understanding* or willing *cooperation* in matters involving *inconvenience* to others, or sacrifice of viewpoint, where the *completion of a relatively minor project* is at stake.	30
5. Requires the ability to *promote understanding* of, and willing *cooperation* with programs, projects, procedures, etc., necessary for the achievement of *entire sectional or of important divisional objectives.*	45
6. Requires the ability to *rally* others to *full support* of *significant* programs, projects, policies, or procedures, etc., affecting *an entire divisional* operation, where there must be *considerable subordination* of individual desires, ideas, or practices.	60
7. Requires the ability to *obtain enthusiastic concurrence and cooperation* with important projects, programs, or policies *affecting several important divisions,* where much inconvenience, additional effort, and/or subordination or revision of other programs or views must be assumed, in support of important overall departmental objectives.	80
8. Requires the ability to *persuade* others to concur in *major* programs and policies having a *strong* effect on overall *bank operations or prestige with the public.*	100

Source: McCurry (1979, p. 138). Used by permission.

176

Figure 8. Skill Requirements—Factor No. 5, Accuracy.
(This factor appraises the extent to which the job requires
dependability for accuracy in the performance of detail work.)

"Detail Work" is defined as practices, operations, and procedures, such as
calculating, counting, balancing, posting, checking, sorting, testing, etc. Assume
errors to be errors of *commission or omission* (and *not* errors in *judgment*)
which result in internal delays, confusion, poor public relations, lowered morale,
etc.

Consider first the difficulty in avoiding errors, and second, the effect of errors.

Effects of Errors	**Difficulty in Avoiding Errors**			
	A Little probability of error	B Some probability	C Good probability	D Errors difficult to avoid
Degree	**Point Value**			
1. *Little or no effect.* Errors easily detected and corrected.	5	10	15	20
2. *Result in irritation and some loss of time. Discovered through established checking* procedures or immediate supervision.	15	20	25	30
3. *Result in considerable internal friction,* confusion, or lost time. *Detection deferred or difficult.* (Some loss of profits result from errors.)	25	30	40	50
4. *Result in a chain of errors* in succeeding operations, reports, etc., leading to serious loss of time or good will, confusion, widespread irritation, and/or significant loss of profits. *Detection feasible* only by *spot check,* general review, or final auditing.	40	50	65	85
5. *Result in serious losses* in prestige, profits and morale, through dissemination of misinformation to governmental agencies, top management, or the public.	60	75	95	120

Source: McCurry (1979, p. 139). Used by permission.

Figure 9. Skill Requirements—Factor No. 6, Manual Dexterity.

This factor appraises *the need on the job* for *special* skill in the use and coordination of the hands and fingers.

Normal physical coordination of the hands is assumed to be incidental to all job performance. Credit is only given where the development of manual dexterity is a *prerequisite* as in operating office machinery and equipment.

Degree	Point Value
1. Only normal physical coordination of the hands and fingers is required.	0
2. *Some deftness required*—Manipulating ability required through some training, as in operating simple equipment such as: addressograph machine; nonproduction operation of typewriter or comptometer; sorting of checks; nonproduction counting of money. (Ability to demonstrate proper use of a number of bank machines, and/or occasionally use adding machine, typewriter, etc. for specific assigned duties.)	30
3. *Moderate amount of manual dexterity required,* for example: experienced production operation of typewriter or comptometer; production counting of money.	60
4. *Considerable manual dexterity required,* for example: first-class skill in use of complex office equipment or machines, requiring a considerable degree of manual dexterity of operation or adjustment.	75

Source: McCurry (1979, p. 140). Used by permission.

values. Interestingly, how many points would a teller receive on this scale? Many tellers (which, incidentally, is a well-known female-dominated job) stand a large part of the work day and suffer body fatigue from this. Evidence reported in Chapter Seven indicates that the Bank of America, which is one of the most important banks on the West Coast, has reconsidered the structure of its job evaluation system so that tellers may receive sufficient point values for the amount of standing they do.

The visual effort and mental effort subscales tap into two important types of job effort required in bank jobs. Neither of these subscales deals directly with stress (nor, as a matter of fact, do most job evaluation plans). We believe that many jobs could be differen-

Figure 10. Responsibilities—Factor No. 7A, Supervisory and Advisory.

Positions requiring managerial responsibilities are considered to be either *supervisory*—involving responsibility for line supervision and control, or *advisory* —involving rendering advice or counsel in a staff capacity. The primary responsibility of line supervision involves determining *which employee* will do *what, when* and *how.* The primary responsibility of staff positions involves serving management or line supervisors in an advisory capacity, rendering technical assistance, furnishing data, reports, or information for the guidance of bank officers and supervisors.

Supervisory or Line Control

In measuring the responsibility for supervisory or line control, consider first the relative complexity of the work supervised and, second, the number of persons supervised.

	Relative Variety and Complexity of Work Supervised		
	A Small variety of routine and repetitive procedures	**B** Variety of procedures, some involved	**C** Wide variety of involved procedures
Number of Persons Supervised*			
Degree	**Point Value**		
1. Non or occasional helper.	0	0	0
2. 1 through 4	20	30	40
3. 5 through 10	50	60	70
4. 11 through 25	65	80	95
5. 26 through 50	80	90	105
6. 51 through 75	90	100	115
7. Over 75	100	115	125

*Includes personnel regularly reporting through subordinates as well as those reporting directly. For an "assistant head" use a rating lowered by one degree.

Source: McCurry (1979, p. 141). Used by permission.

tiated on a scale of stress, because there are many jobs that are notoriously heavy in stress, such as emergency room physicians, air traffic controllers (at certain busy airports during times of intense flight and landing activity), and police officers (on patrol cars in

Figure 11. Responsibilities—Factor No. 7B, Management
Advisory or Staff Capacity.

In measuring the responsibility for performing *management advisory* or *staff* services, consider first the highest level of management served, and second, the complexity and variety of the tasks or subjects involved. Rate on this factor *only when it is a requirement of the job to advise management* concerning *how work should be performed by others* who are not under the direct line of authority of this job (or to assist in determining major management decisions affecting work of others) .

Relative Variety and Complexity

Level of Management Served	A Minor problems involving limited variety and complexity	B Minor problems involving entire system or major problems involving limited groups	C Major problems involving entire system
Degree	**Point Value**		
1. Supervisory personnel (such as section heads)	20	35	50
2. Intermediate levels of management (such as division heads)	40	60	75
3. Higher levels of management (such as department managers or senior officers)	65	90	100

Source: McCurry (1979, p. 142). Used by permission.

urban areas). Such alleged inherent job stress needs to be distinguished from stress that persons in other occupations generate in themselves owing to personality variables. Stress scales do exist for registering the impact of life crises on persons, but to date no pure stress scales designed for job evaluation have ever come to the attention of the author. They clearly are needed.

Working conditions or the job-surrounding conditions that are important in evaluating jobs are found under Factor 13 (physical surroundings) and 14 (personal hazards). In both of these factors the possibility of a zero award exists, which is, of course,

Figure 12. Responsibilities—Factor No. 8, Policy Formulation and Interpretation.

This factor appraises the requirements of the job with respect to responsibility for *determining or formulating polices,* and for the guidance of subordinates and associates inside the bank and for *explanation* and *disposition* of policy matters affecting depositors, customers, and others outside the bank. (Assume that laws, acts, or directives of governmental bodies having jurisdiction, e.g., tax, labor laws, etc., become perforce bank policies.)

Unless interpretation of bank policies is *an actual job* responsibility, it should not be considered in measuring the requirements of a job.

A. Extent to Which Job Requires
Formulation of Policies

Degree

	Point Value
1. *Make changes of minor importance in policies or recommend changes of some significance.*	25
2. *Make changes* in policies of *some significance* or *recommend important changes* in policies.	50
3. *Make important changes* in policies or recommend changes of *major importance.*	75
4. *Make major changes* in policies or *recommend changes in basic bank policies.*	100

B. Degree of Interpretation
of Policies Required

1. *Explanation and limited interpretation* of policies.	20
2. *Explanation and significant interpretation* of policies, i.e., required to make significant interpretations or deviations from general policies.	30
3. *Explanation and important interpretations* of policies, i.e., required to make difficult interpretations of policies including occasional requirement to make rather extensive deviations from general policies, when situation warrants.	40
4. Explanation and major interpretation of policies, i.e., required to make quite difficult interpretations or to make major exceptions to policies when situation warrants.	50

Source: McCurry (1979, p. 143). Used by permission.

Figure 13. Responsibilities—Factor No. 9, Investment of Funds
(Loans, etc.).

This factor measures the responsibility of the job for the effective use of money in equipment, fixtures, supplies, investments, stocks, bonds, or any type of loans (either bank or customer funds). Credit is given only to those jobs charged with the responsibility to determine what investments will be made by *either approving investments on own authority* or *effectively recommending* desirable investments to higher authority.

In determining the appropriate degree of investment responsibility for each job, consider the *significance to the bank* of the *investment decisions* required. Consideration should be given to the *earnings that will accrue* if consistently sound decisions are made and to the *potential losses* possible, as well as to the size and type of investments being made.

Reference is made only to the responsibility to approve investments in the following definitions of investment responsibility. To evaluate jobs that have *only* (or more) responsibility for *recommending* investments, it is necessary to *determine the relative significance* to the bank of *such recommendations,* as compared with the responsibility of other jobs for approving investments of varying significance.

Degree	Point Value
0. Job has *no responsibility* for investment of funds.	0
1. Job has responsibility for approving investment of funds of very minor significance to the bank, i.e., occasional purchase of small amount of office supplies, equipment, and machines.	10
2. Job has responsibility for approving investment of funds of minor significance to the bank, i.e., equipment or office machines for a large section, division, or branch.	25
3. Job has responsibility for approving investments of small significance to the bank.	50
4. Job has responsibility and authority to approve investments of some significance to the bank.	75
5. Job has responsibility and authority to approve investments of considerable significance to the bank.	100
6. Job has responsibility and authority to approve investments of major significance to the bank.	125
7. Job has responsibility and authority to approve investments of greatest significance to the bank charged to any one individual.	150

Source: McCurry (1979, p. 144). Used by permission.

Figure 14. Responsibilities—Factor No. 10, Care of Bank Assets.

This factor measures the responsibility of the job for protecting bank assets. For example, safe storage of finished files, important records; maintenance of buildings, machinery, and equipment to prevent loss or damage beyond normal wear or obsolescences; *safekeeping* (not mere handling) of funds, negotiable documents and papers, money, checks; or protection of collateral pledged or taken over for liquidation (multiple credit should be allowed on this factor *only* when nature of assets requires regular attention of supervisor to insure protection).

	Difficulty of Protecting Assets			
	A	B	C	D
Importance of Assets	Operations where assets are easy to protect.	Operations where normal precautions, care, maintenance, result in adequate protection.	Operations where nature of assets requires extraordinary care.	Operations where nature of assets makes it extremely difficult and important to the bank to exercise proper care.
Degree	**Point Value**			
1. *Little or no* responsibility for care of assets.	5	10	15	20
2. Responsibility for care of assets of *minor value.*	10	15	20	30
3. Responsibility for care of assets of *significant value.*	30	35	40	50
4. Responsibility for care of assets of *considerable value.*	40	45	55	65
5. Responsibility for care of assets of *major value.*	50	55	65	80
6. Responsibility for care of *all* bank assets.	70	75	85	100

Note: Jobs primarily responsible for disposing of assets for cash (i.e., liquidating property or other assets received as collateral on loans) should receive credit on this factor. However, credit on this factor should not be given for such duties if credit has been received under Factor No. 9 for investment of funds.

Source: McCurry (1979, p. 145). Used by permission.

Fair Pay

Figure 15. Effort Demand—Factor No. 11, Physical Demand.

This factor appraises the physical *effort* required by the job in sustaining difficult work positions, lifting, pushing, climbing, walking, standing, and so forth.

Physical effort is expended largely in assuming and maintaining unrestful work positions and in handling heavy or bulky materials. Consider to what extent *strain* is imposed by the *characteristic work position* and the *weight* and *size* of the materials handled *regularly* and *frequently*.

Degree	Point Value
1. *Minimum physical effort.* Characteristic working position: sitting.	0
2. *Light physical effort.* Performing a little physical effort, either sitting or standing. Operate light machines such as typewriter, comptometer, etc.	10
3. *Medium physical effort.* In somewhat straining positions for sustained periods or doing light work under difficult work positions, operations of billing machines continuously, etc.	20
4. *Heavy physical effort.* Strained positions and handling of heavy materials (25-50 pounds).	35
5. *Extreme physical effort.* Handling extremely heavy materials or working for long periods in extremely difficult work position.	50

Source: McCurry (1979, p. 146). Used by permission.

quite realistic in a bank. The degree levels are, again, carefully defined and scaled, culminating in a matrix for Factor 14.

The BAI job evaluation plan represents excellent craftsmanship in plan design and formatting. The design is obviously traditional. A great deal of careful thought was devoted to the factor definitions, degree levels, scaling, and assignment of point values.

An analysis of the maximum total point values in the plan (a theoretical 1,800) shows that about 51 percent of the total point values in the compensable factors are included under skill; 34 percent, under responsibilities; almost 9 percent, under effort; and the remaining 6 percent, under working conditions. Very often, traditional job evaluation plans have about 50 percent of their weight in the skill, education, and work experience area. These appear to be the kinds of things for which employers are quite

Figure 16. Effort Demand—Factor No. 12, Concentration Demand. This factor appraises separately the degree of *mental and visual concentration* which the job requires. Total *concentration* demand is the *sum* of mental and visual *concentration* required.

Consider first the visual concentration required *(A)*, and second, the mental concentration required *(B)*.

A. Visual Effort Required

Degree

1. Visual alertness only to work required.

2. Visual *attention* required. Eyes focused on work, but close concentration not necessary.

3. *Close* visual *concentration* required. Eyes focused on work with close concentration.

4. *Exacting* visual *concentration* required. Eyes intently focused on work demanding the greatest precision or care in handling.

Extent of Effort Required	
A Not Sustained	B Sustained Over 50% of Time
Point Value	
5	10
15	20
25	35
40	50

B. Mental Effort Required

Degree

1. *Little* or no mental *alertness* required —remembering relatively simple instructions, methods, and procedures.

2. Mental *attention* required. Working on somewhat complex procedures or methods.

3. *Close* mental *attention* required. Varied and often complex methods or procedures being handled.

4. *Exacting* and *close* mental *attention* required. Variety of complex methods, procedures, and situations being handled and interpreted.

Extent of Effort Required	
A Not Sustained	B Sustained Over 50% of Time
Point Value	
5	10
15	25
30	40
45	60

Source: McCurry (1979, p. 147). Used by permission.

185

Figure 17. Job Conditions—Factor No. 13, Physical Surroundings.

This factor appraises the *surroundings* under which a job must be performed and the extent to which *unpleasant* conditions affect the employee's *mental and physical well-being.*

In measuring the physical surroundings of the job consider the *presence,* relative *amount* and *continuity* of exposure to:

1. Dust	7. Grease
2. Dirt	8. Wet
3. Heat	9. Cold
4. Fumes	10. Noise
5. Smoke	11. Vibration
6. Oil	12. Any other unpleasant elements

Degree	Point Value
1. *Pleasant working conditions*—None of the above elements readily apparent. Carpeted floors, good light and ventilation, not noisy or crowded. Usual *private office* conditions.	0
2. *Good working conditions*—Good light and ventilation, uncarpeted floors; some noise from machines or crowds, but generally clean surroundings. *Usual general office* conditions.	10
3. *Fair working conditions*—Satisfactory on the whole, but intermittent exposure in moderate degree to such elements as inadequate light or ventilation, heat, cold, dirt, and noises.	20
4. *Unpleasant working conditions*—*Continuous* exposure to *several* disagreeable elements or to one element which is particularly disagreeable.	35
5. *Bad working conditions*—Continuous and intensive exposure to several disagreeable elements.	60

Source: McCurry (1979, p. 148). Used by permission.

willing to pay heavily. This author believes that this common phenomenon is compatible with a theory that can be captured from the well-known employer practice of financially recognizing skill and its components. Specifically, job evaluation is driven substantially by the actual or imputed importance of jobs to the organization *and* the actual or imputed scarcity of talents and competencies believed to exist in the human population. There are more people

Figure 18. Job Conditions—Factor No. 14, Personal Hazards.

This factor appraises the personal hazards inherent in a job, even though all reasonable precautions have been taken by the bank.

The concern here is not with the *possibility* of accidents, but rather with the *probability of their occurring* and the probable degree of *injury* resulting therefrom.

	Probable Degree of Injury			
Probability of Injury	*A Minor—no lost time	*B Result in lost time up to two weeks	*C Result in lost time of 2 weeks to 3 months	*D Result in lost time of more than 3 months
Degree	Point Value			
1. Injury *extremely unlikely.*	0	0	0	0
2. Some *probability of injuries,* but all hazards are safeguarded.	5	10	20	30
3. *Accidents probable* because of conditions that cannot be safeguarded.	10	15	25	35
4. *Accidents likely* due to the nature of the work. Requires alertness at all times.	15	20	30	40

*A—Abrasions, minor cuts or bruises, scratches, etc.
*B—Sprains and strains, crushed hand or foot, loss of finger, deep cuts, eye injuries, etc.
*C—Severe burn, broken arm or leg, serious impairment of vision, etc.
*D—Permanent disability—loss of arm, foot, or eye, etc.

Source: McCurry (1979, p. 149). Used by permission.

that lack competencies and talents than people who possess them to high degrees. Everywhere we look there are more laborers available than electronic technicians, more office receptionists than computer programmers, and more aircraft cabin cleaners than pilots. As a result, electronic repairers are worth more to an electrical machinery manufacturer than are laborers, computer programmers are more important to a high-tech research laboratory than are office receptionists, and pilots have greater worth to a commercial airline than the people who keep the passenger cabin clean. To be sure, all work has dignity, and all jobs rank somewhere on a scale of importance. Some of the latter is actual, as can be seen in the job of piloting an aircraft, and can be perceived objectively. Some of the importance is imputed, as is reflected in a work setting where a company arbitrarily decides that sales and marketing jobs should be generally graded higher in pay than jobs in purchasing, traffic, or production control. The point is that job evaluation tries to reflect the actual or imputed importance of jobs and the actual or imputed scarcity of competencies and talents in the human population. To assert policy-captured theory is not to endorse a simplistic notion of supply and demand of people to industry. Value judgments and concepts of worth appear to play a larger role and get entangled with all the cultural supports that bring about discrimination.

It is easy to understand why at least 34 percent of the worth of a job should be attributed to job duties and responsibilities. These are outputs to a large extent, whereas it could be argued that skills are inputs. Should management be more willing to pay for outputs? It might even be argued philosophically that perhaps skills should be weighted 34 percent and responsibilities 51 percent? Such an argument would be difficult to settle on objective grounds and is best left to custom.

To weight effort 9 percent and working conditions 6 percent may offend some observers who could even argue, Why evaluate effort and working conditions at all if 85 percent of the job is evaluated by skill and responsibility? In a bank, the low weights chosen would seem to fit the ambience rather well. There is no heavy lifting, and bad working conditions would be highly unusual. In an old-fashioned foundry, plating shop, or steel mill, the job evaluation plan for hourly workers would give greater weight to effort and working conditions than would a job evaluation plan for a bank and the typical jobs found there.

Traditional concepts of job evaluation hold that the most useful and adequate plans are those that fit specific work situations: a bank plan for a bank or a factory plan for a manufacturing job family. The idea of designing and constructing one job evaluation plan that would fit nicely for banks, factories, offices, field sales jobs, hospitals, and scientific laboratories was rejected years ago and has never been taken seriously by traditionalists since then. However, as mentioned earlier, since the work of the National Academy of Sciences about a decade ago there has been a strong interest among nontraditionalists in designing and utilizing a single job evaluation plan that could be applied throughout an organization, presumably including even the very large ones (Treiman, 1979).

In broad summary, the point-factor method as exemplified in the BAI plan provides much clarity, ease, and guidance for making consistent and acceptable judgments on jobs. The names of the factors, specifications and identification of degrees, and differences in weights assist greatly in the job evaluation process. The result is an array that lines up the jobs nicely for pricing using a scatter diagram showing dollars on the x axis and points on the y axis. (This procedure was discussed in Chapter One.)

Job evaluation as a field in professional compensation management has evolved to the point that the myriad technical problems involved in deciding on the number of factors and degrees to use, in defining them, in weighting them, and in assigning points to the degrees and factors no longer loom large. Compensation specialists simply use available prototype plans or tailor those known to them for a specific application. The same observation can be made with respect to solving technical problems in the classification method concerning decisions on how many classes are appropriate, what exactly it is that classes should have in common, and how exactly to define a class. Point-factor technology, as we have seen, can be wedded to the classification method to enhance the latter, which was done by the federal government for the GS jobs.

Discrimination may enter in when gender stereotypes affect scale building, weightings, and the selection of factors. For example, to award higher points for lifting and moving heavy products than for working with the assembly of small products— the classical equal pay controversy over heavy and light assembly— may be to affect adversely the value of light assembly jobs, and, if they are female-dominated, to cause the incumbents ultimately to be underpaid. In this way—and others related technically to the construction of job evaluation scales—discriminatory considerations surreptitiously enter the system being used to evaluate jobs.

Factor Comparison Method

The last approach to job evaluation is traditionally discussed in books on compensation planning and administration. The factor comparison method was developed by Edward N. Hay, Samuel L. H. Burk, and Eugene J. Benge in 1926 (Benge, Burk, and Hay, 1941). It has had numerous installations in the past throughout the Eastern part of the United States. This method is an elaboration and modification of the man-to-man rating scale concepts of World War I and focuses on evaluating certain key jobs that are used as anchor points to build an entire structure.

What we do in the factor comparison method is to prepare a key job scale and move from that into placing all the jobs in a structure. Again, we look at rankings but make the ordering more understandable to the human mind by breaking the jobs down into parts. The factor comparison method may thus be viewed as a refinement of the ranking method, because both evaluate whole jobs. But under factor comparison, the evaluator's or job evaluation committee's work is more refined than under ranking.

The evaluator(s) takes all the jobs in an organization that are thought to be key jobs (usually twenty-four to thirty) and tries to rank them directly. (A benchmark job and a key job are about the same in concept.) It is not assumed by the evaluator that these tentative key jobs are truly key jobs. In fact, an interesting aspect of the factor comparison method is the attempt to find out whether provisional key jobs are really key jobs.

The evaluator(s) ranks each key job by each of five factors according to its importance. The five factors in the original Hay-Burk-Benge factor comparison scale are mental requirements, skill requirements, physical requirements, responsibilities, and working conditions, and they relate well to factory production and maintenance jobs paid on an hourly basis.

The different factors are then ranked in order of "importance" and order of value, either in money or by some other unitary consideration, for each job by the persons evaluating the jobs. The compensation analyst next examines the rankings to see how consistent the evaluators have been in reviewing a number of jobs and in ranking them according to money value for each factor and according to "importance" for each factor. The jobs may be set aside and reranked at a later date to ascertain the reliability of the ranking. This same procedure, incidentally, is not uncommon in point and other plans; that is, an evaluation is repeated after a week or a month to determine whether the evaluation judgments are the same. They may drop or they may increase. Another technique used to increase the reliability of job evaluation is to ask two job analysts to evaluate the jobs and then to have both of them perform this task again later. A comparison is made of their independent evaluations in order to determine if there is high or low reliability in the evaluation.

Gross discrepancies in the job evaluations are determined by inspection of the consistency in the rankings. If there are inconsistencies, the jobs in question are probably not key jobs. They are thrown out of the structure until there is a very close consistency between the rankings of the jobs in units and in importance. The final result is an ordering of key jobs and an understanding of what they are worth. These "true key jobs" are then made the anchor points in the job structure.

The final result of factor comparison is the identification of a small number of key jobs, ranging from the most expensive to the least expensive. They are placed in the structure where they are thought to belong. There are various ways of doing this that need not concern us here but that can be pursued (Burgess, 1984). Ultimately, all the other jobs in the organization are considered in small clusters, ranked through the same process described above, and are slotted into the structure in reference to the anchor points. In other words, the evaluator(s) merely needs to look at the anchor points and slot the jobs in the structure in relation to them.

In factor comparison, the evaluated jobs are also priced. The structure is built by studying the units and converting them to cents per hour in the case of factory production and maintenance jobs. In this way all jobs are priced. Thus, the factor comparison method is not only a job evaluation method but also a pricing method.

Let us turn next to the Hay plan, which is the most important type of factor comparison in use today.

The Hay Plan

The Hay Guide Chart–Profile Method of job evaluation (simply called the Hay plan in this book) was developed by Edward N. Hay and later refined by Hay Group and could be considered a variant on the factor comparison method (Bellak, 1984b). The Hay plan is the most important variant and probably comes to mind instantly as the best embodiment of its type. It still follows two factor comparison principles. It requires (1) a thorough understanding of the content of the job to be evaluated and (2) the direct comparison of one job with another to determine relative value.

The Hay plan has been implemented by at least 4,000 organizations in 30 countries all over the world, small and large, public and private (Belcher and Atchison, 1987). Today it is most commonly used for evaluating exempt and nonexempt office jobs in organizations. Although it is a proprietary plan belonging to the Hay Group (and the latter is now owned by Saatchi and Saatchi, a marketing-advertising conglomerate based in the United Kingdom), a great deal of public information concerning the Hay plan has been made available in an up-to-date volume written primarily by Hay experts (Rock, 1984), in a textbook on compensation (Burgess, 1984), and in the National Academy of Sciences study of job evaluation (Treiman, 1979). As a result, managers and compensation specialists often know something about the Hay plan even if it is not used by their current employer.

The Hay plan makes use of three factors in the vast majority of its installations: know-how, problem solving, and accountability (when nonexempt production and maintenance jobs are evaluated, a fourth factor, working conditions, is used). Using job descriptions written either by employees or by a job analyst, the job evaluation committee reviews the duties of the job and slots it into the structure by considering the Hay-plan factors and subfactors one at a time. A Hay consultant helps the committee do its work and can draw upon his or her expertise in other organizations to help the installing organization work through its job evaluations by examining matrices called guide charts for each factor. The matrices are very significant for applying the Hay plan.

Know-how in the Hay plan context is defined to mean the total of all skills and knowledge, no matter how acquired, for acceptable job performance. Table 5 displays the know-how guide chart for the state of Idaho, a state that was the earliest to implement comparable job worth, carrying it out quietly and effectively by use of the Hay plan. Since Idaho is a small state in terms of the size of state government employment, its Hay know-how scale runs up to a maximum of 2,432 points. In a large state the total number of points needed to evaluate a steeper managerial hierarchy would probably be closer to 5,000. Such a scale could be developed ad hoc to meet the needs of organizational size.

As with all evaluations made during the Hay job evaluation process, the focus of the know-how evaluation is a judgment on the content of the job without, of course, considering the characteristics or unique contributions of any particular job incumbent. Know-how is subdivided into three component guide chart dimensions: specialized or technical education and experience know-how, managerial know-how, and human relations know-how. When these variables are analyzed, a total point value is obtained that represents the value of know-how for the job (Burgess, 1984).

The second factor, problem solving, is the degree to which the know-how is applied: the amount of original, self-starting thinking required by the job for analyzing, evaluating, creating, reasoning, and arriving at conclusions. (See Table 6, which was also used in Idaho.) The guide chart for problem solving contains a vertical dimension consisting of degrees of the freedom to think and the horizontal dimension portrays the thinking challenge, such as whether the latter is creative or repetitive or somewhere between. The data in the problem-solving guide chart are stated in percentages rather than points. The percentage chosen for a particular job is multiplied by the points obtained in the know-how charts to arrive at a single point value for problem solving. The rationale for evaluating problem solving as a percentage of know-how is explained by Hay-plan experts as embodying the rationale: "You can think only with what you know" (Burgess, 1984).

The third factor in the Hay plan, accountability, is a measure of the impact of the job on the end results of the organization. It is a payoff factor shown as Table 7. Accountability means being held answerable for what happens to something—that something being an identifiable, measured end result, and accountability is, therefore, effect not cause. Know-how and problem solving produce nothing until they are put to work, and accountability measures the effect the two other factors produce. Viewed in this context, accountability has three dimensions: freedom to act independently, degree of responsibility for end results described in dollars entrusted to or affected by the individual holding the job, and the magnitude of the job in terms of its impact on organizational dollars. The Hay plan emphasizes what the occupant for a position is accountable for rather than the specific duties of the job (Burgess, 1984).

The fourth factor, working conditions, includes any relevant job hazards, unpleasant working conditions, or unique physical demands of the job (Bellak, 1984b). Table 8 displays the working conditions matrix, but unlike Tables 5–7, it was not needed in the Idaho study.

Each of the factors evaluated by the use of the Hay plan is described by means of a matrix, with the component dimensions of the factor shown as rows and columns. The four separate matrices are printed on large, separate spreadsheets and at first blush are imposing to look at. The numbers in the numerous boxes in the matrices represent the point values available for rating the job on that factor. The numbers are arrayed on the guide charts so that the values increase in 15 percent increments going down or across the matrix. In deciding on a rating value for a factor, members of the job evaluation committee are required to determine into which box the job falls for each of the component dimensions, and then they must select one from the two or three possible values on the matrix

(*opposite*) **Table 5. Hay Guide Chart, Know-How.** *Source:* Reprinted from Treiman (1979, p. 161) by permission of the Hay Group, Inc., Philadelphia, Pa.

DEFINITION: Know-How is the sum total of every kind of skill, however acquired, needed for acceptable job performance. Know-How has 3 dimensions: the requirements for:

• Practical procedures, specialized techniques, and scientific disciplines.

•• Know-How of integrating and harmonizing the diversified functions involved in managerial situations (operating, supporting and administrative). This Know-How may be exercised consultatively as well as executively and involves in some combination the areas of organizing, planning, executing, controlling and evaluating.

••• Active, practicing, person-to-person skills in the area of human relationships.

MEASURING KNOW-HOW: Know-How has both scope (variety) and depth (thoroughness). Thus, a job may require some knowledge about a lot of things, or a lot of knowledge about a few things. The total Know-How is the combination of scope and depth. This concept makes practical the comparison and weighing of the total Know-How content of different jobs in terms of: "HOW MUCH KNOWLEDGE ABOUT HOW MANY THINGS".

GUIDE CHART — KNOW-HOW
© Hay Associates 1979

	••• Human Relations Skills →	I. NONE OR MINIMAL (1,2,3)	II. INTERMEDIATE (1,2,3)	III. BROAD (1,2,3)	IV. COMPREHENSIVE (1,2,3)	V. MAJOR (1,2,3)	VI. TOTAL (1,2,3)
A. PRIMARY — Elementary plus some secondary (or equivalent) education, plus work indoctrination.		50 / 57 / 66 ; 57 / 66 / 76 ; 66 / 76 / 87	66 / 76 / 87 ; 76 / 87 / 100 ; 87 / 100 / 115	87 / 100 / 115 ; 100 / 115 / 132 ; 115 / 132 / 152	115 / 132 / 152 ; 132 / 152 / 175 ; 152 / 175 / 200	152 / 175 / 200 ; 175 / 200 / 230 ; 200 / 230 / 264	200 / 230 / 264 ; 230 / 264 / 304 ; 264 / 304 / 350
B. ELEMENTARY VOCATIONAL — Familiarization in uninvolved, standardized work routines and/or use of simple equipment and machines.		66 / 76 / 87 ; 76 / 87 / 100 ; 87 / 100 / 115	87 / 100 / 115 ; 100 / 115 / 132 ; 115 / 132 / 152	115 / 132 / 152 ; 132 / 152 / 175 ; 152 / 175 / 200	152 / 175 / 200 ; 175 / 200 / 230 ; 200 / 230 / 264	200 / 230 / 264 ; 230 / 264 / 304 ; 264 / 304 / 350	304 / 350 / 400 ; 350 / 400 / 460
C. VOCATIONAL — Procedural or systematic proficiency, which may involve a facility in the use of specialized equipment.		87 / 100 / 115 ; 100 / 115 / 132 ; 115 / 132 / 152	115 / 132 / 152 ; 132 / 152 / 175 ; 152 / 175 / 200	152 / 175 / 200 ; 175 / 200 / 230 ; 200 / 230 / 264	200 / 230 / 264 ; 230 / 264 / 304 ; 264 / 304 / 350	264 / 304 / 350 ; 304 / 350 / 400 ; 350 / 400 / 460	400 / 460 / 528 ; 460 / 528 / 608
D. ADVANCED VOCATIONAL — Some specialized (generally nontechnical) skill(s) acquired on or off the job giving additional breadth or depth to a generally single function.		115 / 132 / 152 ; 132 / 152 / 175 ; 152 / 175 / 200	152 / 175 / 200 ; 175 / 200 / 230 ; 200 / 230 / 264	200 / 230 / 264 ; 230 / 264 / 304 ; 264 / 304 / 350	264 / 304 / 350 ; 304 / 350 / 400 ; 350 / 400 / 460	304 / 350 / 400 ; 350 / 400 / 460 ; 400 / 460 / 528	460 / 528 / 608 ; 528 / 608 / 700 ; 608 / 700 / 800
E. BASIC SPECIALIZED — Sufficiency in a technique which requires a grasp either of involved practices and precedents, or of scientific theory and principles, or both.		152 / 175 / 200 ; 175 / 200 / 230 ; 200 / 230 / 264	200 / 230 / 264 ; 230 / 264 / 304 ; 264 / 304 / 350	264 / 304 / 350 ; 304 / 350 / 400 ; 350 / 400 / 460	350 / 400 / 460 ; 400 / 460 / 528 ; 460 / 528 / 608	460 / 528 / 608 ; 528 / 608 / 700 ; 608 / 700 / 800	700 / 800 / 920 ; 800 / 920 / 1056
F. SEASONED SPECIALIZED — Proficiency, gained through wide exposure or experiences in a specialized or technical field, in a technique which combines a broad grasp either of involved practices and precedents; or of scientific theory and principles, or both.		200 / 230 / 264 ; 230 / 264 / 304 ; 264 / 304 / 350	264 / 304 / 350 ; 304 / 350 / 400 ; 350 / 400 / 460	350 / 400 / 460 ; 400 / 460 / 528 ; 460 / 528 / 608	460 / 528 / 608 ; 528 / 608 / 700 ; 608 / 700 / 800	608 / 700 / 800 ; 700 / 800 / 920 ; 800 / 920 / 1054	920 / 1054 / 1216 ; 1054 / 1216 / 1400
G. SPECIALIZED MASTERY — Determinative mastery of techniques, practices and theories gained through wide reasoning and/or special development.		264 / 304 / 350 ; 304 / 350 / 400 ; 350 / 400 / 460	350 / 400 / 460 ; 400 / 460 / 528 ; 460 / 528 / 608	460 / 528 / 608 ; 528 / 608 / 700 ; 608 / 700 / 800	608 / 700 / 800 ; 700 / 800 / 920 ; 800 / 920 / 1056	608 / 700 / 800 ; 700 / 800 / 920 ; 800 / 920 / 1054	1054 / 1216 / 1400 ; 1216 / 1400 / 1600 ; 1400 / 1600 / 1840
H. PROFESSIONAL MASTERY — Exceptional competence and unique mastery in economic, judicial, educational, and/or political affairs.		350 / 400 / 460 ; 400 / 460 / 528 ; 460 / 528 / 608	460 / 528 / 608 ; 528 / 608 / 700 ; 608 / 700 / 800	608 / 700 / 800 ; 700 / 800 / 920 ; 800 / 920 / 1054	800 / 920 / 1054 ; 920 / 1054 / 1216 ; 1054 / 1216 / 1400	920 / 1054 / 1216 ; 1054 / 1216 / 1400 ; 1216 / 1400 / 1600	1400 / 1600 / 1840 ; 1600 / 1840 / 2112 ; 1840 / 2112 / 2432

Managerial Know-How column descriptions:

- **I. NONE OR MINIMAL** — Performance or supervision of a single activity, with appropriate concern for related activities.
- **II. INTERMEDIATE** — Primarily within single field or toward single objective with some integration of, or external integration with, other fields.
- **III. BROAD** — Integration and coordination of diversified activities in an important management area or consulting field.
- **IV. COMPREHENSIVE** — Comprehensive integration and coordination of diversified activities and functions in a major management area.
- **V. MAJOR** — Management at the level of policy making which affects the over-all operation of the state or which directs its most complex and far-reaching components.

Row scale (left margin): PRACTICAL PROCEDURES — SPECIALIZED TECHNIQUES — SCIENTIFIC DISCIPLINES

•• MANAGERIAL KNOW-HOW

••• HUMAN RELATIONS SKILLS

1. BASIC: Ordinary courtesy and effectiveness in dealing with others.	2. IMPORTANT: Understanding, influencing, and/or serving people are important, but not critical considerations.	3. CRITICAL: Alternative or combined skills in understanding, influencing, selecting, developing and motivating people are important in the highest degree.

corresponding to their choices. The result of this aspect of the job evaluation is the choice of a single number representing the job's rated value on that factor. Values on each of the four Hay-plan factors (again: know-how, problem solving, accountability, and working conditions) are then summed up to arrive at the overall measure of the job's value to the organization and to allow for direct comparisons of the different jobs' relative organizational worth (Farnquist, Armstrong, and Strausbaugh, 1983). It should thus be apparent why the Hay plan has an appeal for persons who would like to evaluate all the jobs in an establishment by using one job evaluation plan and use the common yardstick for implementing comparable job worth.

When the points for the Hay-plan job evaluation are summed, the single score for each job allows easy comparisons. The points for know-how are obtained from the guide charts. To obtain the points for problem solving, the percentage on the guide chart is multiplied by the points for know-how. The points for accountability and working conditions are obtained and then when the four are known, simply added. These results obtained from the guide chart are checked by what Hay-plan experts have called *profiling*. The latter is the comparing of a job's total points with the total points of another. The Hay Group has found from working with its clients that it can check each guide chart–profile against standard profiles for (1) all jobs, (2) line jobs, (3) staff jobs, and (4) research jobs. These comparisons are facilitated by a technical characteristic of the guide charts. As noted above, the numbers in the body of each chart represent a geometric progression in which steps are 15 percent apart. For the profiling of jobs, the Hay Group recommends the following conventions or rules:

- For any jobs, points for accountability and points for problem solving should be no more than four steps apart;

(*opposite*) **Table 6. Hay Guide Chart, Problem Solving (State of Idaho, April 1976).** *Source:* Reprinted from Treiman (1979, p. 162) by permission of the Hay Group, Philadelphia, Pa.

PROBLEM-SOLVING GUIDE CHART

GUIDE CHART

© HAY ASSOCIATES 1978

DEFINITION: Problem Solving is the original, "self-starting" thinking required by the job for analyzing, evaluating, creating, reasoning, arriving at and making conclusions. To the extent that thinking is circumscribed by standards, covered by precedents, or referred to others, Problem Solving is diminished, and the emphasis correspondingly is on Know-How.

Problem Solving has two dimensions:

• The environment in which the thinking takes place in terms of the limits on approaches to use in solving problems.

•• The challenge presented by the thinking to be done to solve problems in a given thinking environment.

MEASURING PROBLEM SOLVING: Problem Solving measures the intensity of the mental process which employs Know-How to: (1) identify, (2) define, and (3) resolve a problem. "You think with what you know." This is true of even the most creative work. The raw material of any thinking is knowledge of facts, principles and means; ideas are put together from something already there. Therefore, Problem Solving is treated as percentage utilization of Know-How.

•• THINKING CHALLENGE

• THINKING ENVIRONMENT — Thinking guided or circumscribed by:	1. REPETITIVE — Identical situations requiring solution by simple choice of learned things	2. PATTERNED — Similar situations requiring solution by discriminating choice of learned things	3. INTERPOLATIVE — Differing situations requiring search for solutions within area of learned things	4. ADAPTIVE — Variable situations requiring analytical, interpretative, evaluative, and/or constructive thinking	5. UNCHARTED — Novel or nonrecurring pathfinding situations requiring the development of new concepts and imaginative approaches	
A. STRICT ROUTINE — Simple rules and detailed instructions.	10% 12%	14% 16%	19% 22%	25% 29%	33% 38%	A
B. ROUTINE — Established routines and standing instructions.	12% 14%	16% 19%	22% 25%	29% 33%	38% 43%	B
C. SEMI-ROUTINE — Somewhat diversified procedures and precedents.	14% 16%	19% 22%	25% 29%	33% 38%	43% 50%	C
D. STANDARDIZED — Substantially diversified procedures and specialized standards.	16% 19%	22% 25%	29% 33%	38% 43%	50% 57%	D
E. CLEARLY DEFINED — Clearly defined policies and principles	19% 22%	25% 29%	33% 38%	43% 50%	57% 66%	E
F. BROADLY DEFINED — Broad policies and specific objectives.	22% 25%	29% 33%	38% 43%	50% 57%	66% 76%	F
G. GENERALLY DEFINED — General policies and ultimate goals.	25% 29%	33% 38%	43% 50%	57% 66%	76% 87%	G
H. ABSTRACTLY DEFINED — General laws of nature or science, within a framework of cultural standards and governmental philosophy.	29% 33%	38% 43%	50% 57%	66% 76%	87% 100%	H

STEP VALUES

3200 — 2800 — 2432 — 2112 — 1840 — 1600 — 1400 — 1216 — 1056 — 920 — 800 — 700 — 608 — 528 — 460 — 400 — 350 — 304 — 264 — 230 — 200 — 175 — 152 — 132 — 115 — 100 — 87 — 76 — 66 — 57 — 50 — 43 — 38 — 33 — 29 — 25 — 22 — 19 — 16 — 14 — 12 — 10 — 9 — 8 — 7 — 6

(STEPS BELOW 100%)

Table 7. Hay Guide Chart, Accountability (State of Idaho, April 1976). Source: Reprinted from Treiman (1979, p. 163) by permission of the Hay Group, Philadelphia, Pa.

DEFINITION: Accountability is the answerability for an action and for the consequences thereof. It is the measured effect of the job on end results. It has three dimensions, in the following order of importance:

● Freedom to Act — the degree of personal (or procedural) control and guidance affecting the actions taken needed to achieve desired results.

●● Job Impact on End Results — as defined at upper right.

●●● Magnitude — indicated by the general dollar size of the area(s) most clearly or primarily affected by the job (on an annual basis), stated in terms of Constant Dollars, 1985 Base.

AMI for use in [ ] in [ ]
●●● Magnitude — AMI Equivalent
●● Impact

●● IMPACT OF JOB ON END RESULTS

REMOTE: Informational, recording, or routine services for use by others in taking action.

CONTRIBUTORY: Interpretive, advisory, or facilitating services for use by others in taking action.

SHARED: Participating with others (except own subordinates and supervisors), within or outside the organizational unit, in taking action.

PRIMARY: Controlling impact on end results where shared accountability of others is subordinate.

ACCOUNTABILITY GUIDE CHART
© Hay Associates 1975

Level (Freedom to Act)	(1) VERY SMALL OR INDETERMINATE Under $100 M				(2) SMALL $100 M–$2 MM				(3) MEDIUM $2 MM–$20 MM				(4) LARGE $20 MM–$200 MM				(5) VERY LARGE $200 MM–$2 BB			
	REMOTE	CONTRIB	SHARED	PRIMARY	REMOTE	CONTRIB	SHARED	PRIMARY	REMOTE	CONTRIB	SHARED	PRIMARY	REMOTE	CONTRIB	SHARED	PRIMARY	REMOTE	CONTRIB	SHARED	PRIMARY
A. PRESCRIBED	10	14	19	25	14	19	25	33	19	25	33	43	25	33	43	57	33	43	57	76
	12	16	22	29	16	22	29	38	22	29	38	50	29	38	50	66	38	50	66	87
	14	19	25	33	19	25	33	43	25	33	43	57	33	43	57	76	43	57	76	100
B. CONTROLLED	16	22	29	38	22	29	38	50	29	38	50	66	38	50	66	87	50	66	87	115
	19	25	33	43	25	33	43	57	33	43	57	76	43	57	76	100	57	76	100	132
	22	29	38	50	29	38	50	66	38	50	66	87	50	66	87	115	66	87	115	152
C. STANDARDIZED	25	33	43	57	33	43	57	76	43	57	76	100	57	76	100	132	76	100	132	175
	29	38	50	66	38	50	66	87	50	66	87	115	66	87	115	152	87	115	152	200
	33	43	57	76	43	57	76	100	57	76	100	132	76	100	132	175	100	132	175	230
D. GENERALLY REGULATED	38	50	66	87	50	66	87	115	66	87	115	152	87	115	152	200	115	152	200	264
	43	57	76	100	57	76	100	132	76	100	132	175	100	132	175	230	132	175	230	304
	50	66	87	115	66	87	115	152	87	115	152	200	115	152	200	264	152	200	264	350
E. DIRECTED	57	76	100	132	76	100	132	175	100	132	175	230	132	175	230	304	175	230	304	400
	66	87	115	152	87	115	152	200	115	152	200	264	152	200	264	350	200	264	350	460
	76	100	132	175	100	132	175	230	132	175	230	304	175	230	304	400	230	304	400	528
F. GUIDANCE	87	115	152	200	115	152	200	264	152	200	264	350	200	264	350	460	264	350	460	608
	100	132	175	230	132	175	230	304	175	230	304	400	230	304	400	528	304	400	528	700
	115	152	200	264	152	200	264	350	200	264	350	460	264	350	460	608	350	460	608	800
G. GENERAL GUIDANCE	132	175	230	304	175	230	304	400	230	304	400	528	304	400	528	700	400	528	700	920
	152	200	264	350	200	264	350	460	264	350	460	608	350	460	608	800	460	608	800	1056
	175	230	304	400	230	304	400	528	304	400	528	700	400	528	700	920	528	700	920	1216
H. STRATEGIC GUIDANCE	200	264	350	460	264	350	460	608	350	460	608	800	460	608	800	1056	608	800	1056	1400
	230	304	400	528	304	400	528	700	400	528	700	920	528	700	920	1216	700	920	1216	1600
	264	350	460	608	350	460	608	800	460	608	800	1056	608	800	1056	1400	800	1056	1400	1840
I. GOVERNOR/CHIEF JUSTICE	304	400	528	700	400	528	700	920	528	700	920	1216	700	920	1216	1600	920	1216	1600	2112
	350	460	608	800	460	608	800	1056	608	800	1056	1400	800	1056	1400	1840	1056	1400	1840	2432
	400	528	700	920	528	700	920	1216	700	920	1216	1600	920	1216	1600	2112	1216	1600	2112	2800

Freedom to Act — level definitions:

A. PRESCRIBED — These jobs are subject to: Direct and detailed instructions / Close supervision

B. CONTROLLED — These jobs are subject to: Instructions and established work routines / Close supervision

C. STANDARDIZED — These jobs are subject, wholly or in part, to: Standardized practices and procedures / General work instructions / Supervision of program and results

D. GENERALLY REGULATED — These jobs are subject, wholly or in part, to: Practices and procedures covered by precedents or well-defined policy / Supervisory review

E. DIRECTED — These jobs, by their nature or size, are subject to: Broad practice and procedures covered by functional precedents and policies / Managerial direction

F. GUIDANCE — These jobs are inherently subject only to broad policy and general management guidance

G. GENERAL GUIDANCE — These jobs, by reason of their nature or size, independent complexity and high degree of effect on State operations are subject only to Guidance from the Governor's office or from appointed boards or designated major dept. heads.

H. STRATEGIC GUIDANCE — These jobs receive guidance from the Governor or his appointed boards, are characterized by a comprehensive and controlling effect on operations of the State and on the people of the State.

I. GOVERNOR/CHIEF JUSTICE — These jobs are subject only to the limitations of the State Constitution as it pertains to the Executive or Judicial Branch.

Table 8. Hay Guide Chart, Working Conditions. *Source:* Reprinted from Treiman (1979, p. 164) by permission of the Hay Group, Philadelphia, Pa.

WORKING CONDITIONS

© HAY ASSOCIATES 1979

DEFINITION

Working Conditions are made up of:

●Physical Effort - (defined at right)

●●Environment - (defined at right)

●●●Hazards - The factors taken on the average which increased the risk of accident, as follows:

  I. General absence of hazards.

  II. Moderate hazards, fairly predictable and controllable.

  III. Potentially dangerous and somewhat unpredictable hazards.

● Physical Effort, which involves occasional, intermittent or steady handling of light, medium, or heavy weight materials in normal to difficult work positions, or unusual circumstances which produce physical fatigue.

●● Environment, which includes occasional, intermittent or continuous exposure of varying intensities to such things as dust, dirt, heat, cold, fumes, steam, moisture and noise.

●● ENVIRONMENT

PHYSICAL EFFORT	1. EXCELLENT (General office or other equivalent environment.)			2. GOOD (Occasional variations in temperature, unfavorable atmospheric conditions, rarely unavoidably exposed to outside conditions as part of job.)			3. FAIR (Unfavorable environment factors because of unavoidable need to be in variable weather atmospheric variables, dust, fumes, wetness, etc. Ear protection required.)			4. DIFFICULT (Unavoidable exposure to unfavorable conditions, such as weather, or other undesirable atmospheric conditions, very dusty, fumes.)			5. VERY DISAGREEABLE (Predominant exposure to disagreeable surroundings.)		
	I	M	H	I	M	H	I	M	H	I	M	H	I	M	H
A. BASIC — Physical effort at the level normally found in clerical work or equivalent.	0	6	7	6	7	8	7	8	12	9	12	16	12	16	22
	0	6	8	6	8	10	8	10	14	10	14	19	14	19	26
	0	7	9	7	9	12	9	12	16	12	16	22	16	22	29
B. LIGHT — Physical effort at the level represented by the use of light hand tools and handling fairly light materials manually, such as frequent lifting of light weight objects, with occasional lifting of heavier objects.	6	7	9	7	9	12	9	12	16	12	16	22	16	22	29
	6	8	10	8	10	14	10	14	19	14	19	26	19	26	33
	7	9	12	9	12	16	12	16	22	16	22	29	22	29	38
C. MODERATE — Physical effort at the level represented by climbing and working from ladders, or in awkward positions, or working on incentives or conveyor paced jobs, or frequent lifting of fairly heavy objects and occasional lifting of heavier objects.	7	9	12	9	12	16	12	16	22	16	22	29	22	29	38
	8	10	14	10	14	19	14	19	26	19	26	33	26	33	43
	9	12	16	12	16	22	16	22	29	22	29	38	29	38	50
D. STRENUOUS — Physical effort at the level represented by lifting objects of very heavy weight or necessary to work prolonged periods with very fatiguing motions or positions.	9	12	16	12	16	22	16	22	29	22	29	38	29	38	50
	10	14	19	14	19	26	19	26	33	26	33	43	33	43	57
	12	16	22	16	22	29	22	29	38	29	38	50	38	50	66

- For line jobs, accountability should be two, three, or four steps higher than problem solving;
- For staff jobs, accountability and problem solving should be equal or not more than one step apart either way;
- For research jobs, problem solving should be two, three, or four steps higher than accountability.

Profiling thus becomes a way to develop the relationship among the three scales and provides an additional comparison with the points assigned from the guide charts. Jobs are assumed to have characteristic shapes or profiles in terms of their problem-solving and accountability requirements. Sales and production jobs supposedly emphasize accountability over problem solving. Research jobs stress problem solving more than accountability, whereas staff jobs tend to equate the two (Belcher and Atchison, 1987).

In using the Hay plan (or indeed any plan involving points), the evaluators should be alert to possible problems in sex stereotyping that might enter into their judgments. For example, if their well-considered opinion is that a number of nonexempt female-dominated clerical jobs are properly evaluated but result in very high point values (which might be unexpected), then the job evaluation committee can "sore-thumb" through a stack of jobs as a "logic check." They might find that indeed the sore-thumbing shows that there is a face validity problem: the clerical jobs turn out to have higher point values than previously evaluated office support jobs that have historically been male-dominated and paid more. The job evaluation committee can then (1) recommend that its well-considered point assignments be honored; (2) back off from its decision, adjust the data, and decrease the points assigned to the clerical jobs; or (3) put the job evaluation project on hold and freeze the *status quo*. We would recommend the first approach, the second one should be avoided as patently manipulative and discriminatory, and the third should be used only momentarily in order to develop a successful strategy and organizational development effort for implementing the first tactic. Of course, a well-monitored Hay-plan or point-factor plan installation would prevent the possible sex stereotyping. The consultant or coordinating compensation specialist should be alert to the entry of unlawful subjective judgments. Also, the placement of women on the job evaluation committee could help in this regard.

In pricing the structure, Hay-plan users relate the points assigned to the jobs to commercially available, ad hoc, or Hay surveys expressing H points. The basic pricing approach could be to use the three factors to evaluate jobs and to compare the structure with external pay rates among firms surveyed by Hay so that an internal structure can be built. Companies and agencies can avail themselves of the Hay compensation comparison survey, an annual survey, primarily of management jobs, that updates and compares the salary practices of Hay clients whose jobs have been measured according to the Hay guide chart–profile method of job evaluation (Barker, 1984).

Newer Methods of Job Evaluation

There are several "new" methods of job evaluation that have been reported in the literature since the four basic methods were set in concrete between 1920 and 1940. Common to most of these new directions is an interest in defining one factor so that it can be applied to all levels of jobs in an organization and in evaluating the jobs along this dimension. These are the single-factor theories. Also new are the PAQ (Position Analysis Questionnaire) method of McCormick, Jeanneret, and Mechem (McCormick, 1979; Jeanneret, 1980) and the FJA (Functional Job Analysis) method (Fine, Holt, and Hutchison, 1974). The PAQ and FJA have greater relevance for job analysis than for job evaluation, but they have been used in comparable job worth and EPA litigation; therefore, they are worth brief mention. Neither is on the same plane of importance as the Hay plan in the number of installations in companies or agencies or as a center-stage job evaluation method.

Jaques (1964), Charles (1971), and Paterson and Husband (1970) are associated with the single-factor theories. The actual number of American firms using each is not known and could be close to zero, although the work of Paterson and Husband was adapted by Arthur Young and Company for use in Minnesota counties that are tackling comparable job worth.

Jaques (1972) excoriates job evaluation for being based on

judgment and opinion. He proposes instead the use of the "time span of discretion" exercised on the job as a universal compensable factor. Discretion is measured by the time lapse between the exercise of a substandard discretion and the discovery of the consequent substandard work by the manager in charge. One problem with this method is that the review of work assignments may be subject to considerable variation among supervisors. An incompetent manager could easily distort this factor to such an extent that every position under him would be evaluated incorrectly.

Charles (1971) argues that the functions of coordinating, organizing, and planning are performed by employees at all levels in organizations. The functions are performed to solve problems; therefore, problem solving should be a compensable factor for all types of workers in all kinds of organizations. The distinguishing element among levels of problems is the complexity of the problem. This method, on the face of it, seems better suited to managerial or supervisory positions than to the jobs of hourly production workers. The factor is very broad and obviously not subject to a clear definition.

The essence of the Paterson and Husband (1970) method is the recognition that decision making is common to all jobs. Six levels of decision are identified (policy making, programming, interpreting, routine, automatic, and defined), and jobs are analyzed and graded in terms of these decision levels. The higher the level, supposedly the greater the value of the job to the enterprise and, therefore, the larger the deserved reward. The interesting aspect of this method is that it claims only to provide a framework of grades within each of which pay differentials can be made by whatever method is suitable.

The main weakness of each of the single-factor theories is the belief that the single factor focused upon has universal applicability for complex situations. Single factors obviously fail to fulfill the goal of adequate explanation. In job evaluation, they seem to represent desperate last-ditch attempts to save the field from disrepute as mere judgment. The single-factor reduction fallacy seems to resemble the search for the philosophers' stone in ancient times!

The PAQ is a job analysis tool that can be used in job evaluation and in forensic contexts (Jeanneret, 1980). It consists of a worker-orientated, structured questionnaire containing 187 items called job elements that is usually completed by a worker's supervisor. The specific tasks in a specific job are not inquired into. The items are organized into six generic divisions: information input, mental processes, work output (physical activites and tools), relationships with others, job context (the physical and social environment), and other job characteristics (such as pace and structure). Each of these generic job elements is rated on six scales: extent of use, importance, time, possibility of occurrence, applicability, and a special code for certain jobs. Once the 187 elements are rated, 45 basic job dimensions are derived statistically through factor analysis. These statistics yield job evaluation points that enable comparisons to be made between jobs through an analysis of variance procedure. The PAQ can then supposedly be used for evaluating jobs and establishing comparable job worth because if similar underlying job characteristics (like common denominators) exist between dissimilar jobs, the jobs are probably equivalent in the demands made on the incumbent worker and should therefore be paid at equivalent rates. The process of transferring PAQ responses to pay rates is carried out by obtaining the value of each of the 187 elements through computer analysis. By using multiple regression analysis, it is possible to combine all the job elements for a particular job and to compare this score with going market rates and other jobs within the organization. If two jobs are rated equally using the PAQ yet have substantial differences in pay as shown by their positions in relation to the line of best fit on a scattergram, then we would want to know why. We should then, in turn, reevaluate the administration of the PAQ or the relative worth of each job to the organization or the meaning of the market rate. The PAQ has been shown to have high reliability in job evaluation and to be highly correlated with job evaluation results obtained by other traditional systems. Moreover, 9 of the 187 elements are powerful predictors of a job's value, and these 9 are strikingly similar to the compensable factors found in conventional point-factor plans, such as education, experience, physical effort, communication with others, supervision of others, and initiative (Treiman, 1979; Belcher and Atchison, 1987; Burgess, 1984).

The FJA system is usually thought of in terms of the familiar data, people, and things hierarchies used in the famous *Dictionary of Occupational Titles* (U.S. Department of Labor, 1977). The major concern of FJA in job evaluation is an employee's work activity, which is obtained by a thorough job analysis. Once the information is obtained, the tasks in the job are evaluated in terms of what functional level they are on in the three separate hierarchies: data, people, and things. Each hierarchy has six to eight points on it and is considered comprehensive (see Table 9).

Every job is thought to require a person to function to some degree in relation to data, people, and things (Fine, Holt, and Hutchison, 1974). The functions as listed in the three respective hierarchies are arranged in each instance from the relatively simple to the complex and in such a manner that each successive level includes those that are simpler and excludes the more complex (Miller, Treiman, Cain, and Roos, 1980). Apparently, point values are assigned to the various functional levels in the three hierarchies. The value of a job is determined by summing the total points that apply by functional level to each job. These points express ordinal differences by functional level on the hierarchical scales. However, specific detail on how the mechanics of FJA is used in job evaluation does not appear to have been published, and the conclusions stated are the author's conjecture based on the literature and personal contact with an FJA expert. How FJA ties to job pricing remains unexplained.

Bridging and Pricing

Naive analysts in any field of human endeavor see homogenization in subject matter. More sophisticated analysts see subtleties, identify distinctions, label these differentiations, and ponder over their actual or imputed importance to the functioning of the context in which they are embedded. These analysts perceive a world of differences and inequality first and then afterward seek uniformities, patterns, sequences, commonalities, and comparabilities if such can be justifiably discerned. Scholars of job evaluation are no different from those in other fields with respect to how they study phenomena within their purview: they are likely to perceive subtleties and complexity rather than verisimilitude and simplicity.

Table 9. The Data, People, and Things Hierarchy.

Data	People	Things
0 Synthesizing	0 Mentoring	0 Setting-up
1 Coordinating	1 Negotiating	1 Precision working
2 Analyzing	2 Instructing	2 Operating-controlling
3 Compiling	3 Supervising	3 Driving-operating
4 Computing	4 Diverting	4 Manipulating
5 Copying	5 Persuading	5 Tending
6 Comparing	6 Speaking-signaling	6 Feeding-offbearing
	7 Serving	7 Handling
	8 Taking instructions–helping	

Certainly, they are unlikely to see any body of knowledge as existing on a single plane.

Let us consider job evaluation in the health care field, for the sake of carrying this discussion to an operational context and to illuminate what is meant by bridging. We are likely to observe persons in jobs in the health care field who by the nature of the work they perform and its actual of imputed importance to the employing institution (hospital or nursing home) can be differentiated. Thus, such job titles as nurse aide, student nurse, licensed practical nurse, registered nurse, supervisory nurse, and so on have been created to recognize differences in types of work in nursing.

Why not classify all such persons as nurses and ignore the distinctions in professional preparation for the work, differential job tasks, relative responsibility for administering drugs and medications to patients, and the like? This is, of course, a rhetorical question, and the answer is obvious. There are "natural" inherent "levels" of complexity in nursing. The work by level is incomparable; therefore, there should be unequal pay for unequal work in proportion to the inequality, if a pay policy appropriate to a nursing job family is to be properly framed. Other pay policies are possible, in theory, that could provide a rationale for identical pay for "nurses" generically defined, but we will not consider these. Such policies would sound strange in the United States in view of our prevailing work ethic and democratic ideology, endorsement of job evaluation, and interest in performance motivation.

Let us consider next the issue of comparable job worth in

Table 10. Sample Job Categories in a Large Health Care Institution.

Nursing	Clerical	Maintenance
Nurse aide	= Office clerk	= Laborer/helper
Student nurse	= Clerk/typist	= Apprentice
LPN	= Stenographer	= Electrician
RN	= Secretary	= Electronic technician
Nursing supervisor	= Office manager	= Foreperson

three illustrative, roughly hierarchically arranged jobs in job families in a large health care institution (see Table 10).

The equal signs are important here because they suggest ordinal levels in which unequal jobs have now been comparatively equated across job families. Natural levels have been specified, and the theory of comparable job worth when implemented in practice would call for equal pay for the RN, secretary, and electronic technician (who repairs hospital equipment). The equal pay could be a single rate of pay for all the jobs on the same level or the placing of the jobs in labor grades that provide the same salary range for the three jobs in question (that is, what could be termed labor grade equality). The actual salary of any RN, secretary, and electronic technician could, of course, vary depending on performance (and/or length of service), but the salary "potential" or maximum to which persons in the three occupations could aspire would be identical.

There is a serious problem that arises in job evaluation that would prevent our attaining labor grade parity for an RN, secretary, and an electronic technician. If we were to use a point-factor job evaluation plan, it probably would not fit the three occupations well in relation to their respective job families. The degree points on the scales and the compensable factors themselves could not be specified across the quite different job families and weighted very well to carry out the evaluation task. Moreover, pay survey data from local labor markets would show a dispersion of going rates of pay reflecting supply and demand factors. We would hypothesize that market rates in Miami, San Jose, and Billings would show differences in the going rates for the three occupations. In one city nurses would be paid the highest, secretaries less, and there would be a paucity of electronic technicians, working for random rates. We would have apples, oranges, and pears. In another city there would be several grades of electronic technicians (some being paid handsomely), several grades of secretaries depending on establishment size, and very high paid RNs (most of whom may be found to have B.S. degrees). We might have Baldwin apples, navel oranges, and bing cherries. The complexities of the real world would, in other words, upset our simplistic conception of comparable job worth and at the very least reduce its universality.

Interestingly enough, internal job evaluation using a single point-factor plan and external labor-market rates could be made to work in a specific local health care institution of the type we have been describing—and frequently is made locally applicable on a one-shot basis. Why? How? How well?

It may be desirable to see how the discrepant jobs mentioned above can be evaluated in a well-designed job evaluation plan that could by a small stretch of the imagination be applied to the fifteen jobs listed. See Table 11. The fit of the plan for the jobs encompassed is far from perfect (as can be seen in the point allocation in Table 12), yet it is useful for illustrative purposes. The fit is poorest for the maintenance jobs because ordinarily the compensable factors and scales constructed to evaluate such jobs give greater attention to physical demands, environment/surroundings, unavoidable hazards, and safety of others than is the case in the plan used in this example in Tables 11 and 12. The work of forepersons who supervise maintenance employees is especially difficult to evaluate and could result in a point score inferior to that of other supervisors as well as subordinates. Of course, if we added thirty or forty jobs to the nursing job family, the difficulties in applying the plan in

Table 11. Total Point Scores by Jobs in Job Families.

Nursing		Clerical		Maintenance	
Nurse aide	85	Office clerk	67	Laborer/helper	66
Student nurse	95	Clerk/typist	117	Apprentice	202
LPN	198	Stenographer	167	Electrician	354
RN	330	Secretary	264	Electronic technician	364
Nursing supervisor	388	Office manager	398	Foreperson	332

Table 12. Point Allocation.

Job Title						Job Evaluation Factor											Total
	1*	2	3	4	5	6	7	8	9	10	11	12	13	14	15	16	
Nurse aide	10	0	10	9	10	25	5	5	1	10	0	0	0	0	0	0	85
Office clerk	10	0	10	6	5	25	5	0	1	5	0	0	0	0	0	0	67
Laborer/helper	0	0	5	16	0	25	0	0	0	5	0	0	0	0	5	10	66
Student nurse	10	10	10	9	10	25	5	5	1	10	0	0	0	0	0	0	95
Clerk/typist	10	10	15	6	5	50	10	5	1	5	0	0	0	0	0	0	117
Apprentice (skilled trades)	20	20	20	13	15	75	10	5	1	5	0	0	5	0	3	10	202
LPN	30	20	10	9	10	75	15	5	3	10	3	3	5	0	0	0	198
Stenographer	20	10	20	6	10	75	10	5	1	5	0	0	5	0	0	0	167
Electrician	40	40	40	16	25	100	10	0	5	25	5	0	10	0	3	35	354
RN (nondegreed)	40	40	40	3	20	100	20	5	7	25	10	5	15	0	0	0	330
Secretary	20	30	30	6	20	100	20	10	3	5	5	5	10	0	0	0	264
Electronic technician	40	50	40	16	25	100	10	0	5	25	5	5	15	0	3	20	354
Nursing supervisor	50	50	0	3	25	130	20	10	10	25	10	5	20	30	0	0	388
Office manager	50	50	0	3	25	130	35	15	10	5	15	10	20	30	0	0	398
Foreperson	30	40	5	9	25	75	35	5	10	25	10	5	20	20	3	15	332

*Code to factors:

1. specialized or technical knowledge
2. experience
3. manual skill or dexterity
4. physical effort
5. mental/visual effort
6. complexity/difficulty of duties
7. seriousness of errors
8. contacts with customers or public
9. contacts with other departments
10. responsibility for safety of others
11. responsibility for funds or property
12. responsibility for confidential information
13. responsibility for performance of work without immediate supervisor
14. responsibility for work of others
15. environment/surroundings
16. unavoidable hazards

a practicable way would multiply and result in diminishing an observer's belief in the credibility of the fit of the plan. For example, how would we evaluate the jobs in maintenance such as floor sweeper, carpenter, inhalation therapy machine technician, stationary engineer, ambulance driver, plumber, outside building and grounds worker and the like vis-à-vis a number of clerical and nursing jobs?

The total point scores by jobs in job families show the existence of hierarchies in the job families but considerable differences in the rungs of the ladders looking across the hierarchical job families (see Table 11). To be sure, the rough-and-ready example chosen in this chapter lacks refinement and shows only the grossest of a rank ordering. Perhaps one could argue with the point assignments made, the weights of the factors used in the scales, and other technical issues sidestepped in the illustration. Yet the fact remains that some persons who advocate comparable job worth as a theory seem to have glibly assumed that if there is a will to measure comparability through job evaluation, there are ways available to do so. The means, however, are not always operationally plain and could create as much (or more) injustice, inequity, and mischief as traditional methods of job evaluation. Bridging job families by the use of one job evaluation plan that cannot be readily fine-tuned for this purpose is not the answer to implementing comparable job worth.

The Hay plan apparently could encompass all fifteen jobs. The GS system could handle most, except perhaps only part of the maintenance job family. There may be other plans that could also be applied effectively for the fifteen jobs in the example. But the PAQ and FJA would not seem to be applicable at the establishment level for these jobs, although perhaps only an expert on those specific systems could make a meaningful judgment on that point.

In addition to bridging, there is the problem of pricing in job evaluation and tying an internally evaluated structure of jobs to the external labor market. To review, in the ranking method of job evaluation, the structure of jobs is built like a totempole from top to bottom. The jobs are priced arbitrarily by obtaining market rates in a survey and assigning pay rates or pay grades to them by using judgment and the survey data. The result is a type of direct market pricing. In the classification method the jobs are assigned pay based on what a legislative body allocates and the executive branch decides on, perhaps quite arbitrarily and politically. Both the legislative and executive branches may use surveys of rates in the labor market(s) in their deliberations. In point-factor plans and the Hay plan, surveys and regression analysis are used to relate job points and dollars. The rates are based on an examination of the scatter diagram and decisions about whether to have a single rate structure or a rate range. Management policies and wage and salary administration and rules also influence the pay levels decided on. If the company or agency engages in collective bargaining, the union will have considerable impact on the negotiated wage structure. The types of pricing methods used for orthodox factor comparison are quite recondite and seldom employed; hence, we will skip over them. The pricing methods for the single-factor plans, PAQ, and FJA are skipped for the same reason and also because the latter plans are perhaps more useful for job analysis than for job evaluation.

Pricing is obviously an important matter in job evaluation, and the bottom line in comparable job worth is yielding a fair and equitable paycheck for men and women. Yet it gets less attention than all the necromancy about points, plans, committee action, validity, and the like.

Conclusion

If we are prepared to consider job evaluation as a method of organizational problem solving (or organizational development intervention in a reward system, as the author prefers to conceptualize it), then it can continue in the future to have the value that it has had since the days of the War Labor Board of World War II. Under this concept, we must *not* consider job evaluation as measurement by means of a micrometer but measurement (or better still estimation) by means of a yardstick. This assertion is hoary in the field but does not seem acceptable to many people in adversary roles who have recently entered the job evaluation field in a peripheral way in the wake of the Equal Pay Act and Title VII. Some newcomers, engaging perhaps in wishful thinking, would like job evaluation to be more potent in metrics than it can be, given our limitations in knowledge. An occasional cynic knowing better will nevertheless prostitute himself by evaluating an array of jobs to prove a preexisting notion of worth. The ethical professional will try to be as objective as possible, recognizing that his or her measurement tool is gross and a mixture of the objective and subjective. Our only consolation is that at the present state of the art of work measurement, nothing is scientifically better than job evaluation for many of the tasks we will be asked to observe and assess. Yet we might yearn for a superior tool—and should if we are concerned with the steady improvement or professionalization of the field.

Job evaluation is an imperfect but useful tool for organizational problem solving in a company's or agency's reward system. It works best locally in what is legally viewed as an establishment and when participatively administered in an environment of trust. The author would hypothesize that its chances for being a successful, relatively durable solution to a work organization's pay problems are maximized when management, union, and employees are fed up with perceived inequities, are somewhat demoralized and highly aggravated by inadequate human resource management, and want to do something about the mess! If the grievances over rates of pay are cluttering up the grievance procedures, and EPA and Title VII individual employee and class action lawsuits are being used to intensify industrial conflict, these circumstances need to be dealt with in an early and fundamental way so as to deescalate the level of management, union, and employee aggravation. A litigious atmosphere is inconsistent with the best type of human resource management but may be a necessary stage to pass through before a better day can dawn.

American work organizations need to go back to using job evaluation in the traditional ways but, of course, lawfully and in an ambience of continuing equal employment opportunity. We would also endorse a stronger interest than in the past for seeking (through research and experimentation) improved methods of work measurement, including, of course, better techniques for job evaluation.

7

Managerial Strategies
for Implementing
Pay Equity

Affirmative action as a policy with programs to support its implementation has never been seriously tried on a sufficiently large scale with strong enforcement to significantly reduce sex discrimination in employment in the United States. One reason is that progress in this field is not easy, because it requires changes in behavior patterns. It runs up against deep-seated prejudices and entrenched systems of discrimination. Second, there has been very little political power behind the antidiscrimination initiatives, and the administration of these laws has generally not been energetic or efficient. However, without affirmative action, sex segregation would be prolonged for more years, and young women would be robbed of a chance to choose the most congenial jobs from an array of those in existence. Continued segregation would keep the male-female pay gap open and leave unshared the better jobs men occupy and which symbolize inequality between the sexes (Bergmann, 1986).

If affirmative action were proceeding rapidly, efficiently, and effectively, a pay equity campaign might be redundant. The argument for comparable job worth defined as simple pay equity boils down to an assertion that whatever affirmative action has accomplished, it benefits have not percolated down to women in traditional jobs. Most of the women who have gained entry to the previously male-dominated higher-paying occupations are young, recent entrants to the labor force. The majority of women who entered the labor force years ago and are currently employed have, through choice or lack of a better alternative, already committed themselves to jobs that are stereotyped as female. Most women who are secretaries, nurses, librarians, teachers, social workers, or cleaners will probably continue in these jobs for the remainder of their work lives. Some of these women have invested in lengthy, difficult, and expensive training for placement in the jobs they hold and would be comfortable remaining in them if their pay were increased to male-level wages in comparable jobs. If this is not done, then the efforts to improve women's economic status will benefit only younger women—not working women with long work histories (Bergmann, 1986).

Recent responsible business journalism accounts have shown that there are no women among the world's top fifty chief executive officers in industry (Pare and Woods, 1987). Where women in corporate America are succeeding to top-management positions, they appear to do best in industries rocked by change (such as computers, telecommunications, and financial services) because competition places a premium on managerial talent and ability. However, change brought about by deregulation and corporate restructuring, spinoffs, and leveraged buyouts have opened the way to advancement and put some women within striking distance of the top jobs. Also, women have forged ahead in businesses that historically hired large numbers of women for low-level jobs but then neglected to promote them, such as retailing, publishing, and advertising (Fisher, 1987). In fact, about 37 percent of corporate managers now are women, compared with 24 percent a decade ago. More than one-third of the 70,000 MBAs graduating each year are women, which is up from 12 percent a decade ago and 2 percent in 1967. Women managers have moved beyond the mid-level and staff positions where they staked their claim in large corporations in the 1970s. A survey by *Business Week* ("Corporate Women—They're About to Break Through to the Top," 1987) of the nation's highest ranked female executives from America's top 1,000 companies showed that in contrast to a similar 1976 survey, the new crop of women executives was better educated, more determined to advance, more single-minded about their careers, more confident about their prospects, and more apt to keep mum on gender-related inequities.

There are more women managers in the companies surveyed then in 1976, and they held far more senior positions. Their odds for succeeding in upward mobility were also improved for various reasons. First, the broad economic shift from manufacturing to services (a business sector that had accepted women earlier in America's economic history) gave these women a better chance at landing the top jobs as opportunities expanded. Second, many of the men now moving up corporate ladders are accustomed to having women work as peers in their environments. These men went to business schools and lived in college residence halls with women. They have worked with women as colleagues, subordinates, and superiors. None of this type of interaction was true of the generation of men who now are at the top of corporations in the strategic policy-making positions.

Women executives continue to face many hurdles involving discrimination and prejudice in corporate cultures. They still earn less than their male counterparts, perhaps about 42 percent. Of the top fifty women in *Business Week's* list, nearly one-half have never married or are divorced. Of those who married, almost one-third do not have children; of those who are mothers, many tire of high-pressure corporate jobs or decide to drop out temporarily or permanently. It appears that to make career progress in the corporate world, most successful women have sacrificed something, be it marriage, family, or personal time. Similarly situated men would appear to have sacrificed less. Some women have had to settle for careers where they were pigeonholed into staff jobs rather than enabled to move up in line management ("Corporate Women— They're About to Break Through to the Top," 1987).

Many of these same findings were set forth in a classic in-depth study of the life and career histories of twenty-five women who by 1970 had reached positions as presidents or divisional vice presidents in nationally recognized firms (Hennig and Jardim, 1977). These old and new studies seem to suggest that equal opportunity has aided women in upward mobility and contributed to the better utilization of female human resources in various organizations. Yet much progress needs to be made, and that is a major challenge to management today. How do we arrive at pay equity for tomorrow? What role might a comparable job worth thrust play? Perhaps before answering this question we need to recapitulate the oppositions' arguments to considering the application of comparable job worth concepts and rebut them, as appropriate.

Opposition Arguments: Skeptical Views

The arguments of the opposition can be summed up—and responded to—as follows.

1. There is no inherent objective economic worth to a job; therefore, there is no meaningful global way to define such worth independently of its value *to* someone, such as an employer or employee. The value of a particular job may not be the same for two similarly situated individuals or even the same for a given individual in different sets of circumstances. The value varies (California Employment Law Council, 1985).

To acknowledge the alleged instability in job value across organizations, time, and local circumstances in no way denies that the perceived value of a job can be agreed upon through lawful applications of job evaluation in a particular time and place. It is patent in the history of job evaluation that acceptable job value at the establishment level (that is, within a company or agency or specific location) can be agreed on by the parties involved. Such acceptability is the essence of well-conducted job evaluation.

2. Job evaluation systems are inherently subjective and cannot provide a basis for objectively and consistently comparing the relative worth of different jobs (California Employment Law Council, 1985). Acknowledging the subjectivity inherent in job evaluation should not lead us to conclude that it is necessarily not objective and necessarily inconsistent in comparing the relative worth of jobs within an establishment. Alert, well-trained job evaluation committees are as capable of exercising multiple judgments and achieving a consensus within the parameters of applicable laws and guideposts as are juries of twelve persons subjectively examining objective evidence pertinent to a felony or misdemeanor. Neither job evaluation committees nor juries are

involved in measurement in a puristic sense: they are judging based on facts and ultimately rendering a decision based on logic, reason, and common sense that most of the time solves a problem. The method is human and fallible, yet it works well often enough to be useful and entirely acceptable. Let us not insist on a nonexistent metric as the only alternative to well-conducted job evaluation. Above all, let us not throw out the baby with the bathwater simply because the latter lacks the cleansing power of a caustic wash.

3. Comparable job worth would be an administrative nightmare, especially if by this thought is meant that a federal government agency or worst yet a court of jurisdiction should direct the conduct and detailing of an establishment's job evaluations (California Employment Law Council, 1985). The federal government and the courts cannot and should not attempt this. However, the issue is a red herring when conceived of as an enforcement strategy. There is no necessary connection between comparable job worth and the regulation of business. No serious student of the subject wants the federal government and the courts to aim for a nationwide grand scheme aimed at cross-company, cross-organization pay equity. People want pay equity in the establishment where they work and are not seeking a uniform system bureaucratically applied from Washington or through the courts so that tens of millions of employers are in lockstep. Comparable job worth conceived of as nationwide regulatory controls would fail as surely as wage and price controls have failed in the several times in the twentieth century they have been imposed on business in the United States!

4. Comparable job worth would interfere with the goal of integrating male- and female-dominated jobs (California Employment Law Council, 1985). Crowding is conceived of as a "natural" result of women's entering the occupations traditionally open to them and would result in even greater overconcentration of women in such fields as nursing, teaching, retail sales, and clerical work if rates of pay in these occupations were "artificially" increased further. As we have seen previously in the book, this naive argument sets up the labor market as a sacred cow and warns us not to think about barbeque sauce. Indeed, it is thought proper, democratic, and workable to encourage the movement of women into male-

dominated jobs through equal opportunity and affirmative action programs. Higher wage levels in those jobs are not only a sacred cow but also the most powerful inducements to women who want to be pioneers in integrating male-dominated occupations. However, in reality this argument sidesteps the very essence of pay equity in the name of gender integration by ignoring the problem of underpayment.

5. Intentional sex discrimination in pay is already prohibited by law even where two jobs may be completely different (California Employment Law Council, 1985). The argument made here is that a comparable job worth approach to pay equity is thus redundant when intentional discrimination is present, as was set forth in the *Gunther, AFSCME,* and *Spaulding* cases. What if the discrimination is not proved to be intentional in comparison sets of jobs and yet women experience a disparate impact in the form of underpayment in the work?

6. If federal law is changed, comparable job worth could bring about a huge economic penalty for employers who have tried to pay market rates and have never intentionally engaged in sex-based pay practices (California Employment Law Council, 1985). Culpable discrimination would follow from meeting market rates, and this is held to be "unfair" in some vague, undefined sense. The market defense has generally been supported by the courts and should not be minimized as to its effectiveness. Yet where the external market data seem to reflect values that are incongruent with the employer's internal job evaluation system, simple fairness would suggest that internal judgments should supervene. Market rates usually show great dispersion for the same job, and often the employer or compensation specialist examines the averages of reported pay and tries to relate to them. Averages need not and should not be slavishly followed unless it is management's policy to do so—to have a market wage policy—and it acts accordingly. The level of pay rates chosen by management is its prerogative (or a function of negotiations in a unionized setting), and it should decide on a lawful policy that also coincides with its values, which morally suggests a need to achieve pay equity.

7. In instances where an employer has made all jobs equally available to persons of both sexes, has recruited both sexes, and has

set pay without regard to sex, that employer should not be financially liable for woman's voluntary preference for a traditional woman's job that happens to be relatively low paying (California Employment Law Council, 1985). This argument is much like the one in the previous paragraph, referring to the employer who is sex blind and acts in good faith but must pay more money to women who prefer to work in traditional female-dominated occupations because presumably a new law on comparable job worth enforced nationwide by a federal agency or court would upset the status quo in pay. The argument pits a bogeyman against an employer and suggests that many women who have crowded certain occupational fields are already properly paid and should not and would not receive higher compensation except for pressure from the government or courts. The wistfulness of this argument is appealing; morality is now on the employer's side and government and the courts are seen as high-handed and overriding the labor market(s). Stripped of sophistry, it is an appealing argument for laissez-faire for the employer who acts in good faith with respect to equal opportunity and affirmative action. We need not go back to analyze the sufficiency of that position once again; we have already shown that EEO-AA do not go far enough.

8. Comparable job worth carries enormous costs, which would not be justified by any resulting benefits (California Employment Law Council, 1985). This argument lacks substance in two respects: (a) to date the costs of achieving pay equity have not been shown to be excessive (and available numerical data on the modest costs involved at the establishment or state level have been provided in previous chapters), and (b) the justification of resulting benefits is a matter of personal opinion or morality. Pay inequity and unfair treatment of employees by sex are "benefits" to no one and impossible to justify. Wild estimates of the cost of comparable job worth ranging from $150 billion to more than $300 billion per year are vile and polemical, not grounded in reality and reason.

9. Imposing comparable job worth on business and the American economy can be expected to result in numerous unintended negative consequences (California Employment Law Council, 1985). Any government "imposition" that hampers the lawful activity of business needs to be carefully scrutinized, but regulation need not inevitably lead to increased inflation, higher unemployment (especially among women), and the loss of industry to the state and nation. As has been shown, there is no necessary connection between comparable job worth and oppressive government regulation. Ever since Hildebrand's (1980) gloomy pronouncement and overly rationalistic arguments against comparable job worth appeared, the negative economic bugaboos have been periodically trotted out in an attempt to discredit comparable job worth. Lindsay (1984) and Killingsworth (1985) have tended to carry Hildebrand's banner forward in recent years through their economic reasoning. No solid data support the conclusion of an economic apocalypse, though. Moreover, as we have argued several times, comparable job worth is not inherently connected with government impositions, as many conservative economists seem to imply.

10. Experiences in the United States with wage and price controls confirm that legislation intended to influence wages and prices "artificially" does not work in a free market system (California Employment Law Council, 1985). This argument rehashes the antipathies toward government regulation of wages and prices, which admittedly failed in the past. However, the reasons these fiascoes took place have nothing to do with artificial interventions in a naturalistic free market system. American labor markets are forcefully affected by such institutions as collective bargaining; wage and hour laws; tax laws; health, welfare, and pension plans; transfer payments; the customs and pay practices endemic to various industries; management policies; international competition; and a host of other considerations that suggest it is now and has for decades been anything but the "free" entity espoused in textbooks and by shallow thinking. Moreover, comparable job worth is not merely another predetermined flawed government wage policy and mandatory control.

11. A study by the prestigious Rand Corporation indicates that American women's wages have been improving dramatically in recent years and that the gap between men's and women's average wages will continue to narrow in the future owing to changes in human capital without comparable job worth legislation (California Employment Law Council, 1985). The Rand study is interesting

because of its analysis of the statistics that show the work experience of women in the U.S. labor force has been increasing in recent decades and that the education of women has been rising more rapidly than that of the male segment of the labor force. The movement toward greater pay parity between the sexes is seen by the Rand researchers as caused by changes in female human capital, not governmental affirmative action programs. The Rand study makes the emphatic point that women's market skills have been the primary shaper of their economic status in the past—and will be in the future—rather than legislation, government commissions, or political movements (Smith and Ward, 1984). Any predictions that are so inexorable and inevitable based on statistical trends deserve careful attention for the economy as a whole. Such statistics are very pertinent for thinking about the macroeconomic, long-run, sex-based wage disparity concept of comparable job worth. They are less germane for dealing with short-run pay inequities at the level of the establishment—the work organization, company, agency, or establishment where people are employed. As a policy matter for executives, line and staff managers, and human resource and compensation specialists, employees are caught up in day-to-day living in the short run and the size of their paychecks right now. The sixty-year sweep of future economic history between 1990 and 2050 will probably be at least as important as the sweep from 1920 to 1980, but spans of years that large are more like meat for the statisticians than potatoes for management and the female worker.

12. Comparable job worth is really not necessary. Over time, existing equal employment opportunity laws and the marketplace can be expected to bring about pay equity. Also, vigorous efforts to bring women into traditionally male jobs can speed this progress without the alleged disruptions of comparable job worth (California Employment Law Council, 1985). This twelfth point (and final conclusion) appears redundant and more like a statement of wishful thinking than a prognostication that can be accepted with confidence. The removal of all barriers for women entering traditionally male jobs and destroying the last vestiges of job segregation everywhere are clearly important for implementing equal employment opportunity. In this situation, we are still left with the issue of pay equity for tomorrow, which is not coterminous with equal

employment opportunity today or tomorrow. And this means we must go off on a slightly different tack and look very closely at the real-world issues facing management today in regard to purposefully discriminatory overt acts and circumstantial evidence that might support a judgment of sex-based pay discrimination. What happens "over time" passively is different from what management consciously and actively makes happen now.

The Chances of Litigation and Uses of Job Evaluation

No employer is beyond the scope of some legal theory of wage discrimination today. There can be claims based upon allegations of purposeful discriminatory acts that create a wage differential between male and female employees or claims based purely on circumstantial evidence that suggest sex-based pay inequity. The latter type of claim is more likely to arise and to be proved in organizations where the existence of sex-segregated positions that are paid differently indicates the possibility of a sex-based wage differential (Lorber and others, 1985).

A threshold question that should be asked by an employer concerned about a claim grounded on circumstantial evidence of sex-based wage discrimination is whether fundamental characteristics of the company's work force make it one in which comparable worth pay disparities have practical meaning. Thus, if certain basic characteristics are not present in its work force, a company or agency might reasonably decide that sex-based wage discrimination claims are unlikely. However, if there are at least two sex-segregated jobs (one male- and one female-dominated) and the wages paid employees in these jobs are different, the wise employer should be alert to the possible surfacing of a comparable job worth claim. No such claim based on circumstantial evidence would be likely in the absence of a pay differential between the sexes. Of course, most employers have at least somewhere in their organizations basic conditions that exist in female employment for asserting a theory of comparable job worth that could be grounded on circumstantial evidence. This is because very few firms have a single-sex work force; there is almost always somewhere in the organization a pocket of lower-paid female-dominated workers. In a unionized firm the labor organization may find these pockets and make a case that they are underpaid for apparent sex-based reasons. Hence, through job evaluation, a historical explanation, an analysis of the facts, or perhaps a special study, the employer should prepare to meet charges generated from advocates who have mustered the circumstantial evidence (Lorber and others, 1985). Of these preparations, job evaluation (or a special study that involves it one way or another) deserves the greatest attention.

Job evaluation can be both a problem leading to litigation and a defense useful in litigation. We have already seen in previous chapters how central job evaluation studies were to the *AFSCME v. State of Washington* case, in pinpointing specific point-value differences in the *Lemons* case in Denver and the *Westinghouse* case in Trenton, New Jersey. Beginning about 1977 in the case of *Angelo v. Bacharach Investment Company* [14 F.E.P. 1778 (CA3 1977)], job evaluation was introduced in Equal Pay Act lawsuits. The *Angelo* case established that (1) because they utilize *compensable factors* applicable to jobs rather than specific *tasks carried out in jobs,* job evaluations cannot be used to establish the common content of two jobs; and (2) the total of points in a job evaluation cannot be used to *assess* the *extra duties required in a higher-paid job.* In one of the most extensive uses of job evaluation made by a court (in the case of *Thompson v. Boyle* [21 E.P.D. 30332 (D.C. Col. 1979)], the court refused to give weight to a defendant's expert because his evaluations were based on two days of observation and were therefore considered cursory, but it accepted other, better-founded job evaluation testimony. Interestingly, in this case the court did hold that job evaluation by itself cannot establish the substantial equality of job content but it can establish the equality of the factors required for the performance of two jobs. In the case of *Marshall v. J. C. Penney Company* [19 E.P.D. 9092 (N.D. Oh. 1979)], the court received the results of three different job evaluations but gave little weight to any of them. Instead, the court made its own job comparison from descriptive evidence to conclude that many of the firm's females held positions which were equal to those of higher-paid males. By contrast, in *Wetzel v. Liberty Mutual Insurance Company* [449 F.Supp. 397 (W. D. Pa. 1978)], the court gave substantial weight to a job evaluation prepared by the plaintiff's expert to establish the equality of job qualifications required of the female-dominated job of claims representative compared to the male-dominated job of claims adjustor. Without offering a reason, the same court went on to dismiss as legally insignificant the conclusion of the defendant's job evaluation expert that working conditions for the claims adjustor were more difficult than for the claims representative. The jobs differed in that the claims adjustors used their cars to examine claims in various locations outside, whereas the claims representatives stayed in the office and evaluated claims assigned to them there. In sum, the courts appear to have given little weight to job evaluation evidence of job equality (or inequality) and to have greatly constrained the probative value of job evaluation evidence.

The language of the EPA that defines equal work is quite imprecise and ambiguous. As a result the courts have been forced to make difficult judgments about highly specialized jobs, a task for which they have no special competence and in which many judges have eschewed an opportunity to rule. No accepted standards for judging job equality have been formulated; therefore, litigants can only guess what a court might decide (Fogel, 1984).

In the *Gunther* and *Westinghouse* cases (both of which were settled before a trial involving Title VII charges), the fact patterns strongly suggested that intentional sex-based wage discrimination by the employer existed. If these two employers had not established or used *job evaluation* systems, but had instead simply used the *labor market* to establish wage rates for all of their jobs, no disparate treatment of the women plaintiffs would have existed. Put another way, it may be argued that if employers conduct job evaluations, they should use them in setting wages and salaries or risk the possibility of a lawsuit. Yet it would certainly be unwise for an employer to implement mindlessly the results of a job evaluation study if doubts exist about the adequacy, accuracy, or value of the study. Some employers will probably interpret *Gunther* and the *Westinghouse* cases to mean that they should *not* utilize a formal job evaluation plan in their company or agency. The overall effect of this belief could hurt the cause of wage equity, because despite its many limitations, job evaluation fosters and explicitly supports a pay-for-the-job policy that prevents setting rates of pay according to sex, race, or any other unlawful criterion or policy (Fogel, 1984).

Viewed another way, we could say the group A employers, who have the same job structure and pay the same market rates as group B employers, can be charged with sex-based wage discrimination because their pay rates for women conflict with female employees' job evaluations. At the same time, group B employers can be termed nondiscriminatory under the law because they rely entirely on the market and possess no job evaluations! This situation encourages either eliminating job evaluations or manipulating them to coincide with market rates, fudging the system to create an appearance of objectivity. This situation also raises the issue of whether plaintiff-sponsored job evaluations will compel employers who pay market rates to carry out their own evaluations in order to defend themselves against comparable job worth claims. Some employers have, of course, already done this, and the author has carried out many of these (Patten, 1978; 1985). It is questionable, however, if the courts are likely to permit such bald claims in the first place in the name of comparable job worth. Furthermore, the courts are likely to recognize, as they have in EPA cases, that partisan-sponsored job evaluations are too unreliable to be admitted as evidence for pay discrimination claims. When we consider that a court may be asked to look at a plaintiff's expert's job evaluations that came up with a conclusion that is diametrically opposed to a defendant's expert's conclusion—and both experts are competent and intellectually honest!—we can understand why many courts despair when confronted with conflicting recondite testimony and dismiss the experts as mere hired guns. Yet when males are paid what the employer's job evaluations say they are worth and females are paid less than the job evaluations suggest they are worth, courts are unlikely to let the market legitimize this inconsistency (Fogel, 1984).

Where does this line of reasoning leave us? Women workers in America are underpaid relative to men. The way to change that fact is not by replacing the market system of pay determination with a governmentally or judicially imposed system to change the nation's wage structure. Women themselves through concerted action and (where it pertains) collective bargaining can modify the market-produced structure of wages and salaries. Also important are offering women equal access to all jobs and *especially encouraging private industry to raise the relative wages of predominantly female jobs.* These methods could preserve a market-oriented system of pay determination based upon the decisions of individuals and private parties, a system that our experience with existing law (especially the EPA) demonstrates we should not give up (Fogel, 1984).

In this context, as the National Academy of Sciences has pointed out, it would be unwise to reject the use of job evaluation plans altogether. Despite their numerous limitations, they do provide an orderly and methodical basis for comparing jobs to determine whether they are fairly compensated. Because job evaluation plans as currently implemented are likely to understate the extent of differences in pay based on the sex, race, or ethnic composition of employees, estimates of the amount of discrimination derived from the application of contemporary job evaluation plans are probably low. Nevertheless, using job evaluation scores to determine pay rates will generally help an employer to reduce discriminatory differences in pay when they exist (Treiman and Hartmann, 1981).

The National Academy of Sciences also strongly advocates further experimentation with and the development of job evaluation plans. A part of this effort should be research on the possibility that stereotypes are operating in the evaluation of jobs and on the discriminatory components of pay rates. Importantly, the Academy did *not* recommend requiring the installation of a job evaluation plan in a firm not using one for the purposes of ensuring that the firm's pay system is nondiscriminatory. The reason is that we know of no method of job evaluation that would *guarantee* a fair pay system (Treiman and Hartmann, 1981). Thus, there remains a certain amount of equivocation that persists when we think of litigation and the place of job evaluation in achieving pay equity.

Strategic Options and Policies

In arriving at pay equity for tomorrow, we have set forth earlier in the chapter the opposition's arguments against comparable job worth. Both opponents and proponents may be seen as influenced by two sets of strategic invisible hands. The first of these is a strategy of "wait, watch, and worry," and the second (advocated by the author) is a deliberate policy of "review, revise, and reevaluate" (Rosen, Rynes, and Mahoney, 1983).

As we have seen, "wait, watch, and worry" (or "WWW") is a passive wait-and-see approach with which very conservative managers and observers of comparable job worth feel comfortable. WWW should not be regarded pejoratively because under many of the existing concepts of comparable job worth employers can find a safe harbor for inactivity. For example, employers are free to choose whether or not they want to close the gap in the wage gap between the sexes. Under current law, employers are not obligated to assign equal pay to positions differing in skill, effort, responsibility, or working conditions even if these positions are judged equivalent in overall worth to the organization. Federal government pressure to force such a concept of comparable job worth on the nation as a whole is remote if not downright fatuous to contemplate. However, employers who espouse WWW should keep abreast of lobbying, legislative, case law, and collective bargaining developments so that such a conservative position does not become outmoded or unlawful (Rosen, Rynes, and Mahoney, 1983).

A notch up the ladder in WWW is taking concrete actions to deal with the gender-related wage gap, which amounts to rising above passivity but not becoming proactive. In this intermediate stage the employer concentrates on affirmative actions such as speeding up the selection, training, career counseling, and promotion of women to higher-level positions. This approach raises female employees' pay generally but does nothing to the systems of wage and salary administration that by their usual construction have imported pay discrimination into the company or agency. A prerequisite to such affirmative action is having first identified female-dominated jobs and then taking the aforementioned necessary steps in human resource management. Women's advocacy groups and others point out that more is needed, to which we turn.

A strategy of "review, revise, and reevaluate" proactively suggests the type of organizational development effort that is needed to go beyond affirmative action. A number of corporations and state and local governments have started to reexamine their entire compensation systems. (See Chapter Two.) The motivations for their undertakings are quite diverse. Public-sector employers have often acted out of a strong sense of social responsibility and desire to be model employers by setting a policy example of pay equity. Other employers have learned from experience that the failure to take aggressive voluntary action on politically volatile issues leads to heavy-handed governmental regulation. Still other employers are inspired to be proactive because they enjoy the prestige and challenge of being at the cutting edge of contemporary human resource management. Finally, many managers may be moved in anticipation of growing pressures from employees, unions, and women's advocacy groups (Rosen, Rynes, and Mahoney, 1983).

Organizations that choose to address the comparable job worth controversy probably start by means of a review process in identifying which of their compensation policies and practices need to be revised. The first two Rs—review and revise—of the three Rs of review, revise, and reevaluate thus come into play at an early stage of this organizational development strategy. The review may begin at the very basic level of searching for possible biases in the naming of positions and in the description of job duties. For example, jobs requiring roughly equivalent levels of skill, effort, and responsibility and carried out under very comparable working conditions should not have titles that imply differences in job performance difficulty or prestige. Specifically, male-dominated jobs titled "manager" or "account executive" are often quite similar to but paid considerably more than female-dominated jobs titled "coordinator" or "sales representative." Naturally, all such basic sex-biased language in job descriptions would have long since been changed. Wireman, policeman, foreman, and postmaster would have been replaced respectively by wirer, police officer, foreperson (or supervisor to avoid a seemingly awkward word), and postal service manager (or some appropriate neutral term). While much creativity will have gone into gender-free job titles, it goes without saying the organization would have also long since changed at least superficially the erstwhile work culture that fostered referring to sixty-year-old grandmothers who happened to be employees as "girls" or "gals" and taken other actions to extirpate sexism.

The third of the three Rs in RRR is reevaluate, which embodies the technical reexamination of the organization's job evaluation plan(s) with an eye to studying the number and type of compensable factors, any subtle biases favoring predominantly male jobs, and the best way to evaluate jobs in different job families. Fundamentally, an organization needs to confront the issue of one big tent in job evaluation (as we explained this term in a prior chapter) or the use of disparate job evaluation systems tailor-made to such clusters of jobs as executive, managerial and supervisory, professional and technical, office and clerical, and production/ service and maintenance categories. The other side of the third R is economic reevaluation, the determination of the financial feasibility of comparable job worth. To reevaluate jobs probably means to increase the costs of being in business.

An astute compensation specialist could build a model or simulation by describing a single, comprehensive job evaluation plan and applying it to all positions in existence in an organization. Setting pay rates based exclusively in internal equity considerations would simulate an ideal-type or model comparable job worth system. A comparative analysis of present pay policies and practices with the model comparable job worth system would then show how much of the pay differential between men and women would be reduced by adopting a comparable job worth pay policy. Additional comparisons would approximate the cost effects of these changes. On the basis of the costs and benefits (many of which are moral, as we discuss below), corporate policy-level executives could better judge the kind and extent of compensation policy revisions that will fit and be practicable in their organizations. Open-minded efforts on the part of all line and staff managers to examine the issues and explore the policy options represent an important first step for the implementation of the RRR strategy and ultimately the creation of an equitable reward system for all employees (Rosen, Rynes, and Mahoney, 1983).

Comparable job worth persists as a moral problem that is most effectively addressed by an RRR strategy. The existence of an organizational policy to accomplish the specific purposes for which it was intended, such as pay equity or simple fairness, is increasingly coming to be seen in America as a contractual obligation on the part of employers toward employees. In time, it takes on a morality of its own. The very existence of accepted programs and practices (and the abuses that are alleged when management does not live up to its own rules) arms legislators with the ammunition they need to create laws that focus on these same specific moral obligations. For example, the Employee Retirement Income Security Act of 1974 came about largely because employers were not living up to reasonable standards of funding and vesting that would assure employees a minimum of security and income certainty in the form of retirement pay. Attacks on the doctrine of employment-at-will are growing, and judgments against employers are becoming commonplace because employers' policies of steady employment subject to good performance are being ignored by their actions. The same drift can be expected with respect to the moral and legal future of comparable job worth (Ost, 1985).

Many American business firms seem to realize this and are pragmatically but quietly going about the implementation of comparable job worth in a variety of ways. These organizations include AT&T, BankAmerica, Chase Manhattan Bank, General Electric, IBM, Tektronix, and Motorola. Some of these companies have started to adhere closely to internal comparison in job evaluation even when it means paying employees more than survey data from the relevant labor market(s) would suggest is the going rate. In a few of the high-tech companies (such as Tektronix), the costs of implementing comparable job worth are viewed as negligible because their high-tech jobs do not have a history of being dominated by one gender. Other companies (such as GE) are trying to ensure that the factors used to evaluate jobs do not contain a built-in bias against work usually performed by women. Still others, such as BankAmerica Corporation when it installed a new pay system, have expanded the definition of physical effort to include eyestrain generated by work on video display terminals that is often performed by women. BankAmerica also considers the type of muscle strain experienced by tellers in its job evaluations. IBM and Control Data Corporation have been making statistical studies of the pay of male and female employees in order to determine if sex is a predictor of pay level. Undoubtedly, a great many other organizations are attending to comparable job worth issues and simply do not want to publicize what they are doing and why (*Business Week,* April 28, 1986, pp. 52–56). There is an emerging literature available on how to examine one's organization using various types of logical and statistical methods for this purpose (Risher, 1977; Sullivan, 1985; Bottini, Chertos, and Haignere, 1987). These sources can be very helpful for thinking through concrete data gathering and analyses that can, in turn, form a genuine basis for organizational action.

Organizational Imperatives

The possibilities for strategy and organizational development in the implementation of comparable job worth need to be seen in the context of broad types of organizations and job clusters within organizations. Four types of organizations are very different from one another and present different arrangements of market orientation and internal wage-structure orientation for the purposes of assessing potential for the implementation of comparable job worth.

First, there are organizations whose employees come largely from a well-organized and competitive labor market but are not unionized and have clearly market-oriented wage structures. These types of organizations have only limited choices in building wage structures because the jobs they contain are easily identified and quite uniform throughout the labor market. Examples of such organizations are banks, insurance companies, department stores, and restaurants. Professional employers throughout the country and regardless of industry experience the same forces as the organizations just mentioned. Nationwide, professionals are groups of employees whose jobs have been designed largely by the extent of education they possess. Labor markets recognize this. As a result, there is a nationwide commonality among organizations in the design of and pay for professional jobs (Belcher and Atchison, 1987).

The second category includes organizations having many specialized jobs, dealing in labor markets that are too disorganized to provide adequate job grading and pricing, and lacking unionization. These organizations have internally determined wage structures that may be influenced by product markets but only if labor costs are high relative to total costs. Internally determined wage structures result from managerial decisions and may range from highly rational structures built on job evaluation to systems of almost personalized rates. Organizations of this type often appear in small towns, isolated locations, or nonunion communities, or in unique organizations in larger communities, and in government employment (Belcher and Atchison, 1987). Based on what we have observed to date, these organizations are in the best position to implement comparable job worth and are most likely to do so, as we have seen in the field of public employment and in selected industrial establishments.

The third type consists of most large, unionized organizations that have combined union- and product-oriented wage structures. In these organizations wage structures represent the product of or combination of managerial decisions shaped and restrained by technology, unions, cost-price relationships, and the market for goods and services. Quite often technology provides some uniformity in the job structures of organizations that are engaged in businesses having common products. Unions in these industries, by means of their insistence on traditional pay and job relationships, establish some key jobs and job clusters and generate an upward thrust on the wage structure. Companies react to this upward push by making changes in jobs and job relationships, because they must do so in order to control cost-price relationships and remain competitive in the product market. Organizations in many branches of manufacturing, in mining, and in some service industries typically demonstrate the union- and product-orientated wage structure (Belcher and Atchison, 1987). Their receptivity to implementing comparable job worth probably depends on how effective the union(s) with which they bargain are in demanding comparable job worth. It also depends on how strong the competitive pressures facing the companies are and whether the companies are largely in international business and can avoid the problem of higher labor costs by having their work completed offshore to control labor costs and returned to the United States for sale. It should not be surprising that companies of this type really need to be studied individually to determine if comparable job worth would even be entertained by them.

The fourth type includes the organizations that build wage structures based on custom, and comparable job worth for them is particularly hard to handle because it is an anomaly. In these organizations, management takes its cues in building wage structures from key jobs, clusters of jobs that are important in the industry, and customs and pattern bargaining. The key jobs that interest this management acquire their importance from labor markets, product markets, and comparative rates for these same jobs paid by other organizations, often bid up by union pressure in collective bargaining. The job clusters are accorded importance owing to the technologies and skill mixes among employees in the industry. Customary pay comparisons with other firms are also very important (Belcher and Atchison, 1987). We may hypothesize that management in the organizations characterized as type 4 is not likely to want to implement comparable job worth. Not only is the latter inconsistent with the customs of the industry, but it is also beyond the ken of management. It would take skillful organizational development intervention to have management even consider the morality and desirability of introducing comparable job worth in these establishments.

Although organizations can be classified as having wage structures broadly categorized in the four ways described above, large organizations will have considerable further diversity depending on their employee and work force composition. For example, organizations employing skilled trades employees, unless they are members of an industrial union, usually must conform to external union-oriented wage structures. All organizations employ some clerical workers, and they are mostly paid on a market-oriented basis. Professional employees have salary structures that combine market orientation and internal determinations, regardless of the major activity of the organization. Finally, managerial pay structures are primarily internally determined except in very tight labor markets, regardless of organizational type (Belcher and Atchison, 1987). When the implementation of comparable job worth is contemplated, it must be forged upon the jerry-built wage and job structures of the real world that are resistant to change. Yet there are things that can be done.

Managerial Action

To implement comparable job worth, management in any particular establishment, company, or agency must understand the legal interaction between job segregation, pay disparities, and the presence of discrimination. Then it must plan what to do in coping with pay disparity (Sape, 1985).

The beginning point is ascertaining whether job segregation by sex exists. Female- and male-dominated jobs should be identified. The existence of segregation may not be conclusive of any legal liability. Yet all line and staff managers need to challenge the thinking behind the status quo as well as the status quo itself in the workplace. They must be aware of and sensitive about what they see at work and ask why. What are the peculiarities in gender-based job and work assignments? Why do traditions that are associated with segregation exist? Should they be changed?

Once job segregation has been identified, employers must determine whether the women's jobs are lower paid than similar but not necessarily identical male-dominated job classifications. Other related comparisons should be made, examining employment segregation in the same department, plant, or other organizational component. It might also be well to analyze all salaries in a certain band of pay in the organization and then determine insofar as possible whether sex may have played a role in the placement of employees in those particular bands (Sape, 1985).

The third and most difficult component with which to deal is determining whether discrimination has caused the observed pay disparities. Usually some combination of history, the evolution of the job or job family, job evaluation, and market considerations explains most pay differences. But none of these factors is immune to infection by discrimination. Management may be able to ascribe only a portion of an existing wage gap to lawful or neutral sources that a court or outside agency would accept as nondiscriminatory. The remainder may be presumed to be the result of discrimination and its elimination is tantamount to attainment of comparable job worth (or at least the elimination of pay disparity) (Sape, 1985).

From these legal interactions management can deal with a series of broad policy issues and take a series of actions to improve job evaluation for the purpose of implementing comparable job worth. Let us turn first to what policy-level executives should do in concert with adequate policy development and clarification of personnel practices by human resource managers.

- State policies in pay that endorse the concept of pay equity for jobs of different content but equal worth to the employer.
- Determine from each line and staff manager what financial and budgetary aid is needed to realign the internal organizational worth of jobs where internal inequities are identified, and make such resources available normally over a period of two or three years.
- Acquire external labor-market data on rates of pay for key jobs, but do not slavishly follow it when it conflicts with management's prerogative to pay what it considers equitable internally.
- Identify occupations where jobs seen to be overly concentrated by gender (defined as 70 percent or more dominated by one sex), and where possible break these up by offering upward and meaningful lateral mobility programs, career management and planning, and training to reduce overconcentrations by gender. It is important to ask why this ghettoization took place initially and to plan how to prevent it in the future so that internal placement and career mobility is driven by competence and performance and not by discriminatory variables.
- Enable men to enter female-dominated occupations and women to enter male-dominated occupations when they respectively have the skills, knowledge, and ability to do so, but do not make entry because of cultural or traditional barriers. This policy is not formulated to suggest that unqualified clerks be made professionals or to expect professionals to step down to the lower pay of clerks. Instead the idea is to go beyond affirmative action and equal opportunity minima and, for example, engage in such positive actions as making it possible for a woman to become by promotion a supervisor of production at any

organizational level or males to enter jobs that hitherto have been female-dominated, such as becoming flight attendants. The goal should be the open and unimpeded mobility and free circulation of people in careers based on their competence and levels of performance.

- Remove from their positions those line and staff managers and supervisors who appear incorrigible after training and counseling, and who are given a chance to implement comparable job worth and fair treatment for pay purposes and then fail to generate the desired results. This seemingly peremptory treatment is reminiscent of actions that management was required to take in the early 1980s in order to send out the correct managerial signals that have since halted sexual harassment in many organizations.

- Oppose government intervention and public policies that would require the imposition of a single nationwide job evaluation plan or mandated concept that equally valued jobs in existence at widely different firms should be paid at the same level (regardless of local situational factors and contrary to any given management's lawful exercise of the prerogative to build a reward system as it sees fit).

- Develop private policies that are supportive not only of pay equity but also of modern human resource management concepts related to the facilitation of comparable job worth and the expansion of employment opportunities for women, such as child-care programs for employees, endorsement of educational and information programs offered in public school systems that explain pay equity, open job posting, and mentoring where needed.

The other large area for strategic attention by management is taking a series of actions to improve job evaluation. The focus is on making traditional models of the overall job evaluation process work with a comparable worth goal.

- Examine the organization's job evaluation plan(s) for any explicit or implicit practices that might underevaluate or overevaluate occupations of any type that are male- or female-dominated. Such practices might include the factors selected in the job evaluation, their relevancy, their internal weights (if applicable), and whether the full range of degrees, points, or other items used in the specific evaluations are used properly.

- Reconstitute job evaluation committees if they are dominated by white males in order to include female and minority representation. Also, in general, make sure that line and staff managers who are chosen to serve on such committees are properly trained in the techniques they will be asked to use and in the applicable company or agency policies on pay equity.

- Where more than one job evaluation plan exists in an organization, construct bridges between the plans so that equivalencies in value can be converted from one plan to another and one occupational field to another. To a large extent this is a challenging research and development task for human resource management professionals. Use the line and staff managers' knowledge of the jobs, operations, functions, and organizational structure in order to construct these bridges and conversion charts.

- Install and publicize a complaint review procedure for disputed evaluations of all jobs for all employees. Make adjustments in the pay grades of jobs where warranted.

- Build job structures by the initial use of empirical job analysis and include the views of line and staff managers in these procedures. Make certain that the final working of the resulting job descriptions is regarded by a large sample of job incumbents for each job as at least 90 percent accurate. (If not, executive management should insist on reanalysis of jobs until a 90 percent accuracy acceptance rate is achieved by male and female job incumbents.)

In making use of the proprietary job evaluation plans of commercial consulting firms in order to implement comparable job worth, there are at least two major strategic considerations for policy-level executives as well as human resource managers.

Although many outside consultants are highly aware of sex discrimination and have consciously excised it from their proprietary plans, any user firm should check for remnants of sex discrimination in the plans. It would be highly ironic for an organization to endorse pay equity as a policy and have it thwarted by an outside consultant!

Where outsiders rather than internal line and staff managers evaluate jobs, control over the former is required so that they do not introduce biases into the actual job evaluations or processes used to study, analyze, and describe jobs for the purposes of job evaluation.

As we have noted many times in this book, government (especially at the state and local levels) should be viewed today as a model employer that is actively struggling with the contemporary issues of pay equity. It provides a laboratory for comparable worth implementation and experiences with the traditional tools of human resource management as well as innovations needed to make pay equity work well. It offers a resource: the results of experimentation. The private sector should be prepared and ready to benefit from these and should use them.

Final Thoughts

Pay equity is the American way. Comparable job worth is the rallying cry for fair pay that owing to semantics confuses many managers and people generally who are not pay system experts. But the bands have assembled and the parade has long since started in the states. American industrial management, except for some harbinger establishments that have quietly gone about their pay rectification programs, is not leading the parade and presently stands by the sidelines as an observer. This is a pity, because well-known and proven administrative techniques, existing institutions (including the law), and careful experimentation will enable those organizations that want to find the appropriate managerial ways to extirpate the remaining sex-discrimination in pay in America. The evidence to date indicates that the cost of implementing comparable job worth will be relatively small for most organizations, and the exaggerated financial fears that give so much sensational publicity are clearly unjustified.

The politics of change are hovering over the movements below as the parade takes shape. We can see a new president coming into the White House and a vastly different composition in the

Supreme Court for the 1990s. Congress has been buffeted by compensation equity acts in several of its recent sessions and is contemplating what the American public may demand next in the long war against discrimination. Yet there is almost no likelihood at this writing that the federal government will mandate one job evaluation plan for industrial America or that our court system will generally accept the responsibility for evaluating jobs for the purpose of achieving pay equity. The challenge has been given to management, and a free enterprise remedy is wanted.

Pay equity will come tomorrow. Tomorrow is the 1990s.

Appendix:
Interpreting Regression
Statistics of
Pay Equity Assessment*

In this appendix, we provide an introduction to the interpretation of regression models for the benefit of readers unfamiliar with this technique. We work through a number of hypothetical examples to make clear the interpretation of regression statistics in the context of pay equity analysis, and especially of equations containing "proportion female" and "proportion minority" as variables.

To keep matters simple, let us assume that pay differences among jobs in an enterprise depend on only three factors: how much responsibility each job entails, how much skill it requires, and the extent to which it is regarded as a "woman's job." In fact, the determinants of pay rates typically are much more complex. Also, in an actual analysis we would want to consider whether there is a race as well as a sex effect on pay rates.

Suppose that each of the factors is measured as follows:

The *pay rate (Y)* is measured by the average salary of incumbents of each job title.

*Revised version of an appendix to the *California Comparable Worth Task Force Minority Report* issued by Donald J. Treiman and Phyllis W. Cheng, Aug. 19, 1985. Grateful acknowledgement is given to Dr. Donald J. Treiman of the Department of Sociology, University of California, Los Angeles, who prepared this revised version for the author of this book.

    Responsibility (R) is measured by a combination of items
        put together into a scale with scores ranging from 0 to 10,
        10 high.
    Skill (S) is likewise measured by a combination of items
        aggregated into a single scale with scores ranging from 0
        to 10, 10 high.
    *The extent to which a job title is regarded as "women's
        work" (F)* is measured by the proportion of females
        among all employees with that job.

Assume that each job title in the enterprise has a score on each of
these four variables.

Model 1: Pay Is Based on Skill Only

Let us begin with a very simple model. Suppose we want to know
whether, to what extent, and in what way pay differences among
jobs depend on differences in the skill required to do them, ignoring
for the moment any other determinants of pay differences. We could
estimate the effect of skill differences between jobs on pay rates by
statistically predicting pay rates from our skill variable, specifically
by finding the line relating the two variables that minimizes the
sum of the squared errors in prediction. To see this graphically,
imagine that we had a sample of only five job titles. We could then
plot each job title on a two-dimensional plot, known as a scatterplot, where the horizontal axis represents our skill variable and the
vertical axis represents average salary. Figure 19 (top) gives such a
hypothetical plot. From even a casual glance at Figure 19 (top) it
is evident that as skill requirements increase, salaries tend to
increase. To quantify this relationship, with an estimate of how
large a difference in salary we would expect, on average, for two
occupations that differed by one point on the skill requirements
scale, we would fit the line shown in Figure 19 (bottom).

      Recall from high school algebra that the formula for a
straight line is $Y = a + b(X)$, or, since we have labeled our skill
variable S rather than X, and want to estimate an *expected* or
predicted value of Y, which we designate by $\hat{Y}$ ("*Y*-hat"), $\hat{Y} = a +
b(S)$. The a is the intercept; it gives the value of Y when $S = 0$. The

Figure 19. Examples of Estimating the Relationship
Between Skill Requirements and Average Salary for Five Jobs;
top = Job Plot; bottom = Wage Line

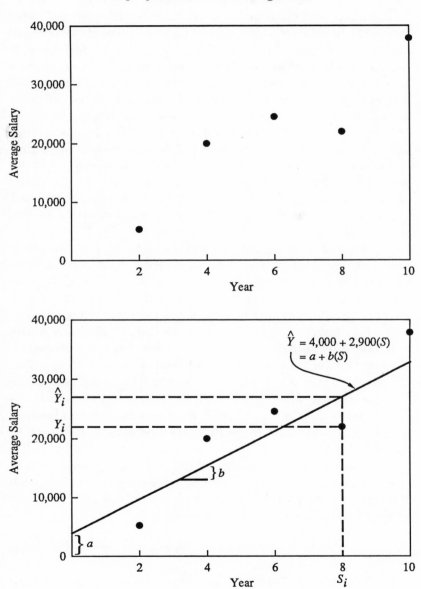

b is the slope; it gives the number of units of change in Y for a one-unit change in S. The point on the Y axis corresponding to any particular point on the S axis is the expected or predicted value of Y, $\hat{Y}$. In Figure 19 the actual value of S, the actual value of Y, and the predicted value of Y are marked for one observation; these are labeled S_i, Y_i, and $\hat{Y}_i$, respectively. Regression analysis is a procedure that finds the best-fitting line relating, in this case, Y to S, where the criterion of "best fit" is that the sum of the squared differences between the actual and predicted values of Y is minimized. That is, regression is a technique for finding the a and b that will result in the smallest value for $\Sigma(Y-\hat{Y})^2$, which is another way of saying that the resulting equation gives the best prediction of the value of Y given that one knows the value of S or, in the present case, the best prediction of the average salary of incumbents of an occupation that can be made from knowledge of the skill requirements of the occupation. The line representing the prediction equation is known as the *regression line*.

The square of the correlation coefficient, r^2, is a measure of how good the prediction is. Obviously, the smaller the scatter of observed points around the regression line relating the two variables, the better the prediction. Formally, r^2 is defined as $r^2 = 1 - \Sigma(Y-\hat{Y})^2/\Sigma(Y-\bar{Y})^2$, that is, as 1 minus the ratio of the variance around the regression line to the total variance in Y, which is why r^2 is a measure of the proportion of the variance in Y explained by another variable, in this case S. From this definition, it is evident that if prediction is perfect, $r^2 = 1$, and if there is no association between the two variables, $r^2 = 0$. (If prediction is perfect, each $Y_i - \hat{Y}_i = 0$ and so their sum = 0, and if there is no association between S and Y, the regression line will be flat and each $\hat{Y}_i = \bar{Y}$, so $\Sigma(Y-\hat{Y})^2/\Sigma(Y-\bar{Y})^2 = 1$.)

Now, suppose we estimated the relationship between skill requirements and average salary not for the five hypothetical job titles in the scatterplot but for all job titles in a large enterprise, and obtained the following prediction equation:

$$\hat{Y} = 4{,}000 + 2{,}900(S) \qquad (1)$$

with an associated r^2 of .60. These results would tell us, first, that sixty percent of the variance across job titles in average salaries can be explained by variations in the skill requirements of jobs. Second, jobs with the lowest skill level (a score of 0) would be predicted to pay an average of $4,000 per year, and each additional point on the skill scale would result in a predicted increase of $2,900 per year. Thus, job titles with the highest skill level (a score of 10) would be predicted to pay incumbents an average of $33,000 per year (= 4,000 + 2,900(10). Of course, some jobs might actually pay even more, presumably because they not only require a high degree of skill but also great responsibility, and so on. For such jobs, relying on skill as the only measure of job content would underestimate their value. Similarly, some jobs not only require low skill but entail little responsibility, and so forth. For such jobs, relying on skill as the only measure of job content would overestimate their value. For this reason, we need to be able to measure the simultaneous effect of a number of different aspects of job content. To do this, we would estimate a *multiple regression* equation, which is a straightforward extension of the two-variable regression example we have just worked through.

Model 2: Pay Is Based on Both Skill and Responsibility

Suppose we wanted to know the effect of both skill requirements and responsibility demands on salary level. To discover this we would estimate a multiple regression equation analogous to Eq. (1) above, which might yield the following:

$$\hat{Y} = 3,400 + 1,400(S) + 1,900(R) \tag{2}$$

with an associated R^2 of .70.

R^2 ("multiple R-square") is a measure of how good the prediction is; it is exactly analogous to r^2 in the example above, but the convention is to capitalize r in the multiple regression case. An R^2 of .70 indicates that 70 percent of the variability ("variance") in pay rates across job titles can be attributed to variability in the responsibility and skill the jobs entail. The other 30 percent is due to factors that have not been measured. Typically, studies of this kind are able to explain around 90 percent of the variance in pay rates among jobs in an enterprise, or in a state or local civil service system, on the basis of a relatively small set of job characteristics, which means that they have successfully captured almost all of what differentiates the pay rates of jobs.

Now let's interpret the equation. The $\hat{Y}$ is the salary that would be expected for a job given its level of skill and responsibility if each job were paid only on the basis of responsibility and skill and if each of these factors were worth exactly the same for each job.

The 3,400 is the intercept, and is exactly analogous to the intercept in the two-variable case described above. It indicates the predicted average salary of job titles that have scores of 0 on each of the factors—that is, jobs that have the lowest scores on both the responsibility and the skill factors. One way to think of it is that it is the component of pay that all jobs share regardless of their levels of responsibility and skill.

The 1,400 is the weight, or coefficient, associated with the skill factor. It indicates that two jobs that have the same scores on the responsibility factor but that differ by one point on the skill factor would be predicted to differ by $1,400 per year in average salary. Another way of putting this is to say that the *net* regression coefficient associated with skill is $1,400. Note that the net regression coefficient associated with skill in Eq. (2) is substantially smaller than in Eq. (1). The reason for this is that skill and responsibility tend to be highly correlated; jobs that require a great deal of skill also entail a great deal of responsibility. Thus when both variables are included in the equation, their effect tends to be divided. Each one-point increase in skill results in a predicted increase of $1,400 in average salary and each one-point increase in responsibility results in a predicted increase of $1,900. So two job titles that differ by one point in skill requirements *and* by one point in responsibility level would be expected to differ by $3,300 (= 1,400 + 1,900) in average salary, compared to a difference of $2,900 predicted from skill alone in Eq. (1).

The 1,900 is the weight, or net regression coefficient, associated with the responsibility factor. It is interpreted in the same way as the coefficient for the skill factor.

These results allow us to predict the salary grade of jobs with different combinations of skill and responsibility. Jobs with both the lowest skill level and the lowest responsibility level would be predicted to have an average pay rate of $3,400 (= 3,400 + 1,400(0) + 1,900(0)). Jobs with the highest levels of both skill and responsibility would be predicted to pay an average of $36,400 (= 3,400 + 1,400(10) + 1,900(10)). A job title with a skill level of 3 and a responsibility level of 5 would be predicted to pay an average of $17,100 (= 3,400 + 1,400(3) + 1,900(5)); and so on. Predicted pay rates can be computed for each job title and compared to the current average pay rate. If the predicted pay rate for a job is higher than the actual average salary, the job would be said to be undervalued relative to its skill and responsibility requirements. Of course, if the predicted pay rate is lower than the actual average salary, the job would be said to be overvalued relative to its skill and responsibility requirements.

Correcting the Effect of the Sex Composition of Jobs

Equations such as Eq. (2) are conventionally used in job evaluation studies to determine the relative worth of jobs. They have one major limitation, however. Insofar as job content variables, such as skill and responsibility, or—more pertinently, physical effort, and so on—are correlated with the sex composition of jobs, the regression procedure will attribute to these characteristics part of what might in fact be due to sex composition. For example, if jobs done mainly by women tend to pay less than jobs done mainly by men *because* of sex discrimination and if the jobs done mainly by women require low levels of physical effort relative to the jobs done mainly by men, the regression procedure will incorrectly attribute heavy weight to a physical effort factor, even if physical effort has no effect on pay rates within the set of jobs done mainly by men or within the set of jobs done mainly by women. To correct for this difficulty, a modified regression model can be estimated, namely:

Model 3: Pay Is Based on Skill, Responsibility, and Proportion Female

In this approach, an equation similar to that of Eq. (2) is estimated, but with one additional variable, the proportion of incumbents in each job title who are female. The inclusion of this variable does two things: first, it provides a direct estimate of the extent to which the sex composition of jobs affects their pay rates, net of other factors; and, second, it provides estimates of each of the other effects net of sex composition—that is, it tells us how skill, responsibility, and so on affect pay among jobs with equal proportions of women among incumbents, thus giving unbiased estimates of the effects of these variables.

Again, let us work through a concrete example. Suppose that we estimated a regression equation predicting average salary from our measures of skill and responsibility and also a measure of gender composition, the proportion female among incumbents of the job title, with the following result:

$$\hat{Y} = 3,300 + 1,300(S) + 1,800(R) - 2,000(F) \tag{3}$$

and the associated $R^2 = .80$.

Here the interpretation of the coefficients associated with skill and responsibility is the same as for Eq. (2). Job titles that differ by one point on the skill scale but that are identical on the responsibility scale *and have identical proportions female among incumbents* would be predicted to differ by $1,300 in average salary; and job titles that differ by one point on the responsibility scale but that are identical on the skill scale and have identical proportions female among incumbents would be predicted to differ by $1,800 in average salary.

The -2,000 is the coefficient associated with the "femaleness" factor. It indicates the predicted difference in average salary between job titles that have identical scores on the responsibility and skill factors but that differ by 1.0 in their proportion female. That is, it indicates that the predicted difference in the average salary of two job titles, one of which is 100 percent male and the other of which is 100 percent female but which have identical scores on the skill and responsibility variables, is $2,000. Note that since the coefficient is negative, this equation indicates that predominantly female job titles tend to have *lower* average salaries than predominantly male job titles with similar skill and responsibility requirements.

To see how these weights are used, let us consider the predicted salary levels for two jobs, typist and truck driver. Suppose that typists have a score of 4 on the skill factor, a score of 3 on the responsibility factor, and are 100 percent female; and that truck drivers have a score of 4 on the skill factor, 4 on the responsibility factor, and are 0 percent female. Then the predicted pay rate for typists would be

$$\hat{Y} = 3,300 + 1,300(4) + 1,800(3) - 2,000(1.0) = 11,900 \qquad (4)$$

while the predicted pay rate for truck drivers would be

$$\hat{Y} = 3,300 + 1,300(4) + 1,800(4) - 2,000(0) = 15,700 \qquad (5)$$

From these two equations we see that of the $3,800 (= 15,700 - 11,900) difference in the predicted salary grades of truck drivers and typists, only $1,800 (= 1,800(4) - 1,800(3)) is due to what we would regard as a legitimate basis of pay differentials, the fact that truck driving involves more responsibility than typing, while $2,000 (= -2,000(1.0) - (-2,000)(0)) is due to the fact that truck driving is a male job while typing is a female job.

The "gender effect" can then be removed from the equation (and from the enterprise's job evaluation system) by setting the coefficient associated with "femaleness" to zero and estimating a predicted pay rate from the legitimate factors—responsibility and skill in the Eq. (3) example. These predicted pay rates can be interpreted as "equitable job worth" scores since they indicate what the employer would pay if responsibility and skill differences between job titles were taken into account but differences in gender composition were not. The utility of this strategy is that it provides an ordering of jobs with respect to their evaluated worth that is free of any sex bias but that otherwise conforms as closely as possible to the current job hierarchy of the enterprise. That is, the relationship between skill and responsibility, on the one hand, and pay rates, on the other, that emerges from an exercise of this kind is precisely the relationship that *already exists in the enterprise,* adjusted only insofar as is necessary to remove sex as a basis of pay differentials. By capturing the current compensation policy of the enterprise, and insisting only that it be sex (and race) neutral, or made so if it is not, pay equity can be achieved without having to enter into the difficult and divisive debate about what makes one job worth more than another.

References

Aaron, H. J., and Lougy, C. M. *The Comparable Worth Controversy*. Washington, D.C.: Brookings Institution, 1986.

Abbott, E. *Women in Industry*. New York: Appleton, 1910.

Aldrich, M., and Buchele, R. *The Economics of Comparable Worth*. Cambridge, Mass.: Ballinger, 1986.

Angrist, S. A. "The Study of Sex Roles." *Journal of Social Issues*, 1969, *15*, 215–232.

Ashenfelter, O., and Rees, A. (eds.). *Discrimination in Labor Markets*. Princeton, N.J.: Princeton University Press, 1973.

Barker, L. "Acquiring Competitive Information from Surveys: The Hay Compensation Information Center." In M. Rock (ed.), *Handbook of Wage and Salary Administration*. (2nd ed.) New York: McGraw-Hill, 1984.

Barrett, G. V., and others. "Frequently Encountered Problems in the Application of Regression Analysis to the Investigation of Sex Discrimination in Salaries." *Public Personnel Management*, 1986, *15*, 143–157.

Baruch, I. *Position-Classification in the Public Service*. Chicago: Civil Service Assembly of the United States and Canada, 1941.

Becker, G. S. *The Economics of Discrimination*. Chicago: University of Chicago Press, 1957.

Belcher, D. W. *Compensation Administration*. Englewood Cliffs, N.J.: Prentice-Hall, 1974.

Belcher, D. W., and Atchison, T. J. *Compensation Administration.* (2nd ed.) Englewood Cliffs, N.J.: Prentice-Hall, 1987.

Bell, C. S. "Comparable Worth: How Do We Know It Will Work?" *Monthly Labor Review,* 1984, *108,* 5–12.

Bellak, A. O. "Comparable Worth: A Practitioner's View." In U.S. Commission on Civil Rights, *Comparable Worth: Issues for the 80's.* 2 vols. Washington, D.C., 1984a.

Bellak, A. O. "The Hay Guide Chart–Profile Method of Job Evaluation." In M. Rock (ed.), *Handbook of Wage and Salary Administration.* New York: McGraw-Hill, 1984b.

Bellak, A. O., Bates, M. W., and Glassner, D. M. "Job Evaluation: Its Role in the Comparable Worth Debate." *Public Personnel Management,* 1983 *12,* 418–424.

Bem, S. L. "The Measurement of Psychological Androgyny." *Journal of Consulting and Clinical Psychology,* 1974, *42,* 155–162.

Benge, E. J., and Burk, S. L. H., and Hay, E. N. *Manual of Job Evaluation.* New York: Harper & Row, 1941.

Bergmann, B. R. *The Economic Emergence of Women.* New York: Basic Books, 1986.

Bianchi, S. M., and Spain, D. *American Women—Three Decades of Change* (Special Demographic Analyses CDS-80-8). Washington, D.C.: Bureau of the Census, U.S. Department of Commerce, 1984.

Blau, F. *Equal Pay in the Office.* Lexington, Mass.: Heath, 1977.

Booker, S., and Nuckolls, L. C. "Legal and Economic Aspects of Comparable Worth." *Public Personnel Management,* 1986, *15,* 189–206.

Bottini, M. L., Chertos, C. H., and Haignere, L. *Initiating Pay Equity: A Guide for Assessing Your Workplace.* Albany: Center for Women in Government, State University of New York at Albany, 1987.

Brownmiller, S. *Femininity.* New York: Simon & Schuster, 1984.

Buford, J. A., Jr., Burkhalter, B. B., and Wilmoth, J. N. "Auditing the Compensation Function for Sex-Based Salary Differences: Some Needed Refinements." *Compensation and Benefits Review,* 1983, *15,* 33–41.

Burgess, L. R. *Wage and Salary Administration: Pay and Benefits.* Columbus, Ohio: Merrill, 1984.

Burkhalter, B. B., and others. "Auditing the Compensation Function for Race- and Sex-Based Salary Differences: Further Needed Refinements." *Compensation and Benefits Review*, 1986, *18*, 35–42.

California Comparable Worth Task Force. *Report to the Legislature, August 1985*. Sacramento: California Comparable Worth Task Force, 1985.

California Department of Finance. *California Statistical Abstract*. Sacramento: California Department of Finance, 1987.

California Employment Law Council. *Why CELC Supports Pay Equity, Job Mobility, Affirmative Action and Nondiscrimination in Employment, but Opposes the Controversial Concept of Comparable Worth*. Los Angeles: California Employment Law Council, Jan. 1985.

Campbell, J. G. "Equal Pay for Work of Equal Value in the Federal Public Service of Canada." *Compensation and Benefits Review*, 1983, *15*, 42–51.

Cascio, W. F. *Applied Psychology in Personnel Management*. (2nd ed.) Reston, Va.: Reston Publishing Co., 1982.

Charles, A. W. "Installing Single-Factor Job Evaluation." *Compensation and Benefits Review*, 1971, *3*, 9–21.

Commons, J. R., and Andrews, J. B. *Principles of Labor Legislation*. (4th ed.) New York: Harper & Row, 1936.

Comptroller General of the United States. *Options for Conducting a Pay Equity Study of Federal Pay and Classification Systems*. Washington, D.C.: General Accounting Office, Mar. 1, 1985.

Cook, A. H. *Comparable Worth: A Case Book of Experiences in States and Localities*. Honolulu: University of Hawaii Press, 1985.

Cook, A., Daniels, A. K., and Lorwin, V. R. *Women and Trade Unions in Eleven Industrial Countries*. Philadelphia: Temple University Press, 1984.

Corcoran, M., and Duncan, G. J. "Work History, Labor-Force Attachment, and Earnings Differences Between the Races and Sexes." *Journal of Human Resources*, 1979, *14*, 3–20.

"Corporate Women—They're About to Break Through to the Top." *Business Week*, June 22, 1987, *3004*, 78–86.

Council on the Economic Status of Women. *Pay Equity and Public*

Employment. St. Paul, Minn.: Council on the Economic Status of Women, 1982.

Crompton, R., and Jones, G. *White-Collar Proletariat: Deskilling and Gender in Clerical Work*. Philadelphia: Temple University Press, 1984.

Danielson, J. L., and Smith, R. "The Application of Regression Analysis to Equality and Merit in Personnel Decisions." *Public Personnel Management*, 1981, *10*, 126–131.

Davies, M. *Women's Place Is at the Typewriter*. Philadelphia: Temple University Press, 1982.

DeBeauvoir, S. *The Second Sex*. New York: Knopf, 1953.

DeForrest, S. "How Can Comparable Worth Be Achieved?" *Personnel*, 1984, *61*, 4–10.

Durkheim, E. *The Division of Labor in Society*. New York: Macmillan, 1933.

Ehrenberg, R. G., and Smith, R. *Modern Labor Economics*. (3rd ed.) Glenview, Ill.: Scott, Foresman, 1988.

Ehrenreich, B. *The Hearts of Men: American Dreams and the Flight from Commitment*. Garden City, N.Y.: Doubleday, 1983.

England, P. "The Failure of Human Capital Theory to Explain Occupational Sex Segregation." *Journal of Human Resources*, 1982, *17*, 358–370.

Epstein, C. F. *Women in Law*. New York: Basic Books, 1981.

Eyde, L. D. "Evaluating Job Evaluations: Emerging Research Issues for Comparable Worth Analysis." *Public Personnel Management*, 1983, *12*, 425–444.

Fallows, D. *A Mother's Work*. Boston: Houghton Mifflin, 1985.

Farnquist, R. L., Armstrong, D. R., and Strausbaugh, R. P. "Pandora's Worth: The San Jose Experience." *Public Personnel Management*, 1983, *12*, 358–368.

Fine, S. A. "A Structure of Worker Functions." *Personnel and Guidance Journal*, 1955, *34*, 66–73.

Fine, S. A. *The 1965 Edition of the Dictionary of Occupational Titles—Content, Contrasts, and Critique*. Kalamazoo, Mich.: W. E. Upjohn Institute for Employment Research, 1968.

Fine, S. A., and Heinz, C. A. "The Estimates of Worker Trait Requirements for 4,000 Jobs." *Personnel and Guidance Journal*, 1957, *36*, 168–174.

Fine, S. A., and Heinz, C. A. "The Functional Occupational Classification Structure." *Personnel and Guidance Journal,* 1958, *37,* 180–192.

Fine, S. A. and Holt, A. M., and Hutchinson, M. F. *Functional Job Analysis: How to Standardize Task Statements.* Kalamazoo, Mich.: W. E. Upjohn Institute for Employment Research, 1974.

Finkelstein, M. O. "The Judicial Reception of Multiple Regression Studies in Race and Sex Discrimination Cases." *Columbia Law Review,* 1980, *80,* 737–754.

Finn, M. "The Earnings Gap and Economic Choices." In P. Schlafly (ed.), *Equal Pay for Equal Work: A Conference on Comparable Worth.* Washington, D.C.: Eagle Forum Education and Legal Defense Fund, 1984.

Fisher, A. B. "Where Women Are Succeeding." *Fortune,* Aug. 3, 1987, *116,* 78–86.

Fisher, F. M. "Multiple Regression in Legal Proceedings." *Columbia Law Review,* 1980, *80,* 702-736.

Fogel, W. *The Equal Pay Act: Implications for Comparable Worth.* New York: Praeger, 1984.

Friedan, B. *The Feminine Mystique.* New York: Norton, 1963.

Friedman, J. W., and Strickler, G. M., Jr. *Cases and Materials on the Law of Employment Discrimination.* (2nd ed.) Mineola, N.Y.: Foundation Press, 1987.

Fulgham, J. B. "The Employer's Liabilities Under Comparable Worth." *Personnel Journal,* 1983, *62,* 400–412.

Gael, S. *Job Analysis: A Guide to Assessing Work Activities.* San Francisco: Jossey-Bass, 1983.

Gasaway, L. N. "Comparable Worth: A Post-Gunther Overview." *Georgetown Law Journal,* 1981, *69,* 1123–1169.

Gatewood, R. D., and Feild, H. S. *Human Resource Selection.* New York: CBS College Press Publishing, Dryden, 1987.

Gilmour, R. M. *Industry Wage and Salary Control.* New York: Wiley, 1956.

Gold, M. E. *A Debate on Comparable Worth.* Ithaca: New York State School of Industrial and Labor Relations, Cornell University, 1983.

Goldin, C. "The Earnings Gap in Historical Perspective." In U.S.

Commission on Civil Rights, *Comparable Worth: Issues for the 80's.* 2 vols. Washington, D.C., 1984.

Gutek, B. A. *Sex and the Workplace: The Impact of Sexual Behavior and Harassment on Women, Men, and Organizations.* San Francisco: Jossey-Bass, 1985.

Hacker, H. M. "Women As a Minority Group." *Social Forces,* 1951, *30,* 60–69.

Hartman, H. I., Kraut, R. E., and Tilly, L. A. (eds.). *Computer Chips and Paper Clips.* 2 vols. Washington, D.C.: National Academy Press, 1986.

Hayden, D. *Redesigning the American Dream.* New York: Norton, 1984.

Heilbroner, R. *The Worldly Philosophers.* New York: Simon & Schuster, 1953.

Hennig, M., and Jardim, M. *The Managerial Woman.* Garden City, N.Y.: Anchor Press/Doubleday, 1977.

Hewlett, S. A. *Lesser Life: The Myth of Women's Liberation in America.* New York: Warner Books, 1986.

Hildebrand, G. "The Market System." In E. R. Livernash (ed.), *Comparable Worth: Issues and Alternatives.* Washington, D.C.: Equal Opportunity Advisory Council, 1980.

Hills, F. S. "Comparable Worth: Implications for Compensation Managers." *Compensation and Benefits Review,* 1982, *14,* 33–43.

Hutner, F. C. *Equal Pay for Comparable Worth: The Working Woman's Issue of the Eighties.* New York: Praeger, 1986.

International Association of Machinists. *What's Wrong with Job Evaluation.* Washington: International Association of Machinists, 1954.

Janes, H. "Union Views on Job Evaluation: 1971 vs. 1978." *Personnel Journal,* 1979, *58,* 80–85.

Janeway, E. *Man's World, Women's Place: A Study in Social Mythology.* New York: Morrow, 1971.

Jaques, E. *Measurement of Responsibility.* London: Tavistock, 1956.

Jaques, E. *Equitable Payment.* New York: Wiley, 1961.

Jaques, E. *Time-Span Handbook.* London: Heinemann, 1964.

Jaques, E. "Equity in Compensation." In H. L. Tosi, and others (eds.), *Managerial Motivation and Compensation.* E. Lansing: Michigan State University, 1972.

Jeanneret, P. R. "Equitable Job Evaluation and Classification with the Position Analysis Questionnaire." *Compensation and Benefits Review*, 1980, *12*, 32–42.

Job Evaluation and Pay Review Task Force. *Report to the United States Civil Service Commission, January 12, 1972.* Washington, D.C.: U.S. Government Printing Office, 1972.

Jongeward, D., and Scott, D. *Affirmative Action for Women: A Practical Guide.* Reading, Mass.: Addison-Wesley, 1973.

Kamalich, R. F., and Polachek, S. W. "Discrimination: Fact or Fiction? An Examination Using an Alternative Approach." *Southern Economic Journal*, 1982, *49*, 450–461.

Kanter, R. M. *Men and Women of the Corporation.* New York: Basic Books, 1977.

Kanter, R. M. "From Status to Contribution: Some Organizational Implications of the Changing Basis for Pay." *Personnel*, 1987, *64*, 12–37.

Katz, M., Lavan, H., and Malloy, M. S. "Comparable Worth: Analysis of Cases and Implications for HR Management." *Compensation and Benefits Review*, 1986, *18*, 26–38.

Kerlinger, F. N., and Pedhazur, E. J. *Multiple Regression in Behavioral Research.* New York: Holt, Rinehart & Winston, 1973.

Kessler-Harris, A. *Out to Work: A History of Wage-Earning Women in the United States.* New York: Oxford University Press, 1982.

Killingsworth, M. R. "The Economics of Comparable Worth: Analytical Empirical, and Policy Questions." In H. I. Hartman (ed.), *Comparable Worth: New Directions for Research.* Washington, D.C.: National Academy Press, 1985.

Klein, E. *Gender Politics: From Consciousness to Mass Politics.* Cambridge, Mass.: Harvard University Press, 1984.

Kurtz, M., and Hocking, E. C. "Nurses v. Tree Trimmers." *Public Personnel Management*, 1983, *12*, 369–381.

Lindsay, C. M. "The Simple Analytics of Wage Disparity." In P. Schlafly (ed.), *Equal Pay for Unequal Worth: A Conference on*

Comparable Worth. Washington, D.C.: Eagle Forum Education and Legal Defense Fund, 1984.

Ling, C. C. *The Management of Personnel Relations: History and Origins.* Homewood, Ill.: Irwin, 1965.

Livernash, E. R. (ed.). *Comparable Worth: Issues and Alternatives.* Washington, D.C.: Equal Employment Advisory Council, 1980a.

Livernash, E. R. "An Overview." In E. R. Livernash (ed.), *Comparable Worth: Issues and Alternatives.* Washington, D.C.: Equal Employment Advisory Council, 1980b.

Lorber, L. A., and others. *Sex and Salary: A Legal and Personnel Analysis of Comparable Worth.* Alexandria, Va.: ASPA Foundation, 1985.

Lott, M. R. *Wage Scales and Job Evaluation.* New York: Ronald, 1926.

Maccoby, E. E. (ed.). *The Development of Sex Differences.* Stanford: Stanford University Press, 1966.

Maccoby, E. E., and Jacklin, C. N. *The Psychology of Sex Differences.* Stanford: Stanford University Press, 1974.

McCormick, E. J. *Job Analysis: Methods and Applications.* New York: AMACOM, 1979.

McCurry, C. M. *Bank Personnel Administration: A Basic Plan.* Rolling Meadows, Ill.: Bank Administration Institute, 1979.

MacKinnon, C. *Sexual Harassment of Working Women: A Case of Sex Discrimination.* New Haven, Conn.: Yale University Press, 1979.

McWilliams, C. *Southern California: An Island on the Land.* Salt Lake City, Utah: Peregrine Smith Books, 1983. (Originally published 1946.)

Mahoney, T. A. "Approaches to the Definition of Comparable Worth." *Academy of Management Review,* 1983, *8,* 14–22.

Mahoney, T. A., Rosen, B., and Rynes, S. "Where Do Compensation Specialists Stand on Comparable Worth?" *Compensation and Benefits Review,* 1984, *16,* 27–40.

Majeske, P. K. "Research Findings." In *Report of the Comparable Worth Task Force to the Michigan Civil Service Commission.* Lansing, Mich., 1985. (Duplicated.)

Marshall, R., and Paulin, B. "The Employment and Earnings of Women: The Comparable Worth Debate." In U.S. Commission on Civil Rights, *Comparable Worth: Issues for the 80's.* 2 vols. Washington, D.C., 1984.

Marx, K. *The Eighteenth Brumaire of Louis Bonaparte.* New York: International Publishers, 1963.

Mead, M. *Sex and Temperament in Three Primitive Societies.* New York: New American Library, 1950. (Originally published 1935.)

Michigan Department of Civil Service, "Pay Equity Provisions." *Civil Service News,* 1986, *26,* 1-2.

Milkovich, G. T. "The Emerging Debate." In E. R. Livernash (ed.), *Comparable Worth: Issues and Alternatives.* Washington, D.C.: Equal Opportunity Advisory Council, 1980.

Milkovich, G. T., and Broderick, R. "Pay Discrimination: Legal Issues and Implications for Research." *Industrial Relations,* 1982, *21,* 309-317.

Mill, J. S. *Principles of Political Economy.* New York: Augustus M. Kelley, 1965. (Originally published 1909.)

Miller, A. R., Treiman, D. J., Cain, P. S., and Roos, P. A. (eds.). *Work, Jobs, and Occupations: A Critical Review of the Dictionary of Occupational Titles.* Washington, D.C.: National Academy Press, 1980.

Mincer, J., and Polachek, S. W. "Family Investments in Human Capital: Earnings of Women." *Journal of Political Economy,* 1974, *82,* S79-S108.

Money, J., and Ehrhardt, A. E. *Man and Woman, Boy and Girl.* Baltimore: Johns Hopkins University Press, 1972.

Mulcahy, R. W., and Anderson, J. E. "The Bargaining Battleground Called Comparable Worth." *Public Personnel Management,* 1986, *15,* 233-247.

Murphy, W. P., Getman, J. G., and Jones, J. E., Jr. *Discrimination in Employment.* (4th ed.) Washington, D.C.: Bureau of National Affairs, Inc., 1979.

Myrdal, G. *An American Dilemma: The Negro Problem and American Democracy.* New York: Harper & Row, 1944.

National Committee on Pay Equity. *Pay Equity: An Issue of Race, Ethnicity, and Sex.* Washington, D.C.: National Committee on Pay Equity, 1987.

Nelson, B. A., Opton, E. M., Jr., and Wilson, T. E. "Wage Discrimination and Title VII in the 1980's: The Case Against

'Comparable Worth.'" *Employee Relations Law Journal*, 1981, 6, 380–405.

Newman, W., and Vonhof, J. M. "'Separate but Equal'—Job Segregation and Pay Equity in the Wake of *Gunther.*" *University of Illinois Law Review*, 1981, 2, 269–331.

Northrup, H. R. "Wage Setting and Collective Bargaining." In E. R. Livernash (ed.), *Comparable Worth: Issues and Alternatives.* Washington, D.C.: Equal Opportunity Advisory Council, 1980.

Olney, P. B., Jr. "Meeting the Challenge of Comparable Worth: Parts I and II." *Compensation and Benefits Review*, 1987, 19, 34–44, 45–53.

O'Neill, J. "An Argument Against Comparable Worth." In U.S. Commission on Civil Rights, *Comparable Worth: Issues for the 80's.* 2 vols. Washington, D.C., 1984.

Ost, E. "Comparable Worth: A Response for the '80s." *Personnel Journal*, 1985, 64, 64–70.

Pare, T., and Woods, W. "The World's Top 50 Industrial CEOs." *Fortune*, Aug. 3, 1987, 116, 23–66.

Paterson, T. T., and Husband, T. M. "Decision-Making Responsibility: Yardstick for Job Evaluation." *Compensation Review*, 1970, 2, 21–31.

Patten, T. H., Jr. *Pay: Employee Compensation and Incentive Plans.* New York: Free Press, 1977.

Patten, T. H., Jr. "Pay Discrimination Lawsuits: The Problems of Expert Witnesses and the Discovery Process." *Personnel*, 1978, 55, 27–35.

Patten, T. H., Jr. "Pay Cuts: Will Employees Accept Them?" *National Productivity Review*, 1981, 1, 110–119.

Patten, T. H., Jr. "The Role of the Forensic Expert in Management Consulting." In R. Robinson and J. Pearce (eds.), *Proceedings of the Academy of Management, 1985.* San Diego, Calif.: Academy of Management, 1985.

Perrin, S. M. *Comparable Worth and Public Policy: The Case of Pennsylvania.* Philadelphia: Industrial Research Unit, Wharton School of Finance, University of Pennsylvania, 1985.

Phelps, E. S. "The Statistical Theory of Racism and Sexism." *American Economic Review*, 1972, 62, 659–661.

Pleck, J. H. *Working Wives, Working Husbands.* Newbury Park, Calif.: Sage, 1985.

Polachek, S. W. "Occupational Self-Selection: A Human Capital Approach to Sex Differences in Occupational Structure." *Review of Economics and Statistics,* 1981, *58,* 60–69.

Rehnquist, W. H. *The Supreme Court: How It Was, How It Is.* New York: Morrow, 1987.

Reichenberg, N. "Pay Equity in Review," *Public Personnel Management,* 1986, *15,* 211–232.

Remick, H. "The Comparable Worth Controversy." *Public Personnel Management,* 1981, *10,* 371–383.

Remick, H. (ed.). *Comparable Worth and Wage Discrimination.* Philadelphia: Temple University Press, 1984.

Report of the Comparable Worth Task Force to the Michigan Civil Service Commission. Lansing, Mich., 1985. (Duplicated.)

Reskin, B. F., and Hartmann, H. I. (eds.). *Women's Work, Men's Work: Sex Segregation on the Job.* Washington, D.C.: National Academy Press, 1986.

Risher, H. "On Determining Back Pay Awards." *Compensation and Benefits Review,* 1977, *9,* 39–53.

Risher, H., and Cameron, M. "Pay Decisions: Testing for Discrimination." *Employee Relations Law Journal,* 1982, 7, 432–453.

Roberts, H. V. "Statistical Biases in the Measurement of Employment Discrimination." In E. R. Livernash (ed.), *Comparable Worth: Issues and Alternatives.* Washington, D.C.: Equal Opportunity Advisory Council, 1980.

Rock, M. (ed.). *Handbook of Wage and Salary Administration.* (2nd ed.) New York: McGraw-Hill, 1984.

Rosen, B., Rynes, S., and Mahoney, T. A. "Compensation, Jobs, and Gender." *Harvard Business Review,* 1983, *61,* 170–190.

Ross, M. *All Manner of Men.* New York: Reynal and Hitchcock, 1948.

Rutherglen, G. "Sexual Equality in Fringe Benefit Plans." *Virginia Law Review,* 1979, *65,* 199–256.

Sape, G. "Coping with Comparable Worth." *Harvard Business Review,* 1985, *63,* 145–152.

Schechter, J. H. "The Retirement Equity Act: Meeting Women's

Pension Needs." *Compensation and Benefits Review*, 1985, *17*, 13-21.

Schlafly, P. *The Power of Positive Women*. New York: Harcourt, Brace, Jovanovich, 1977.

Schwab, D. P. "Job Evaluation and Pay Setting: Concepts and Practices." In E. R. Livernash (ed.), *Comparable Worth: Issues and Alternatives*. Washington, D.C.: Equal Opportunity Advisory Council, 1980.

Sibson, R. E. *Compensation*. (Rev. ed.) New York: AMACOM, 1981.

Sjoquist, D., Schroeder, L., and Stephan, P. *Interpreting Linear Regression: An Heuristic Analysis*. Morristown, N.J.: General Learning Press, 1974.

Slichter, S. H., Livernash, E. R., and Healey, J. J. *The Impact of Collective Bargaining on Management*. Washington, D.C.: Brookings Institution, 1960.

Smith, J. P., and Ward, M. P. *Women's Wages and Work in the Twentieth Century*. Santa Monica, Calif.: Rand Corporation, 1984.

Sorenson, E. "Effect of Comparable Worth Policies on Earnings." *Industrial Relations*, 1987, *26*, 227-239.

Spelfogel, E. J. "Equal Pay for Work of Comparable Value: A New Concept." *Labor Law Journal*, 1981, *32*, 30-39.

Spence, J. T., and Helmreich, R. L. *Masculinity and Feminity: Their Psychological Dimensions, Correlates, and Antecedents*. Austin: University of Texas Press, 1978.

Steel, B. S., and Lovrich, N. P., Jr. "Comparable Worth: The Problematic Politicization of a Public Personnel Issue." *Public Personnel Management*, 1987, *16*, 23-36.

Steinberg, R. J. "Identifying Wage Discrimination and Implementing Pay Equity Adjustments." In U.S. Commission on Civil Rights, *Comparable Worth: Issues for the 80's*. 2 vols. Washington, D.C., 1984.

Stieber, J. *The Steel Industry Wage Structure*. Cambridge, Mass.: Harvard University Press, 1959.

Sullivan, J. F. "Comparable Worth and the Statistical Audit of Pay Programs for Illegal Systemic Discrimination." *Personnel Administrator*, 1985, *30*, 102-111.

Taft, P. *Organized Labor in American History*. New York: Harper & Row, 1965.

Taft, P. *Labor Politics American Style: The California State Federation of Labor*. Cambridge, Mass.: Harvard University Press, 1968.

Treiman, D. J. *Job Evaluation: An Analytic Review*. Washington, D.C.: National Academy of Sciences, 1979.

Treiman, D. J., and Cheng, P. W. *California Comparable Worth Task Force Minority Report*. Los Angeles, Aug. 19, 1985. (Duplicated.)

Treiman, D., and Hartmann, H. (eds.). *Women, Work, and Wages: Equal Pay for Jobs of Equal Value*. Washington, D.C.: National Academy Press, 1981.

Treiman, D. J., and Terrell, K. "Sex and the Process of Status Attainment: A Comparison of Working Men and Women." *American Sociological Review*, 1975, *40*, 174–200.

U.S. Commission on Civil Rights. *Comparable Worth: Issues for the 80's*. 2 vols. Washington, D.C., 1984.

U.S. Department of Labor. *Dictionary of Occupational Titles*. (4th ed.) Washington, D.C.: U.S. Government Printing Office, 1977.

Van Riper, P. P. *History of the United States Civil Service*. New York: Harper & Row, 1958.

Wallace, P. (ed.). *Equal Employment Opportunity and the AT&T Case*. Cambridge, Mass.: MIT Press, 1976.

Weber, M. "Class, Status, and Party." In H. H. Gerth and C. W. Mills (eds.), *From Max Weber: Essays in Sociology*. New York: Oxford University Press, 1958.

Weitzman, L. J. *The Divorce Revolution*. New York: Free Press, 1985.

Williams, R. E., and McDowell, D. S. "The Legal Framework." In E. R. Livernash (ed.), *Comparable Worth: Issues and Alternatives*. Washington, D.C.: Equal Employment Advisory Council, 1980.

Wirth, L. "The Problem of Minority Groups." In R. Linton (ed.), *The Science of Man in the World Crisis*. New York: Columbia University Press, 1945.

Witte, E. E. "Economics and Public Policy." *American Economic Review*, 1957, *47*, 1–21.

Zellner, H. "A Report on the Extent and the Nature of Employment Discrimination Against Women." In C. Lloyd and B. Neimi (eds.), *The Economics of Sex Differentials.* New York: Columbia University Press, 1979.

Index

Relationships: customer and public, 175; job, 176

Report of the Comparable Worth Task Force to the Michigan Civil Service Commission, 86, 87, 88

Republic (Plato), 29

Responsibilities: pay based on, 243–245; in point-factor plans, 171, 179–183

Retirement Equity Act of 1983, 42–43

"Review, revise, and reevaluate" (RRR) strategy, 226–228

Rinehart v. *Westinghouse Electric Corporation,* 46–47, 222, 223

Risher, H., 230

Roberts, H. V., 25

Rock, M., 76, 192

Roos, P. A., 204

Roosevelt, F. D., 37

Rosen, B., 13, 14–15, 226, 227, 228

Ross, M., 37

Rynes, S., 13, 14–15, 226, 227, 228

S

Saatchi and Saatchi, 192

San Francisco, California, 100

San Jose, California, 99, 108–109, 114–124

Sape, G., 233, 234

Schwab, D. P., 11

Scott, D., 39, 42, 43, 45

Second Sex (Beauvoir), 29

Secretary of Labor, 45

Segregation, identification of, 233

Service Employees International Union (SEIU), 98, 99, 100, 101, 106, 109, 110, 113

Sex composition of jobs, correcting effect of, 245–248

Shreveport, Louisiana, 63–64

Shultz v. *Wheaton Glass Company,* 51

Sibson, R. E., 145

Single-factor theories, in job evaluation, 201–202

Skill requirements: in Hay plan, 193–194, 195, 197; pay based on, 240–245; in point-factor plans, 171, 172–178

Slichter, S. H., 152

Smith, A., 139

Smith, J. P., 220

Smith, R. S., 16, 17, 19, 20, 21, 22

South Carolina, 80

Spain, D., 32

Spaulding et al. v. *University of Washington,* 56–57, 83

Special Task Force of the Connecticut Business and Industry Association, 81

Staff responsibilities, 180

Stanton, E. C., 29

State governments. *See names of specific states*

Statistical research, 18–25

Statistics: on legal cases, 69–72; and regression analysis, 18–25, 239–248; on working women, 31–32, 213–214

Stieber, J., 151

Strategies, 225–237

Strausbaugh, R. P., 114, 115, 116, 117, 118, 120, 121, 123, 196

Strickler, G. M., Jr., 40, 42, 45

Strikes: San Jose, 114–124; Yale University, 124–128

Sullivan, J. F., 230

Supervisory responsibilities, 179

Supreme Court. *See* U.S. Supreme Court

T

Taft, P., 96

Taft-Hartley Act. *See* Labor-Management Relations Act

Task Force on Pay Equity (Minnesota), 84

Task Force on State Compensation and Classification Equity (Oregon), 83

Taylor v. *Charley Brothers*, 51-52, 60

Teamsters Union, 110

Tektronix, 229

Texas, 80

Thomas v. *Anchorage Telephone Utility*, 63

Thompson v. *Boyle*, 222

Time span of discretion, 155-156

Title VII of the Civil Rights Act of 1964, 5, 36, 40-44; disparate treatment cases involving, 49-57; early cases involving, 58-60; and Equal Pay Act, 43, 44; and job evaluations, 139; pay equity cases involving, 46-49; recent cases involving, 60-69, 72

Treiman, D. J., 76, 146, 148, 151, 161, 162, 189, 192, 194-195, 196-199, 203, 204, 225, 239

Truman, Harry S, 38

U

Uniform Guidelines on Employee Selection Procedures, 140

Unions, 106-136; in California, 91-92, 96; and international business, 111-114; involvement of, 109-111; and job evaluation, 151-154; responsibilities of, 70; and San Jose strike, 114-124; and Yale University strike, 124-128. *See also names of specific unions*

United Automobile Workers (UAW), 88, 90, 110, 166

University of California, 93-94

University of Houston, 54-55

University of Washington, 56-57

U.S. Circuit Courts of Appeal, 71, 72; on disparate treatment and disparate impact, 52-53, 54-55, 56-57; early cases in, 57-59; on pay equity, 46-48, 49; recent cases in, 60, 61, 63-64, 67-68

U.S. Department of Labor, 204; Revised Order No. 4 (affirmative action), 45

U.S. District Court, 44, 70, 71; on disparate treatment and disparate impact, 52, 53, 54, 55-56; early cases in, 58, 59-60; on pay equity, 46; recent cases in, 60-61, 62-63, 66-67, 68, 69, 93

U.S. Office of Personnel Management, 159-163

U.S. Supreme Court: cases accepted by, 46; changes in, 73; on pay equity, 46, 48-49, 72; on sex discrimination in compensation, 41

Utah, 80

V

Van Riper, P. P., 159

Versatile Job Analysis System (VERJAS), 140

Virginia, 80

W

Wagner Act (National Labor Relations Act), 70, 107, 129

"Wait, watch, and worry" (WWW) strategy, 226